Constructing Local Theologies

ROBERT J. SCHREITER, C.PP.S.

ORBIS BOOKS
Maryknoll, New York 10545

Eleventh printing, September 2003

Copyright © 1985 by Robert J. Schreiter
Published by Orbis Books, Maryknoll, NY 10545
All rights reserved
Manufactured in the United States of America

Manuscript Editor: Lisa McGaw

Library of Congress Cataloging in Publication Data

Schreiter, Robert J.
  Constructing local theologies.

  Bibliography: p.
  Includes index.
  1. Theology—Methodology.   2. Catholic Church—
Doctrines.   I. Title.   II. Title: Local theologies.
BR118.S365   1985   230′.01′8   84-14797
ISBN 0-88344-108-X (pbk.)

Contents

FOREWORD

Since 1977 Robert J. Schreiter has been Dean of the Catholic Theological Union in Chicago, where he is also Associate Professor of Theology. Chicago, with its many universities and its cluster of theological schools, is an international center for study that attracts students from all parts of the world. This fact offered Professor Schreiter the opportunity to gather under his direction a group of students from ten different countries for the sake of undertaking a common search for the relation between theology and its concrete sociocultural context. For such a manner of theologizing, the input of the social sciences, and especially the study of cultures and their significant (and economic) nodal points, is necessary. For the analysis of culture, the author makes special use of semiotics, albeit (and rightly so) with some reservation.

Previously, one almost took for granted that the theology of the Western churches was supraregional and was, precisely in its Western form, universal and therefore directly accessible for persons from other cultures. But especially with the emergence of liberation theology, as in Latin America for example, Western theologians came to the realization that their own theology has just as much sociocultural bias as any other. That theology, too, is a "local" theology that, although in this (particular Western) social and cultural context, nonetheless wants to bring *the Gospel* to expression. How can this selfsame Gospel, which is given only in a societal and cultural context (even in the New Testament, for that matter) and can never be wholly extricated from any culture, be allowed to speak the language of an entirely different culture? That is the chief concern of this book.

The author comes to the realization that what we call "the great Christian tradition" consists of a series of "local theologies." Thus, theologizing today also has to deal with the problem of a "culture shock" and not merely with the analysis and comparison of theological concepts. This then raises the question about Christian identity in the polycentric and yet one Catholica. In this same connection questions are raised about the peculiar nature of folk religion and the favorable and unfavorable meanings of syncretism.

This book is really about the many-faceted inculturation of the one Christian faith; it asks questions which previously were scarcely thought about. In my opinion, the book is very important for missiologists, but also for any theological enterprise. Hermeneutics and interdisciplinary research work hand in hand here; of this I heartily approve. Moreover, whenever this approach and method is placed in the service of a responsible option for the emancipatory promotion of the "humanum" and the Christian liberation of humanity and society (an option which the author would certainly endorse, but which is not worked out here), then one finds here, in my opinion, the necessary basis for an emerging form of theology which will be fruitful for *people*.

EDWARD SCHILLEBEECKX, O.P.

Preface

The German theologian Karl Rahner in 1979 called the attention of the theological community to an important shift that has occurred within the church. The dramatic growth of the Christian community in Latin America, Africa, Asia, and Oceania during the twentieth century was already evident at Vatican Council II where, for the first time, a significant proportion of the world's Roman Catholic bishops were coming from outside the North Atlantic community. For Rahner this meant not only a shift in population, but a dramatic shift in outlook: the church found itself moving from a predominantly Hellenistic world-view into the era of a world church, characterized by a pluralism in world-view and multiplicity of new pastoral and theological problems unprecedented in Christian history.[1]

There is now a greater pluralism in world-view. The well-known intellectual frameworks that shaped Christian theology through most of the last two millennia are now suddenly but a few among many. New pastoral and theological problems and issues present themselves in a variety and magnitude bewildering in their number. The churches in Latin America, Africa, Asia, and Oceania are not satisfied to repeat the tradition as it has come to them, in rote fashion. They are anxious to take their place alongside the churches of older origin in contributing their response to the gospel to the great stream of Christian tradition. They are joined by many communities in the North Atlantic ambit, who are seeking new ways of giving voice to their experience of Christ in a rapidly changing world.

In the midst of this tremendous vitality that today's Christians are showing, one set of problems emerges over and over again: how to be faithful both to the contemporary experience of the gospel and to the tradition of Christian life that has been received. How is a community to go about bringing to expression its own experience of Christ in its concrete situation? And how is this to be related to a tradition that is often expressed in language and concepts vastly different from anything in the current situation?

These problems are the subject of this book. An attempt is made here to bring together some of the problems that are recurring in a variety of different contexts, and to reflect on answers to those two problems of fidelity to the present and the past. In many ways the reflections here are provisional and incomplete, since many of these problems have rarely been the object of direct reflection in Christian history. The reflections are not shaped into any single system, since every indication is that such a move would be premature;

we are still at a very early stage of understanding more clearly the relation of theology to its context. The theologian reading these pages will note that many of the underlying theological questions remain unanswered. Again, we are still trying to get hold of the issues, and are still some distance from being able to set out a complete theological methodology shaped by a single theological approach. What is presented here tries to lay the groundwork for future development. Hints of an approach can be discerned, but the theologian must have some patience in awaiting the kind of theology of culture that will have to emerge from this new situation for the Christian church.

The approach taken here bespeaks some of the directions now being taken in this new theological situation. The approach is as interdisciplinary as a single writer is able to muster. There is less of the more familiar philosophical substratum than a theologian might be inclined to expect. The social sciences play the principal role of dialogue partner with the theology being shaped here. Anyone familiar with what is happening on many of the continents of the world will not be surprised by this. Such an approach still leaves many questions of method unanswered. But without plunging in, it seems that we shall not even be able to clarify what the issues are.

Second, the approach is consciously ecumenical. "Church" here refers to the entirety of the Christian church. Attempts are made throughout to address problems faced by all the Christian churches. At the same time any work such as this concerned with theology in its concrete context is bound to come down more heavily within one church than others, and the author's Roman Catholic background and commitment will be evident throughout.

Finally, this work is more collaborative than the single name on the title page might indicate. This book began as a series of lectures given in a seminar on local theologies at Catholic Theological Union in Chicago in 1976. The dozen participants in that seminar, who have since scattered to ten countries, formed the core group for discussion and criticism of those lectures, which were revised and given a second presentation in 1977. That 1977 version circulated on every continent, and was the subject of much useful criticism and suggestion during the intervening years. In the meantime the 1977 version continued to be the basis of seminars that have involved several hundred participants, who in turn added their own comments. There have even been several publications devoted to commenting on the ideas presented in that version.[2] As a result that version has been completely rewritten for this present book. I owe thanks to all of these many people, who have taken the time to share their comments, encouraged me to rewrite parts of this book, and urged me to get this into print. It is my hope that the appearance of this book will not be the end of what has been a stimulating exchange over the past number of years.

In a special way, thanks are due to my colleagues at Catholic Theological Union (CTU) who encouraged me to keep at this project despite administrative responsibilities. Thanks also to Kenneth O'Malley, C.P., who compiled the Index for this book. Special thanks too are due to the students at CTU, who provided the forum for so much of what appears here and urged clarification of many of the points included herein. Besides the faculty and students of CTU, three other locations helped bring this book into final form and deserve mention here: the Sheil Center at Northwestern University, where the chapter on the study of culture was completely rewritten in the summer of 1981; I thank the Rev. John Krump and the staff there for their help. The Center for Mission Studies at Maryknoll provided the location for the development of my thought on popular religion, which resulted in the drafting of the chapter on that subject in 1982; my thanks to the Rev. Frank McGourn, M.M., and the staff and students there for their assistance. Finally, thanks to my congregation, the Society of the Precious Blood, whose Generalate in Rome was the location for my rewriting of the entire manuscript in August 1983. To all of these people, my sincere thanks.

1

What Is Local Theology?

There has been an important shift in perspective in theology in recent years. While the basic purpose of theological reflection has remained the same—namely, the reflection of Christians upon the gospel in light of their own circumstances—much more attention is now being paid to how those circumstances shape the response to the gospel. This focus is being expressed with terms like "localization," "contextualization," "indigenization," and "inculturation" of theology. Despite slightly different nuances in meaning, all of these terms point to the need for and responsibility of Christians to make their response to the gospel as concrete and lively as possible.

This first chapter will wander over the terrain being staked out as of prime concern to this kind of theology and will explore some of the issues involved. Specifically, four broad questions will be pursued, with the hope of our getting to know the concerns of this kind of theology in more detail: (1) What has led to this shift in perspective in theology, and what issues are important to it? (2) What are some of the main approaches being taken? (3) Who is making these approaches? (4) How would one define this new perspective in light of other approaches in theology?

The purpose of this investigation is a synthetic one. In other words, rather than a region-by-region or country-by-country approach, we shall focus upon issues and concerns that have become common among a number of geographical areas. An analysis by region has already been taken up by others.[1]

A SHIFT IN PERSPECTIVE

A shift in perspective, concentrating on the role that circumstances play in shaping one's response to the gospel, first became evident in regions where Christianity was relatively new. It started coming to the world's attention in the 1950s in parts of Africa and Asia. There was a growing sense that the theologies being inherited from the older churches of the North Atlantic community did not fit well into these quite different cultural circumstances.

1

In Roman Catholic circles, the need to adapt theological reflection to local circumstances began receiving official support with Vatican Council II, where in the Decree on the Church's Missionary Activity *Ad Gentes* such adaptation received explicit approbation. In the subsequent years the missionary theology of Pope Paul VI developed this thought, especially in his address to the bishops of Africa in 1969 and in his apostolic exhortation *Evangelii Nuntiandi* in 1975.[2] The latter not only continued his own thought, but grew out of what he had heard in the Synod of Bishops devoted to the question of the mission of the church.

A similar movement was taking place in Protestant circles and was becoming evident by the early 1970s. Krikor Haleblian has chronicled the rise of this concern in and among Protestants.[3] Terms like "contextualization," "localization," "indigenization," "inculturation," and "adaptation" began to be used by Catholics and Protestants alike in referring to this shift in perspective.

At the same time another movement was also afoot, rooted especially in Latin America. By the time of the gathering of Roman Catholic bishops at Medellín in 1968, it was becoming known as "theology of liberation." The publication in English of a book of that title by Peruvian theologian Gustavo Gutiérrez in 1973 helped to bring this approach to the world's attention.[4] The theology of liberation shared an important concern with the shift in perspective going on in Africa and Asia: an attempt to find a Christian voice in quite different circumstances from those more commonly known in Europe and North America. In all these instances, however the theology coming from them might be understood, there was that common concern: making sense of the Christian message in local circumstances. Specifically, three recurring concerns threaded their way through all the different theologies that were emerging in the southern hemispheres and among marginated peoples of Europe and North America.

First, *new questions* were being asked, questions for which there were no ready traditional answers. Indeed, so many new questions were emerging that the credibility of existing forms of theology was weakened. For example, questions about the eucharistic elements: How was one to celebrate the Eucharist in countries that were Muslim theocracies and forbade the production or importation of fermented beverages? What was one to do in those cultures where cereal products such as bread were not known, in which the unconsecrated bread itself became a magical object because of its foreignness? Or how was one to celebrate baptism among the Masai in East Africa, where to pour water on the head of a woman was to curse her with infertility? How was one to understand Vatican Council II's opening to non-Christian religions in countries in southern Asia where Christianity seemed destined to remain a minority religion?

How was one to understand church-state conflict in the repressive regimes of parts of Latin America, where the church was not a power equal to the state, but was now a church of the poor? Or what was one to do with the discipline of celibacy among the clergy in cultures where not to marry and have children was a way of cursing one's parents? Or how was one to understand polygamy in rural Africa, where it seemed to be more a matter of economic security for women than a matter of male lust? Churches in cultural settings vastly different from those of traditional Christianity in the North Atlantic area were not only raising new questions, but asking questions that traditional frameworks of theology could not answer. It was becoming increasingly evident that the theologies once thought to have a universal, and even enduring or perennial character (such as neo-scholastic Thomism in Catholicism or neo-orthodoxy in Protestantism) were but regional expressions of certain cultures.

Second, *old answers* were being urged upon cultures and regions with new questions. People outside the North Atlantic communities felt that the older churches were not taking their questions seriously, or were trying to foist their own agenda upon them. They detected a continuing and consistent colonialism and paternalism on the part of the North Atlantic churches, which seemed to be insisting that, if they wished to be considered full-fledged Christian communities, they would have to come to think and respond like the older churches. The older churches, often the source of much of the financial support, and certainly held up as the mature Christian ideal, wittingly and unwittingly were imposing their problems and their solutions upon the newer churches. As recently as the Sixth General Assembly of the World Council of Churches at Vancouver in 1983 this was again evident: the North Atlantic churches' agenda was dominated by the question of peace and nuclear war, while that of the rest of the churches had to do with hunger, poverty, and political repression. Despite honest efforts to accommodate the agenda of the southern hemisphere, the agenda of the North Atlantic churches continued to have the upper hand in the proceedings.

The problem of old answers was also being felt in the North Atlantic churches. Blacks in the United States detected racism in the patterns of theological response traditional to much of Christianity. Women discovered widespread exclusion of their experience from the mainstream of Christian reflection. And many men and women in ministry found the theology they had learned inadequate to the questions that they now faced in their work. The pluralism that had come about in post-Enlightenment thought kept raising questions about the philosophical underpinnings deemed appropriate to Christian theology. Not only were there competing philosophical systems, but social and natural sciences were now giving more shape to the culture than any philosophy was. A deepening dissatisfaction with existing approaches to theology became more and more widespread.

Third, the realities of new questions and old answers pointed to a concern that recurred in churches around the world: *a new kind of Christian identity* was emerging apart from much of the traditional theological reflection of historical Christianity. The theology emerging out of this new identity had particular sensitivity to three areas: context, procedure, and history.

Rather than trying, in the first instance, to apply a received theology to a local context, this new kind of theology began with an examination of the context itself. In contexts where issues of oppression and conflict were paramount, a lengthy analysis of relationships of power and injustice was clearly called for. Social, economic, and political questions engaged the energies that had once been devoted to philosophical or metaphysical questions. It has gradually become unthinkable in many Christian churches to engage in any theological reflections without first studying the context in which it is taking place. Without such an initial analysis, a theology readily can become either irrelevant or a subtle tool of ideological manipulation. There is now a realization that all theologies have contexts, interests, relationships of power, special concerns—and to pretend that this is not the case is to be blind.

This awareness of how context shapes reflection, how it gives urgency to questions and shape to answers has led to greater attention to a second aspect of this new theology: procedure. In cultures where ideas emerge and decisions are made on a communal basis, one now sees theology developing in that same way. While the professionally trained theologian continues to have a role in relating the experience of other Christian communities to the experience of a local group, the community itself takes much more responsibility in shaping theological response. Much or even most of this theology never comes to be written down as it emerges from the reflection of those myriad small Christian communities in Latin America, the Philippines, or East Africa. But then ideals of individuality and publication again merely reflect certain cultural contexts and preferences. By the same token, in developed capitalist countries such as the United States where more individualist ideals prevail, autobiography or one's personal story has become an important procedural pathway for the development of a theology. Theological procedures, therefore, follow to a great extent the patterns of production of meaning within a given cultural context. What has counted for theology since the thirteenth century in Western Christianity has been dominated by a university model, with its emphasis on clarity, precision, and relation to other bodies of knowledge, about which more will be said in chapter 4. But other ways of engaging in theological reflection are available and are giving shape to how Christians understand themselves in their situations.

A third sensitivity in this new identity is to history. While the timeless and enduring realities of grace are not overlooked, special attention is given to all the ambiguities of history. Racial, economic, sexual, and ideological dominations of many types are never far from the awareness in this new identity. Histories of suffering cannot be forgotten. This is leading not only to a transformation of the present, but also to a reconstruction of our understanding of the past. Women in many churches are discovering both a hidden and forgotten history as well as one distorted to meet male interests.[5] Blacks in the United States and South Africa discover a church that condoned slavery on the basis of race. The poor discover a history of the rich, but find their own families consigned to anonymity. Rarely have Christian communities been more sensitive to the incarnate character of the church, in its moments of grace and abject sinfulness, in its times of prophetic witness and shameful betrayal. All of these factors have been combining to create an important shift in perspective in Christian self-awareness and theology, both among the churches in the southern hemisphere, and among the churches of the North Atlantic communities. But the newness of the approaches, coupled with the heightened sensitivities, raise many questions, some of which are the subject of this book.

The concerns begin with what to call this shift in perspective. A number of different terms are being used, somewhat interchangeably.

One of the first terms for this new perspective was *indigenous theology* which emphasizes the fact that theology is done by and for a given geographical area—by local people for their area, rather than by outsiders. It aims at focusing upon the integrity and identity of the enterprise. It is contrasted with a universal or perennial theology, which attempts to speak for all places over a long period of time. The difficulty with this term, at least in some places, is the history of the word "indigenous." In those parts of the world that once made up the British empire, "indigenous" connotes the old policy of replacing British personnel in colonial government with local leadership. The term, therefore, has a distinctively colonialist ring in East Africa and in India and is unsuited to the new perspective in theology. The term continues to be used in other parts of the world, however.

In some evangelical Protestant circles the term *ethnotheology* was put forward, referring both to the biblical concept of *ta ethnē* (the nations) and to parallel usages in European social sciences (ethnopsychology, ethnopsychiatry, etc.). While the term does help to focus upon the specificity of theology for a given cultural area, it also carries for many ears a slightly unsavory ring. The biblical allusion connotes for some a reference to pagans or the heathen, somehow inferior to the chosen people. The social-science reference suggests that this kind of theology is somehow different from (and probably inferior to) the theology done for Western churches, much as "sociology" is done in technologically advanced cultures, while only "cultural anthropology" is done in less advanced cultures. The term "ethnotheology" has not received widespread acceptance.

Inculturation, as a noun, is often used of this shift in theological process as well. A combination of the theological principle of incarnation with the social-science concept of acculturation (adapting oneself to a culture), the term has come to be used widely in Roman Catholic circles and appears in many documents of congresses and episcopal conferences. It refers to the wider process of which theology is an expression. While widely accepted in church circles, it causes some difficulties in dialogue with social scientists in that it seems to be a dilettantish kind of neologism on the part of non-scientists.[6] When referring specifically to theology, it has no accepted adjectival form.

Contextual theology is a widely used term for this shift in perspective, focusing especially on the role of context in this kind of theology. As a neologism, it has the advantage of not having many previous associations and of being readily used in translation into a wide variety of languages.

Local theology reflects especially English-language usage, emphasizing the circumscribed context of the logical reflection and having also some ecclesial overtones through its association with "local church," the most common form of English translation for Vatican Council II's *ecclesia particularis*.Its principal disadvantage is that the use of the word "local" does not translate well into Germanic languages, where *lokal* has a much different meaning.

The lack of consistent terminology, the need for neologisms, and the problem of conflicting connotations suggest something of the state of this shift in theological reflection. It is still new; many of the problems involved have not yet been thought through; and there is still no consensus about some basic and important issues.

Throughout this book the term "local theology" will be the one used most commonly. While this does present certain problems in translation, there are advantages to recommend it. First, it allows the overtone of the "local church" to be sounded. Second, as we shall see, not all attempts in theology are equally sensitive to the context; indeed, they can take quite different approaches to it. This allows keeping the term "contextual" for those theologies that show greater sensitivity to context. And finally, it avoids undue use of neologisms.

THE VARIETIES OF LOCAL THEOLOGY

In the large number of theological reflections now available to wider audiences (not even beginning to take into account those that are never written down or published), one can easily become disheartened about how to approach them, let alone engage in some kind of evaluation. What follows is an attempt to provide one kind of way of looking at the variety of local theologies emerging. Different classifying principles could be used. The one employed here rests upon how each approach relates to its cultural context.

Three broad categories or types are suggested here: translation, adaptation, and contextual approaches. These approaches suggest not only a relation between a cultural context and theology, but also something about the relation between theology and the community in which it takes place.

TRANSLATION MODELS

The three approaches just suggested can be understood as models for engaging in local theology, a concept now familiar in theological circles.[7] "Model" suggests not only a procedure for engaging in theological reflection, but also some specific interests or principles that help to guide the use of the procedure.

The most common model for local theology has been what could be called a translation model, which sees the task of local theology as one that calls for a two-step procedure. In the first step, one frees the Christian message as much as possible from its previous cultural accretions. In so doing, the data of revelation are allowed to stand freely and be prepared for the second step of the procedure, namely, translation into a new situation. An underlying image directing this procedure is one of kernel and husk: the basic Christian revelation is the kernel; the previous cultural settings in which it has been incarnated constitute the husk. The kernel has to be hulled time and again, as it were, to allow it to be translated into new cultural contexts.

The translation model has often been utilized in Christian history. In the past century in Europe and North America, from Harnack onward, one has heard calls for the "de-Hellenization" of Western Christianity, by which is meant a removal of Greek categories from the biblical revelation. The guidelines for liturgical renewal among Roman Catholics following the Vatican Council are directed by a translation approach: taking the basic Roman liturgy and adapting it to local custom in those matters not deemed "essential" to the rites. In many Protestant settings, the continuing efforts to remain faithful to biblical teaching have prompted the use of translation models in new and different settings.

Notable among these has been the "dynamic-equivalence" method of Bible translation, whereby biblical imagery is first translated into concepts, the equivalents of which are then sought in the local language. These concepts are then translated into imagery specific to the culture. For example, in cultures that do not know sheep or shepherds, an attempt is made to discern the theological concepts conveyed by the sheep imagery, in order to find out how the same concepts might be conveyed in the new culture, albeit with different imagery. Charles Kraft has suggested that the dynamic-equivalence approach might be extended beyond Bible translation to become a theological procedure.[8]

Translation models are generally the first kind of model to be used in pastoral settings, because pastoral urgency demands some kind of adaptation to local circumstances in ritual, in catechesis, and in the rendering of significant texts into local languages. The basic principle behind the translation model would begin with the church tradition and adapt it to a local cultural setting. It calls in many ways for more familiarity with what has been done in the church tradition than what is done in the local cultural setting. For that reason it can be done by persons foreign to the local setting, thereby allowing for some initial missionary adaptation to the local culture. Older forms and music can be adapted to accommodate or include local custom and music in liturgy; linguistic equivalents for great theological categories (grace, salvation, sin, justification) can be sought in local languages. An immediate and pressing pastoral need is met, whereby Christianity is allowed to be incarnated in some measure in the local context.

But while translation models provide for some immediate adaptation to local circumstances, they manifest two major weaknesses, which gradually become more evident over the longer term. Both of these weaknesses have to do with how these models understand culture.

The first of these major weaknesses is a positivist understanding of culture. This approach assumes that patterns in a culture are quickly decoded and understood by foreigners. Thus in making decisions about translation, the missionary, the theologian, the liturgist, the Bible translator do a cultural analysis to a given point, but thereafter it comes to an end. Cultural analysis is done not on the terms of the culture investigated, but only to find parallels with patterns in previously contextualized Christianity. Questions are rarely asked as to whether there really are such parallels, whether the parallels have the same place of significance in the new culture, or whether other more significant patterns might better be drawn upon. More attention is given to the surface patterns of a culture than to its deeper meanings or to the inter- connections between different cultural patterns.

For example, after the call to renewal in liturgy among Roman Catholics, some expatriate pastors in Zambia decided to use drums rather than bells for summoning the people to services, since bells were considered European ac- cretions. They met great resistance among local people, since the drums which they used were associated with particularly erotic dances in the minds of the local Christians. Thus, while the principle of drums rather than bells may have been a good one, the cultural analysis did not go far enough to reveal another important set of meanings.

What this points out is the importance of taking the culture much more seriously than is the case in translation models. The translation model as- sumes that there is a direct equivalent in the local culture for the cultural pattern coming from another church setting.

The second major weakness of the translation approach is the underlying kernel-and-husk theory. It assumes, ultimately, that biblical revelation, con- ciliar pronouncement, or magisterial statement occurs in some privileged, supracultural sphere, which allows for immediate translation into any given culture. Rarely, however, is any information given in such a cultural vacuum. A closer examination would show that kernel and cultural husk are given together, even in the Bible, and they come to have a profound effect on each other over a period of time. Rather than the kernel-and-husk image of an incarnate Christianity, which allows for a ready hulling to reveal the kernel of divine revelation, perhaps the image of an onion would be more appropriate: the kernel and husk are intimately bound together.

Many theological problems, when pursued, reveal this dilemma. Mention was made above of the common eucharistic problem: Do bread and wine constitute essentials (kernel) or accidentals (husk) in the celebration of the Eucharist? Different Christian groups are answering this question in dif- ferent ways. If one takes one line of analysis, the Lord Jesus Christ took the staples of his culture and sanctified them; we, in turn, should do the same with the staples in the respective cultures. Many protestant denominations have followed this line. On the other hand, the Eucharist is the prime symbol of Christian unity; hence the elements that make that union possible should be the same everywhere. And historically, divergence from the use of those elements (e.g., the use of water instead of wine by some early Gnostic sects) has been found only among heterodox groups. Following this line of analysis, the elements of bread and wine should be the same everywhere. This line of analysis has been pursued in official Roman Catholic circles.

How is one to decide? And equally important, who is to decide? The strength of the translation model is its concern to remain faithful to the received tradition of Christian faith. But without a more fundamental encounter with the new culture, that faith can never become incarnate. It remains an alien voice within the culture. It needs to engage in a more fundamental encounter between Christianity as it has been elsewhere, and the culture in question.

A more fundamental encounter takes a good deal of time, and often pastoral urgency does not permit that luxury. Translation approaches are often necessary in the first instance. But in the long run, such a local theology can be called contextual only in a limited sense.

ADAPTATION MODELS

A second kind of approach is found in what might be called adaptation models. These models realize some of the difficulties and long-term weaknesses of the translation models, and seek a more fundamental encounter between Christianity and culture.

Often the adaptation models appear in a second stage of development of a local theology. They try to take the local culture much more seriously. There are three adaptation models that are used quite commonly.

In the first model, expatriates in consort with local leaders will try to develop an explicit philosophy or picture of the world-view of the culture. This picture that develops will be parallel either to philosophical models or to cultural anthropological descriptions used in Western theologies as a basis for developing a theology. Placide Tempels' *Bantu Philosophy*, first published in 1944 from his experience in the Belgian Congo, is an early and good example of this approach. In this book Tempels takes the then prevalent Neo-Thomistic philosophical framework and redevelops it with equivalent categories from Bantu peoples. The understanding was that this could form the basis for a sub-Saharan Christian theology much as Neo-Thomism had formed the basis for a European theology.[9]

In subsequent years this method was refined. In some places (this has happened in southern Peru and in northern Papua New Guinea[10]) local leaders are trained to use Western categories to give expression to the factors shaping the world-view of their people. In some instances (this has happened among an Amazonian people in Bolivia) the local leaders felt that this helped them to come to understand their own culture more profoundly.[11] In other instances local leaders are trained in Western educational centers and themselves set about creating such philosophical models, drawing upon local cultural materials. The early work of Tanzanian theologian Charles Nyamiti is an example of this. He called for the use of local materials to construct a philosophical system parallel to those Neo-Thomist ones he had learned at the University of Louvain.[12]

This kind of adaptation approach has some obvious strengths. Especially when wielded in the hands of local leaders, it can quickly help to achieve the twin goals of some authenticity in the local culture and respectability in Western church circles. The theology that emerges from such a model is replete with the categories, names, and concerns of a local culture, yet looks like Western theology and is relatively easily understood by Westerners. Moreover, it makes dialogue between North Atlantic and other churches much easier, since fundamentally similar frameworks are in use. It can give younger churches a sense of equal status with the older, more established churches.

But the weaknesses begin to appear as well. The basic problem is this: the adaptation model presented here presumes a method in theology whereby an articulated philosophical foundation forms the basis for a systematic theology. This method of understanding what constitutes genuine theology derives from the thirteenth century in the West, and as such has been an important though limited approach to Christian theology. It is a theology addressed principally to the academy. However, church and academy are not coextensive institutions, serving the same communities. While such a theology presents particular strengths in dealing with problems such as secularization, science and religion, and the relation of theology to other forms of knowledge, it has difficulty explaining the role of local communities in theological process. This is probably why so many local leaders continue to experience difficulty in trying to elicit a theology from a community; we have either forgotten how or find the results to be "unscientific," that is, not yielding the kind of sure knowledge we are used to seeking.

Thus this adaptation approach does take the culture more seriously than do translation approaches, but often will try to force cultural data into foreign categories. Many Asian cultures can deal with contradictory data in a conjunctive (both/and) fashion that to Westerners, with their disjunctive (either/or) modes of thought, seems dangerously relativistic. Must Asia bow to these Western considerations? The problems of this kind of adaptation approach are found most often among Roman Catholics who, perhaps more than most Protestants, have relied on explicit philosophical frameworks. The parallel problem in Protestant (especially Calvinist) communities is the concept of the "New Testament church" as the fundamental philosophical framework. Contemporary biblical exegesis has shown that there is no unified New Testament church, except in the minds of later Christians. The New Testament reveals to us a variety of different kinds of communities, animated by different christologies and engaging in a variety of church orders.

While such a more biblical approach assures a greater fidelity to New Testament witnesses, how that New Testament church is understood often owes more to twentieth-century (or sixteenth-century) Christianity than to the first-century variety. It also assumes that the New Testament somehow itself stands above culture, and does not witness to differing cultural settings in the Mediterranean basin of the first century.

There is a third kind of adaptation approach, which does not rely on philosophical models from the West, or upon Reformation concepts about the early church. Pope Paul VI, in an address to the African bishops assembled in Kampala, Uganda, in 1969 eloquently and succinctly presented this kind of adaptation approach:

> The expression, that is, the language and mode of manifesting this one Faith, may be manifold; hence, it may be original, suited to the tongue, the style, the genius, and the culture, of the one who professes this one Faith. From this point of view, a certain pluralism is not only legitimate, but desirable. An adaptation of the Christian life in the fields of pastoral, ritual, didactic and spiritual activities is not only possible, it is even favoured by the Church. The liturgical renewal is a living example of this. And in this sense you may, and you must, have an African Christianity. Indeed, you possess human values and characteristic forms of culture which can rise up to perfection such as to find in Christianity, and for Christianity, a true superior fulness, and prove to be capable of a richness of expression all its own, and genuinely African. This may take time. It will require that your African soul become imbued to its depths with the secret charisms of Christianity, so that these charisms may then overflow freely, in beauty and wisdom, in the true African manner.[13]

Vincent Donovan, in his account of evangelization efforts among the Masai in East Africa, makes something of the same point.[14] Here the approach is not one of taking a philosophical framework as a grid for understanding another culture, but a different kind of adaptation approach. Here the method is one of planting the seed of faith and allowing it to interact with the native soil, leading to a new flowering of Christianity, faithful both to the local culture and to the apostolic faith. Paul VI and Donovan would no doubt have seen the process happening somewhat differently, but the fundamental principle is the same.

The obvious strength of this approach is that it takes the local culture, with its own categories, much more seriously than any of the other approaches examined thus far. It is willing to take the time needed to permit this kind of development. It tries to respect both the integrity of the apostolic tradition and the traditions of the local culture. In ideal circumstances it should allow for the development of a theology that is not only local, but deeply contextual.

The weakness of this kind of adaptation approach is that rarely, if ever, are those ideal circumstances present. Except in those instances where there has never been any contact with Christians, certain patterns of Christianity are already lodged in the culture, for better or for worse. Over a period of time some of these cultural patterns have come to be associated with the fundamentals of Christianity. Thus the only place where one can see the Tridentine Mass still celebrated on a widespread basis is in the cities of the People's Republic of China. Latin hymnody is more readily heard today in Nigeria than in its home in western Europe. Moreover, rarely are Christians living in such isolated circumstances that such a development can come about without conflicting elements from both inside and outside the culture. Worldwide communication has invaded all but the most isolated of cultures. An image repeated in many cultures of the world comes from Latin America: an elderly Quechua man, riding along on his donkey on a trail in northern Peru, with a transistor radio clasped to his ear. He does not understand the Spanish being broadcast, but the noises and the status of having such a contraption are changing his life. Even within a culture, the ideal circumstances assume that there is never a coercive exercise of power whereby pathways of meaning come to be determined. And this is not only a problem in churches with centralized authority. Those in free-church traditions in Protestant Christianity know that, even without the centralized authority of Roman Catholic Christianity, local members of a community will come to exercise power by seizing it.

This model presents an ideal that is almost always skewed by human circumstances. It assumes that the Holy Spirit works in a community in ways basically disengaged from normal human events. It has a stronger theology of unfettered grace than of human sin.

With this adaptation model, we are coming close to the third set of models that we wish to consider, the contextual models. As will become evident, these models share much with this last kind of adaptation model, but try to address more directly the interaction between received apostolic faith and traditions of culture.

CONTEXTUAL MODELS

The third set of models to be investigated here shows a close relation to the adaptation models especially. The differences are more subtle than those between translation and adaptation models. The contextual models, as the name implies, concentrate more directly on the cultural context in which Christianity takes root and receives expression. Whereas the adaptation models continue to emphasize somewhat more the received faith, contextual models begin their reflection with the cultural context. Contextual models are seen increasingly as embodying the ideals of what local theology is to be about, even though the working out of those ideals often proves difficult in the practice.

Two kinds of contextual models will be examined here. They differ principally in how they read the dynamics and dominant needs of their social contexts. In terms of dynamics, both models recognize that almost all cultures in the world undergo continuing social change. To base a local theology entirely upon patterns in traditional religion found in rural West Africa or in the island cultures of the South Pacific ignores some basic facts: the world population is becoming more and more urban. The median age of most of the Third World population is less than twenty. These two factors of urbanization and youthful population indicate that much of that traditional religion and culture is being forgotten or not even learned. In many areas of the world, cultures are not only subjected to rapid social change due to technology and urbanization, but are also subjected to oppression, poverty, and hunger. Change is not only rapid, it is oppressive and dehumanizing.

The two kinds of contextual models to be considered here emphasize either one or the other of these basic social factors. Those concerned with cultural identity have been called (at least in Africa and among the Ecumenical Association of Third World Theologians) "ethnographic approaches"; those concentrating on oppression and social ills, the need for social change, "liberation approaches."

If the social concerns of human communities can be grouped around concerns for identity and for social change, the ethnographic approaches are particularly concerned with identity. They often become evident in the final stages of colonialism or in the reassertion of an identity and dignity that has been denied them. *Négritude* in western Africa, Black Power in the United States and southern Africa, *la raza* among Chicanos in the United States—all are examples of the need to reconstruct an identity that has been denied or considered inferior. Issues of identity are not always on racial lines; women around the world are struggling to understand themselves in their own right, and not be satisfied with the identity given them by men. In countries until recently controlled by North Atlantic nations, the need to forge nationhood out of diverse peoples, to create supratribal identities and loyalties has also been a task for this kind of theology. And finally, maintaining some semblance of traditional family connection and ritual in the midst of dislocation, for refugees or for newly urbanized peoples, becomes the paramount task in many areas.

The difference between these concerns and those of the adaptation approaches is that a local theology begins with the needs of a people in a concrete place, and from there moves to the traditions of faith. How is a Haitian refugee to live in New York City? Or a Croatian immigrant worker in Berlin? How will an Amazonian Indian live in the *favelas* of São Paulo? And what will those left behind in villages in the New Guinea highlands do as their children migrate to Port Moresby? Local theologies of the ethnographic variety of contextual approach strive to answer questions of identity especially. Their particular strength lies in beginning with the questions that the people themselves have—not those posed immediately by other Christian churches or those necessary for a systematic understanding of faith. In other words,

Questions of the people

they try to initiate a dialogue with Christian tradition whereby that tradition can address questions genuinely posed by the local circumstances, rather than only those questions that the Christian tradition has treated in the past. The small Christian community movement has been a vehicle in many parts of the world for this theological reflection leading to a theology enhancing the identity of a local community.

What are the weaknesses of the ethnographic approach? A number can be mentioned. First, the development of a contextual local theology is often set out as a project, but even more often not carried beyond the first couple of steps. Thus problems may be identified, questions may be addressed to the Christian faith as found in other cultural traditions, but there has not been time to continue the dialogue. Second, the ethnographic approach, in its concern with identity and stability, can often overlook the conflictual factors in its environment for the sake of maintaining harmony and peace. It can become a conservative force in situations where change is called for. Third, in its close analysis of traditional factors shaping the life of a culture, the ethnographic approach can become prey to a cultural romanticism, unable to see the sin in its own historical experience. It cannot remain outside the often vigorous dialogue that needs to take place with gospel values as they have been experienced in other cultures. Dealing with this problem can create enormous difficulties. For example, the taking of the heads of one's enemies in battle provided much of the bonding symbolism among the Asmat people in Irian Jaya. When this was forbidden, the culture disintegrated rapidly. How does one deal with a situation wherein the principles maintaining the integrity of the culture come into what seems to be direct conflict with the gospel? Fourth, inasmuch as good and workable models of cultural analysis are still being developed, much of the cultural analysis can now be done only by experts, thereby excluding to a great extent precisely those who need to be involved in the process: the communities themselves.

These weaknesses of the ethnographic approach appear to be formidable. Some of them have emerged out of the struggle to create a contextual and a local theology along lines of identity. Yet when a close working dialectic between gospel traditions and local cultural traditions is maintained, many of these difficulties can be overcome. No other approach takes the problems of identity as seriously as does the ethnographic approach. In view of its great importance for human community, it remains an important form of local theology.

Liberation approaches, on the other hand, concentrate especially upon the dynamics of social change in human societies. In view of the fact that so many cultures are being subjected to social change, or are being denied necessary change through patterns of political, economic, and social oppression, it is not surprising that liberation approaches are probably the most common form of contextual model in the world today. They are associated especially with Latin America, but they can be found wherever Christians are experiencing political, economic, and social oppression. The focus or emphasis may be different from region to region, but certain of the dynamics are parallel.

If ethnographic models look to issues of identity and continuity, liberation models concentrate on social change and discontinuity. Put theologically, liberation models are keenly concerned with salvation. Liberation models analyze the lived experience of a people to uncover the forces of oppression, struggle, violence, and power. They concentrate on the conflictual elements oppressing a community or tearing it apart. In the midst of grinding poverty, political violence, deprivation of rights, discrimination, and hunger, Christians move from social analysis to finding echoes in the biblical witness in order to understand the struggle in which they are engaged or to find direction for the future. Liberation models concentrate on the need for change.

So much has been written about liberation theology that it need not be set out in detail here. Even more of what is important about liberation models never appears in print. It remains in the songs, in the Bible reflection groups, in the hearts of oppressed people. The special strength of liberation models has been what can happen when the realities of a people are genuinely and intimately coupled with the saving word of God. The energies that are released, the bonds of community and of hope that are forged, the insight into the divine revelation received and shared have already enriched the larger Christian community immensely and have challenged the older churches to a more faithful witness.

As in any model, there are shortcomings evident in the liberation approaches as well. Often they are better at hearing the cries of the people than at listening to the biblical witness or to the testimonies of other churches. The problem of one of the most powerful tools for social analysis, the Marxist model, being so directly tied to antireligious and oppressive societies historically, has not yet been adequately resolved. The early disdain for the religion of the people, often seen as superstitious and enslaving, has been gradually resolved. The possibility of reflecting only after action has been taken, rather than making reflection a basis for action, remains an abiding temptation. The too close concentration on ill and the inability to see intermediate manifestations of grace can also be a problem. Safeguarding the intensity of struggle from the pitfalls of a fanatic apocalypticism becomes problematic in desperate situations, often with the result that armed violence comes to pose itself as the only answer.

The potential shortcomings of liberation approaches are well known and have been documented by liberation theology's friends and by its opponents. But to note shortcomings alongside strengths of any human undertaking is simply to be realistic. Liberation theologies are a major force, if not the major force, in contextual models of theologies today. Their ability to speak the language of Christian communities attests to their power and importance.

In summary, a diverse number of models can be grouped together as attempts at constructing local theologies: translation models, adaptation

summary

models, contextual models. Translation models and some adaptation models are concerned in the first instance with the transmission of faith; some adaptation models and the contextual models are concerned in the first instance with the context into which the apostolic faith is received. Given the circumstances in which a community finds itself, one or other model may be the more useful at a given time. My own reading would suggest, however, that contextual models are the most important and enduring in the long run. It will be on those models that the rest of this book concentrates. Translation and adaptation models raise important theological questions as well; but all of these questions eventually come together in a consideration of contextual models.

With this, we turn to another question important for a preliminary consideration of local theologies: Who is engaged in developing local theologies? This is an important question because the author of a theology says something about the nature and purpose of that theology. Out of this should emerge a working definition of local theology that will take into account the concerns of a genuinely contextual theology.

WHO IS A LOCAL THEOLOGIAN?

The theology that is emerging out of new contexts is engaging the energies of more than professional theologians. Liberation theologies in particular emphasize the role of the entire believing community in the development of a local theology. This same movement, however, has been raising questions about precisely who it is that brings about the development of a local theology. Behind that question lurks a second concern, namely, what are we to call theology itself? This section surveys some of the issues involved with these questions.

THE COMMUNITY AS THEOLOGIAN

The experience of those in the small Christian communities who have seen the insight and the power arising from the reflections of the people upon their experience and the Scriptures has prompted making the community itself the prime author of theology in local contexts. The Holy Spirit, working in and through the believing community, gives shape and expression to Christian experience. Some of these communities have taught us to read the Scriptures in a fresh way and have called the larger church back to a fidelity to the prophetic word of God. What happened over a period of years to the fishing village of Solentiname in Nicaragua is one of the best-known examples of this.[15]

The role of the community in developing theology reminds us also for whom theology is, in the first instance, intended: the community itself, to enhance its own self-understanding. The experience of the development of this kind of theology, especially in liberation models, has prompted others to define theology as the emancipatory praxis freeing an oppressed people. Theology then becomes more than words; it becomes also a pedagogical process liberating consciousness and inciting to action.

If one considers the concrete situation and the expression of faith in situations of oppression, it is hard not to agree with such a contention about the community as author of local theology. Theology is certainly intended for a community and is not meant to remain the property of a theologian class. The expression of faith in theology should make a difference in people's lives; otherwise it is a mere beating of the air. Reflection for its own sake may lead to contemplation, but contemplation should lead to action as well.

Understanding the role of the community in the development of theology shows how the poor become the subjects of their own history. It allows us to understand the special preference the God of Israel, the God of Jesus Christ, has had for the poor in their understanding of the Good News. Through the activity of those communities of the poor on virtually every continent, the whole Christian church has been profoundly enriched.

Any conception of what is local theology and who brings it about needs to be carefully balanced with a variety of factors. Not everything any community says or does can be called theology: otherwise theology itself becomes an empty concept. The emphasis on the role of the community as theologian has been an important one in correcting the idea that only professional theologians could engage in theological reflection.

In many instances it is helpful to make a distinction between the role of the whole community of faith, whose experience is the indispensable source of theology, and whose acceptance of a theology is an important guarantor of its authenticity, and the role of smaller groups within the community who actually give shape to that theology. In other words, the role of the whole community is often one of raising the questions, of providing the experience of having lived with those questions and struggled with different answers, and of recognizing which solutions are indeed genuine, authentic, and commensurate with their experience. The poet, the prophet, the teacher, those experienced with other communities may be among those who give leadership to the actual shaping into words of the response in faith. Gifted individuals, within the community and working on its behalf, give shape to the response, which then in turn is accepted or not by the community. Looked at in this way, local theologies can thereby more easily avoid the romanticist fallacy, common among folklorists of the early nineteenth century, who saw whole communities actually composing folk songs and epics. More recent research into oral traditions indicates that it is individuals capturing the spirit of those communities who do the actual shaping. [16] This does not play down the important role of those communities; it only puts it in a clearer context.

In sum, then, the community is a key source for theology's development and expressions, but to call it a theologian in the narrow sense of authorship is inaccurate. Significant members within the community, often working as a group, give voice to the theology of the community. Being a theologian is a gift, requiring a sensitivity to the context, an extraordinary capacity to listen, and an immersion in the Scriptures and the experience of other churches. It remains with the community, however, not only to initiate the theological process, but also to rejoin the process of theology in the act traditionally known as reception.[17]

THE ROLE OF THE PROFESSIONAL THEOLOGIAN

Ordinarily, when one asks the question of who engages in theology, it is the professionally trained theologian who comes to mind. Such a person, schooled in the traditions of a faith community, provides a unique and privileged resource for the shaping of the experience of a believing community.

The problem has been, however, that the requirements of time and energy for immersing oneself in those traditions have often led to a separation of the theologian from the experience of living communities. This problem becomes a hard one for a community to challenge because of the extensive knowledge a theologian needs of Scripture and subsequent Christian tradition, which takes years to develop and is in need of constant upgrading. Yet communities have instinctively felt that such isolation ultimately did not serve the purposes for which theology was intended. How is one to understand the role of the professional theologian in the development of local theologies?

To ignore the resources of the professional theologian is to prefer ignorance over knowledge. But to allow the professional theologian to dominate the development of a local theology seems to introduce a new hegemony into often already oppressed communities. In the development of local theologies, the professional theologian serves as an important resource, helping the community to clarify its own experience and to relate it to the experience of other communities past and present. Thus the professional theologian has an indispensable but limited role. The theologian cannot create a theology in isolation from the community's experience; but the community has need of the theologian's knowledge to ground its own experience within the Christian traditions of faith. In so doing, the theologian helps to create the bonds of mutual accountability between local and world church.

PROPHETS AND POETS IN LOCAL THEOLOGY

What about the prophetic dimension of the experience of a Christian community? Does not the voice of the prophet suffice for giving expression to the gospel in the community? When one hears the songs, reads the pamphlets, and witnesses the testimony of struggling Christians around the planet, one can honestly wonder whether or not more need be done by way of theology. Is not the voice of the prophet and the praxis of the prophetic community all we need?

The poets in the community, who can capture the rhythm and contour of the community's experience—cannot their work be considered a genuine local theology? Is not some of the more authentic theology, especially that which captures the imagination of the majority of people, to be found in their work rather than in theological monographs or church documents? What role does the poet play in capturing the soul of a community?

Both prophets and poets are essential to the theological process, but that process cannot be reduced to either one of them. Prophecy is often the beginning of theology, and it often exercises judgment on a theology that has developed or been accepted by a community. The poet has the task of capturing those symbols and metaphors which best give expression to the experience of a community. Because a theology is not simply any experience of a community, but that experience of believers coming into encounter with the Scriptures and the authentic experiences of other believing communities, past and present, more is needed. Theology and prophecy are not entirely the same thing. The task of a theology is to expand a prophetic insight in order to engage the full range of issues. Prophetic calls to faithfulness must be tested also on the touchstone of other churches' experience of the Spirit. By the same token, the validity of poetic insight has to be tested on more than aesthetic criteria or resonance with a community's experience. Were a community incapable of sin, this would not have to be the case.

All of this, again, is not to play down the role of the prophet or the poet. Rather, it is meant to help situate their tasks within the larger theological process.

OUTSIDERS AND INSIDERS IN LOCAL THEOLOGY

The intense experience of communities often leads them to question the role of outsiders in the shaping of their theologies. In many parts of the world, expatriates have for too long dominated local communities, keeping them (often unwittingly) in a dependent position. Anyone who has worked in another culture knows that parts of that culture will always remain mysterious. One can never know that culture as one does one's own. This has led many cross-cultural ministers to step back from the theological process in local communities, or to be asked to do so by those communities.

Despite the obvious and real problems of paternalism and colonialism, which have frequently marked the expatriate's presence in a culture, the expatriate's role in the development of local theologies has often been quite significant. One wonders if the liberation theologies and the small Christian communities could have developed as rapidly in Latin America without the help of those foreign religious leaders. The expatriate can also be the bearer of the lived experience of other communities, experience that can challenge and enrich a local community. Without the presence of outside experience, a local church runs the risk of turning in on itself, becoming self-satisfied with its own achievements. The expatriate, as an outsider, can sometimes hear things going on in a community not heard by a native member of that community.

In the same way, being a life-long member of a local community does not guarantee insight. One of the disappointments in many local communities has been that having locally born leadership does not guarantee its effectiveness. And local leadership with experience elsewhere often can disdain its own roots and become more oppressive than outsiders. This has sometimes happened with leadership educated outside the local context to the ideals of North Atlantic cultures.

Again, both the insider and the outsider are needed, but they need to be situated within a larger process. What all of this shows is that the task of the development of local theology cannot be committed to one individual or even to one group. The experience of a community can remain amorphous without spokespersons in the prophet and the poet. Yet there is no prophet or poet without a community. The professional theologian can provide essential links to the larger Christian tradition; but local theology has to be more than a mere repetition of that tradition. Outsiders bring important experience, but by themselves can come to exercise hegemony over the community. A rootedness in the community is essential for a local theology, but does not in itself guarantee insight.

All of this underlines how much the theology emerging in local contexts is a communal enterprise. It takes the work of many individuals and groups to be truly effective. This look at some of the individuals and groups is intended to help situate the various roles within that communal undertaking. It helps also to see how complex the development of local theologies is likely to be.

TOWARD DEFINITION OF LOCAL THEOLOGY

In light of all the things just discussed, is it possible to define more exactly just what is local theology? Obviously it is a complex process, aware of contexts, of histories, of the role of experience, of the need to encounter the traditions of faith in other believing communities. It is also obvious that contexts are complex, that histories can be variously read, that experience can be ambiguous, that the encounter in faith is often dimly understood.

But how do all of these factors interact? I would suggest that their relationship be seen as a dialectical one, using the notion of dialectic in a broad sense. Dialectic is to be understood as a continuing attention to first one factor, and then another, leading to an ever-expanding awareness of the role and interaction of each of these factors.

These factors can be seen as roots feeding the development and growth of a local theology. They must interact to produce the full and living reality. The three principal roots beneath the growth of local theology are gospel, church, and culture.

"Gospel" here means the Good News of Jesus Christ and the salvation that God has wrought through him. This includes, and reaches beyond, the proclamation of the Scriptures. This includes the worshiping context of the local community and the presence of its Lord there. It includes those aspects of the praxis of the community announcing the Good News. It includes that Word which missionaries find already active in the culture upon their arrival. It refers to the living presence of the saving Lord that is the foundation of the community, the spirit of the risen Lord guiding that community, the prophetic Spirit challenging the culture and the larger church.

But the gospel does not fall from the sky. Our faith is also a *fides ex auditu*, a faith we have heard from others. The gospel is always incarnate, incarnate in the reality of those who bring it to us, and incarnate in those who help us nurture the beginnings of faith. Church is a complex of those cultural patterns in which the gospel has taken on flesh, at once enmeshed in the local situation, extending through communities in our own time and in the past, and reaching out to the eschatological realization of the fullness of God's reign. Thus there is no local theology without the larger church, that concrete community of Christians, united through word and sacrament in the one Lord. The gospel without church does not come to its full realization; the church without gospel is a dead letter. Without church there is no integral incarnation of the gospel.

Culture is the concrete context in which this happens. It represents a way of life for a given time and place, replete with values, symbols, and meanings, reaching out with hopes and dreams, often struggling for a better world. Without a sensitivity to the cultural context, a church and its theology either become a vehicle for outside domination or lapse into docetism, as though its Lord never became flesh.

It takes the dynamic interaction of all three of these roots—gospel, church, culture—with all they entail about identity and change, to have the makings of local theology. Both living spirit and the network of traditions that make up living communities need to be taken into account. How this interaction of gospel, church, and culture takes place will be the subject of the next chapter.

2

Mapping A Local Theology

The previous chapter set out some of the questions that arise around the shift in perspective that has been going on in theology. This chapter continues that discussion, focusing more upon the relationships among some of the factors involved in the development of local theology.

Local theology was defined in the previous chapter as the dynamic interaction among gospel, church, and culture. That dynamic interaction was seen to be a dialectical one, moving back and forth among the various aspects of gospel, church, and culture. That movement raises questions that need to be addressed if local theology is to become an authentic and compelling voice in local churches.

The *gospel* raises questions about the community context. What is the quality of the community's praxis, its worship, its other forms of action? Who speaks for the community and brings to expression its response to the gospel? We saw that such a bringing to expression needs different actors involved in the theological process: the action and experience of the community itself; the prophet's sensitivity to the challenge of the gospel and the poet's sensitivity to the experience of the community; the professional theologian's knowledge of the experience of other churches; and the unique perspectives of both insiders and outsiders. All of these, guided by the presence of the Spirit within the community, need to come together for the Good News to be truly alive in the community.

The *church* raises questions about the relation of the local church to other churches, for instance, how does the local church interact with the experience of other Christian communities past and present? Put another way, the question of tradition is being raised here. While the sensitivity to the community-based nature of theology, rooted in concrete circumstances, is a hallmark of local theology, one must at the same time relate this to the larger circumstances of the church. Questions about the ascertaining of Christian identity, the normativeness of the Scriptures and subsequent Christian history, issues of orthodoxy—all must be faced in some theory of tradition, in order to test, affirm, and challenge the authenticity of the local church's response.

Gospel and church find themselves interacting within *culture,* the third root feeding into local theology. Questions both of identity and of social change come quickly to the fore: What is unique in this cultural configuration, and where is it to be located within the streams of social change? One has to have a way of perceiving culture, how it reacts to traditions both inside and coming from outside the culture, what are the resources for innovation and conservation, for coping with change and adjudicating dissonances arising from that change.

There is more than one set of answers possible to each of the questions arising from this interaction of gospel, church, and culture. Concrete circumstances may dictate one set of answers as being more helpful than another. This chapter will try to give attention in a broad fashion to the nature of those relationships among gospel, church, and culture. Subsequent chapters then take up some of the individual questions, about developing theories of culture and church tradition, as well as issues arising from the encounter of culture and church.

The way of giving attention to these relationships will be to present a map (see p. 25) charting their interactions. A map is not a recipe for successfully confecting local theology. To present such a recipe would presume that there was but one way to do it and, therefore, one paradigmatic set of cultural circumstances from which all other societies and cultures could be derived. A map functions in a somewhat different fashion. Its purpose is to allow anyone engaged in the development of local theologies to locate where his or her work stands relative to the entire enterprise. As we shall see, circumstances may require entry into the process of constructing local theologies at different places. And experience shows that local theologies tend to move by fits and starts, that they are carried out by persons who can work at it only part-time. More and more, local theology is pointing the way to a return to theology as an occasional enterprise, that is, one dictated by circumstances and immediate needs rather than the need for system-building.

The use of a map to chart the relationships in local theologies serves two important purposes: orientation and evaluation. The orientation function helps a community locate where it is in the overall process of developing a complete theology. The evaluation function, which builds upon the orientation function, helps to ascertain the strengths and weaknesses in what has been done: perhaps the theology has not dealt adequately with church tradition, or has inadequately reflected on the cultural context. It thus becomes easier to provide adjustments to the process and to find what it still must seek out to round out its own theological process.

The notion of mapping proposed here owes its origins to developments in field and systems theory, which has extended the concept of "map" into a variety of different areas.[1] In some ways its use here is intended to help a community learn to make its own map as it develops its theology. Each of the areas has been numbered, to aid in reference (see p. 25). The arrows indicate what would be an ideal flow in the process of constructing a local theology, realizing at the same time that ideal circumstances rarely prevail. Each of the areas will be discussed, with some of the attendant issues and problems raised by interactions in that area.

SPIRIT AND GOSPEL: THE COMMUNITY'S CONTEXT

One cannot speak of a community developing a local theology without its being filled with the Spirit and working under the power of the gospel. Unless the community accepts the free gift of God's grace, unless that community gathers for its own nourishment in word and sacrament, unless this experience of grace moves the community both into a praxis consonant with the gospel and into deeper communion with the other churches, we are not talking about an adequate locale for the expression and development of theology. It cannot be forgotten that theology is the work of God through a human, graced community.

Many of the small Christian communities have experienced again and again the power of the word of God as they gather to reflect upon the Scriptures. However, many of those, especially those part of the Catholic communion, have come to feel keenly the imbalance of receiving the freedom of the word of God but being denied eucharistic participation. The revised Code of Canon Law promulgated for Roman Catholics in 1983 speaks of the right of Christians to the sacraments. How will this right be met under the current disciplines governing clergy and the celebration of the Eucharist? In Roman Catholic ecclesial tradition, Eucharist has been central to nurturance of the Christian life. How to deal with an incompleteness, now to be defined as a deprivation of rights, is a vexing problem.[2]

Another way of speaking about this context created by the movement of the Spirit and by the power of the gospel in a community is that it creates a certain spirituality among the believers. A way to God is charted out, a pathway to deeper faith and commitment opens out before the community. This pathway provides the essential context within which the local theology is then developed. Theology has to be more than an acute analysis of culture and tradition. It is always done for the sake of a community.

That spirituality, lived out over a period of time, provides in itself a kind of history or heritage, which helps to orient the community. The remembering of God's favor and judgment helps the community, like the ancient Israelites, to make its decisions in the current situation.

That spirituality, lived out over a period of time, quite manifestly informs many local churches today. A theology so strongly suffused with this kind of spirituality not surprisingly begins to take on the contours of a wisdom theology, reminiscent of patristic times. This kind of theology will be explored in more detail in chapter 4. Suffice it to say here that perhaps the majority of theologies emerging in these new contexts favors the wisdom style

Spirit and Gospel: Shaping the Community Context

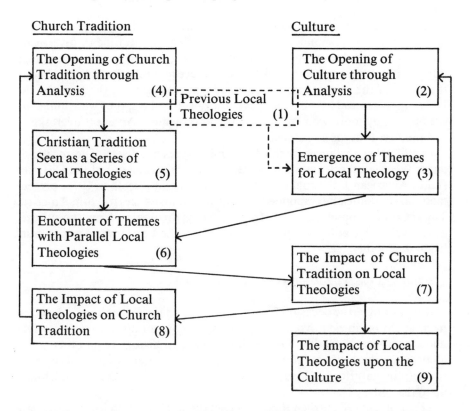

of theology *(sapientia)* over the sure-knowledge style *(scientia)* preferred in academic settings. In many ways these communities are taking important steps toward once again giving this form a special place of honor among churches of Western provenance. As will also be indicated in chapter 4, this phenomenon does not only hold for those contextual theologies of the ethnographic type. It can be fairly stated that liberation theologies are wisdom theologies turned outward to social conditions.

From the questions of the overall context in which local theology is developed, we turn to individual factors in the process of the interrelation of gospel, church, and culture.

THE DIFFICULTIES OF THE BEGINNING POINT

How does a local theology begin? Ordinary life rarely admits of those times when a clear and simple beginning can be made. One of three possibilities often occurs. In the first possibility, a community wishing to engage in the development of its theology will find itself confronted with other theologies already in place, of greater or less value to the community. For example, a religious leader in Nigeria interested in a more truly contextual liturgy finds a long-standing tradition and predilection for chant and Latin hymnody among the people.

At other times a different situation is present: an event overtakes a community and must be responded to immediately, leaving no time to investigate what might be the best point of departure for a local theology. For example, a number of years ago, a long lockout took place at a mine in Bolivia. Finally the wives of the miners gathered at the local cathedral on the Feast of the Holy Innocents and began a fast. Over the next few days, they were joined by the bishop, by more women, and finally also by men. An event overtakes a community. It needs a response.

In still other instances, a third possibility presents itself. The results of larger theological efforts, such as the documents arising out of the CELAM (Latin American Episcopal Conference) meeting in Puebla in 1979, present materials that must be responded to in local circumstances in Latin America. Thus beginning points can arise from previous theologies, from the culture, or from church tradition. All three of these need to be examined as potential beginning points.

PREVIOUS LOCAL THEOLOGIES (AREA I, SEE P. 25)

Rare would be the occasion for a community where its theological development could begin *de novo*. As any Christian community grows, it receives understandings of God and the action of God in history from others. The ability to begin the theological process within a community marks its coming to a certain maturity and assumes that it has been fed by other local theologies up to that time.

The problem arises when those received theologies are no longer adequate or even become an obstacle to a local church's development. This occurs especially when a community has wrapped up its identity in one particular theological expression. Examples of this are myriad. The experience of renewal after Vatican Council II presented one such occasion when many a local church found itself between a theology that had given it identity for years and the challenge coming from the council to move into new possibilities.

In many of the younger churches, which had sacrificed much to take on the local theology of its missionaries, the challenge to develop a local theology of its own has proved paradoxical, puzzling, and painful. Among many Asian Christians, their having become Christian caused painful separations from their families. Early in the twentieth century it was said in China that every time the church gained a convert, China lost a citizen. When people who have made a courageous decision to leave all things are then told that it is no longer necessary to give up veneration of ancestors and other customs, they often respond with utter incredulity.

In other situations the local theologies of the outsiders adopted in local communities became a special mark of distinction and identification. In parts of rural Africa the strange music and vesture of European Christianity bestowed a special status on those who came to Christianity, since the colonial message was one of Western things being superior to anything African. Thus even the Independent Churches would continue to employ Western vestments, music, and ritual to some degree. In the United States, as black people moved up the economic ladder, they often changed church affiliation accordingly, choosing liturgical traditions further and further away from the enthusiastic and thaumaturgical ways of the urban storefront or Holiness church. To be asked to rid African liturgy of its Western accoutrements, or to introduce gospel music into a middle-class, United States, black Episcopal or Roman Catholic church service has often met with resistance. The resistance often stemmed from a suspicion on the part of the people that this was another trick of the powerful whites to take away their access to a better economic world by keeping them clearly black (i.e., inferior). Calling it contextualization or inculturation was perceived as simply a way of concealing the actual motives of the white leadership.

An experience similar to these could be found in the early stages of the development of liberation theology in Latin America. Eager, committed Christians interested in conscientizing the poor often found themselves confronted with the massive, unmoving reality of the *religiosidad popular* of the villages and barrios. The first inclination of those committed Christians was to reject this reality. But to do so would have been to reject the actual context of their work. And so for many years thinkers had to ponder the relation between the religion expressed in the theology of liberation and the religion of processions, blessings, and favors.

How does one respond to these realities of previous local theologies? Ordinarily they are perceived as obstacles to the development of genuine local theologies. And obstacles they indeed are. But to try to remove them as one tries to remove an obstacle from a roadway may not be the best approach to dealing with the problem.

Previous local theologies can indeed be obstacles, but they are also powerful reminders. They remind us of what a local church has struggled with in the past. They remind current local leaders how their predecessors (or sometimes they themselves) may have created these obstacles as part of the conversion process. To admit persons in polygamous marriages in rural East Africa to Christian baptism will not sit well with those Christians who not long ago had to turn out their wives (or as women, were turned out) in order to embrace the fullness of Christian faith. We must be reminded of who created the obstacles in the first place. And we should not be surprised if those people see in this a new paternalistic ploy. Patience, a lot of listening, and careful dialogue will be necessary in order to lay the groundwork for possible removal of those previous local theologies.

Previous local theologies can not only be obstacles and reminders; they can also have revelatory aspects. Those parts of previous local theologies which are woven into the very warp and woof of local Christian identity need closer investigation. What really led to the formation of the *religiosidad popular?* What do these realities say about the patterns of need in the culture where the local church finds itself? In other instances, Christianity has often had its greatest initial success among the marginated people in a culture: Japanese intellectuals, Indian no-castes, slaves and wealthy women in the Roman empire. Often Christianity gives them a sense of worth and status denied them by the culture. What would "fully inculturate" mean to such people? What will the alternate source of their identity derive from? When asked to make this change by a leader who does not share their plight, the discrepancy is revealed in all its poignancy.

Previous local theologies may become obstacle, reminder, revelation. Strategies for dealing with those previous local theologies will have to keep in mind which factor is uppermost. What does that fiercely contested communion railing mean for the feuding parties in a church: a boundary that helps to establish identity or an obstacle to full participation? Perspectives become important: For whom is it important that previous local theologies change? Does the intransigence of the elders mean the driving out of the young? Or is it simply a matter of pride for the expatriate pastor?

THE OPENING OF CULTURE (AREA 2, SEE P. 25)

Ideally, for a genuinely contextual theology, the theological process should begin with the opening of culture, that long and careful listening to a culture to discover its principal values, needs, interests, directions, and symbols. Only in this way can the configurations of a culture become apparent of themselves, without simply responding to other kinds of needs extrinsic to the culture.

Important to preparing for this discipline of listening is to have a theory of culture with an attendant methodology for uncovering the realities of a culture. How to listen to culture is the subject of chapter 3, but a few things should be mentioned here.

There is certainly more than one way to go about analyzing a culture, as we shall see, and, depending upon what issues are before a community, different approaches can contribute to an analysis of a situation. Thus, if there are overriding economic issues, materialist approaches may be the most helpful. If there are issues of interaction in social roles, functionalist approaches may be the most useful. Semiotic approaches (to which much of chapter 3 is devoted) are thought to be the most helpful in terms of the symbolic development of a community.

Listening to the culture calls for what American anthropologist Clifford Geertz has termed the "thick description" of culture.[3] Only through trying to catch the sense of a culture holistically and with all its complexity will we be in the position to develop a truly responsive local theology.

An inherent danger for local theology in giving such attention to the question of culture is a certain cultural romanticism. Reminiscent of Enlightenment concepts of the natural person, this cultural romanticism will tend to see only good in a culture and to believe that the ideal state of the culture would be reached if it were left untouched by the outside world. To be sure, the more intimately acquainted anyone becomes with a culture and the more one sees its delicate balancing of forces, the more one can become entranced by its beauty. But to fall prey to this kind of romanticism assumes that there is no sin in the world, that people cannot be and are not often cruel to one another, and that culture contact is always a bad thing. One should remember that, if Christianity is alive at all in a situation, it will certainly change things about the culture. The Christian message, after all, is about change: repentance, salvation, and an eschatological reality to be realized. To think that Christianity will not change a situation is to rob the Christian message of its most important part.

Cultural romanticism on the part of Christian communities is often prompted by the lack of proper cultural sensitivity in the past. But to correct a lack of cultural sensitivity by creating an atmosphere inimical to any critique simply produces a new set of problems.

Beneath this approach suggested for understanding culture—listening, developing a thick description, finding the balance between respect of the culture and the need for change within culture—lies a theological position that is characteristic of many contextual theologies. When described from a christological point of view, it can be stated thus: the development of local theologies depends as much on finding Christ already active in the culture as it does on bringing Christ to the culture. The great respect for culture has a christological basis. It grows out of a belief that the risen Christ's salvific activity in bringing about the kingdom of God is already going on before our arrival. From a missionary perspective there would be no conversion if the grace of God had not preceded the missionary and opened the hearts of those who heard. It grows too out of those cautious reflections found in Vatican Council II's Declaration on the Relation of the Church to Non-Christian Religions, wherein the saving activity of God is discerned as active outside the visible Christian church.[4] What this stance means is that a local community must listen to its culture in order to complement its past experience of Christ. It must be able to recognize the signs of Christ's presence in its midst. How those signs are to be recognized the council only hints at indirectly. One of the ways suggested elsewhere in this book is through an understanding of Christ out of the wisdom tradition of the Bible. To see Christ as the Wisdom of God—certainly no new representation of the Lord—is a way of reading the divine presence in a culture that is already working out the saving activity.[5]

CULTURE TEXTS: THE EMERGENCE OF THEMES (AREA 3, SEE P. 25)

From the analysis of the culture comes the emergence of what we shall call culture texts, in which are contained themes that in turn are the cultural nucleus around which a local theology develops. Depending upon the mode of cultural analysis used and to the extent that emphasis is placed either on identity or on social change, the way these themes emerge will differ.

Which themes emerge seems to be determined by two principal factors: (1) a current and often urgent need in a culture; (2) the larger patterns that determine how things are done in a culture. Examples of the first kind can be found in many liberation theologies. Current needs often point to need for social change. Land and water rights, unemployment, life crises of death or separation—these all have a profound impact on a community. They need to be taken up into the larger pattern of meaning that the gospel can provide, not only to provide guidance for action, but also to integrate these jarring data into a larger framework of meaning. The symbolization of these activities becomes important. For example, the Sri Lankan theologian Tissa Balasuriya showed some years ago how the themes of self-giving and self-emptying of Christ in the Eucharist became symbols that helped to give shape to the social struggles of his people.[6] In a struggle over land ownership in the southern Philippines, a local community decided at one point henceforth to use only a single loaf at the Eucharist, rather than the traditional individual hosts. The single loaf represented their union with Christ and unity in struggle against the injustices of the absentee landowners. Or to use another, well-known example: the cross of Christ has long served Christians undergoing trial as a sign that could give shape to their own suffering.

Sometimes the symbols that draw together the concerns of a people do not represent so much a single need or crisis as a larger way of doing things. Roman Catholic theology has often looked at the world through the prism of a theology of creation. A bit of reflection shows why this would be the case. In a religious tradition concerned about inclusivity and the salvation of whole sectors of the population, one needs to reach as wide as creation itself. In cross-cultural theologies spanning quite diverse experiences, creation theologies are often the best way to proceed with developing a local theology. Wisdom theologies in Judaism were evidence of this already before the time of Christ. On the other hand, theologies more concerned with emphasizing the word of prophecy in the message of the New Testament have often turned to a more christocentric approach in theology, emphasizing salvation more than creation. Western neo-orthodox theology and many theologies of liberation have taken this tack. Again, where salvation is the central need and theme, it is not surprising that the Savior should take central place. In many places in the world where community and family form the basis of identity and relation to God, ecclesiology becomes the prism through which theology is seen. This makes sense in those areas where extended family is important and permeates every aspect of existence. Japan is a good example. There, where even the place of employment can be seen as an extension of the family, to begin one's theology around themes of the redeemed community seems natural. In all those areas of the world where the family is being disrupted by migration, it is also a likely candidate. In many parts of the world, ecclesiology or Christian community as a starting point for theological reflection is already taking its place along more traditional starting points of creation and redemption. Western theologians are less used to such a starting point; but such a starting point is becoming more common and is leading to a different organization of the great themes of Christian faith.

Not only the major themes but the forms of theology can be profoundly affected by cultural patterns. Not only is it a matter of how meaning is organized in a culture, but also how it is to be communicated. In much of the history of Christian theology, East and West, the written treatise or the commentary on another written text has been the most common medium for the communication of theology. But all this assumes the primacy of literacy, of access to written texts, and to a cultural assumption that such are important. Since theology was for a long time the preserve of the educated clergy, this was considered legitimate. But radio and television have made even those cultures with majority literacy less dependent upon written texts as the medium for communicating cultural meaning. And in other cultures in the world, while literacy may be widespread, it is of such recent origin that it still has no strong influence. Literacy may mix with other forms; one thinks of the tremendous distribution of comic books in East and South Asia, which mix pictures and text.

We certainly are not arguing against literacy, but the point we are making here is an important one: we cannot presume written texts—with all they in turn assume about argumentation—as the sole form for communicating cultural meaning, and therefore theology. Perhaps more African theology will be done via proverbs, which are important in communication in sub-Saharan cultures.[7] James Cone has already argued for the use of the spirituals and the blues as the medium for black theology in the United States.[8] The use of poetry in Japan, the *singsing* in Melanesia, movies and music among the young in the United States—these all suggest that local theologies will often reach to local media for the communication of religious meaning. This important question will be taken up again in chapter 4.

Movies

THE OPENING OF CHURCH TRADITION (AREA 4, SEE P. 25)

Parallel to the opening of culture is an opening of the church tradition. If church tradition is the beginning point of the development of a local theology, then one is most likely dealing with a translation model of local theology rather than a contextual one. As was indicated above, there are times when translation models are necessary because of reasons of pastoral urgency or because of events in the larger church. A traditional ritual gives the wrong message, and so an adaptation needs to take place. Or a movement in the larger church calls local communities to renewal and development, and this needs to be taken into the life of the local community. To the extent that such translations resonate with realities in the local church they can become effectively contextualized. And the ability of messages to come from other Christian communities is important to the catholicity of the church, to the communion among the churches (a matter to be taken up in chapter 5).

Even in those situations in which translation of theology is called for, how the church tradition is opened up to a local community is important. Too often this has been done in a positivist way through a surface reading of church texts. Often, too, it is done through the monocultural lenses of the expatriate leadership in a community, without reflection on how much they might have been westernizing a people as they Christianized them. For a young church, the weight of two millennia of Christian tradition is formidable, even monolithic. For churches used to relating to other churches in colonialist patterns of domination and submission, any utterance of the dominating churches comes as immutable law. For those Roman Catholics whose experience extends only to the uniformities of the Tridentine reforms and two centuries of strong centralized church authority, church tradition may seem to have been all cut from the same cloth.

Alongside the need for a theory of culture, it becomes obvious that there must be a theory of the role of tradition in communities. As long as one has but a single tradition with no outside interference, one can live with a tradition in a positivistic fashion. But once there are multiple traditions or conflicting interpretations of the same tradition, one must formulate a theory about the role of tradition in the community. The Enlightenment in Western Europe raised this question for Western Christianity in the seventeenth and eighteenth centuries, and it is now a question for Orthodox Christianity as well. Factors involved in shaping a theory of tradition will be explored in chapter 5.

TRADITION AS A SERIES OF LOCAL THEOLOGIES (AREA 5, SEE P. 25)

It is not surprising that contextual local theologies would see tradition as a series of local theologies, that is, theologies growing up in response to needs in certain contexts. A little reflection makes this obvious. Any catechist who has tried to explain to a religion class the complexities of Chalcedonian christology will realize that some of the Chalcedonian questions are no longer questions to many contemporary local churches, even though these may be normative for them. Yet those theologies that have survived down to the present time have survived for a reason: they expressed with some degree of adequacy the experience of believers. That gives them some measure of enduring validity for local communities today, as touchstones and sometimes as measuring rods for their own experience.

This contextual theological reflection commits itself to seeing the theological tradition passed on through the centuries as a series of local theologies. Such a procedural commitment, however, still leaves two important questions unanswered: (1) How shall we come to see the tradition as a series of local theologies? (2) What is the relative normative value of each of the theologies that emerges?

Chapter 4 takes up the first question, and suggests applying the sociology of knowledge to the history of Christian theology as a way to see the relation of context to the form and content of the theology which developed. The second question is of prime importance for every Christian church. All the churches have always accorded more normative value to the theologies of certain churches than to others. All Christians would give high normativeness to the churches of the New Testament. The major ecumenical councils of the first five centuries also hold a special place for most churches. The great confessions from the sixteenth century are important for Reformation Christianity, and magisterial and additional conciliar statements have played the same role in Roman Catholic Christianity. How does this way of reading the tradition mesh with seeing the tradition as a series of local theologies, particularly as historical research uncovers more of the contexts in which each of these first appeared? This question, so important both to the authenticity of the witness in the local church and to the catholicity of the larger church, will be addressed in chapter 5.

THE ENCOUNTER OF CHURCH TRADITION
AND LOCAL THEMES (AREA 6, SEE P. 25)

encounter

In the encounter of church tradition and local themes, the actual development of a local theology takes place. Local theologies in the church tradition are sought out that parallel the local theme or need, either in content, in context, in form, or in all three.

When liberation theology sought to clarify its christology in Latin America, it found kinship in some of the New Testament synoptic christologies, more so than in the Johannine and Pauline christologies, which have been the prime determinant of the larger tradition. Much of the post-Vatican II reform found patristic parallels in matters of liturgy, sacramental praxis, and church order as a way of developing new local theologies. As a result, much contemporary Western eucharistic theology sounds more like the eucharistic theology prior to the great theological debates on the Real Presence of the tenth century than it sounds like subsequent theology.

The seeking out of parallels in the tradition, the similar experience of other communities in similar contexts at other times helps to shape the newer local theologies in a number of important ways. First, it reduces to a significant degree the problems of paternalism. A local church has a better chance of approaching the tradition on an equal footing, inasmuch as a local church, according to Vatican Council II, can represent in itself the fullness of the church.[9] Second, this kind of parallelism allows for a more genuine encounter of the tradition with the local church, both to aid in the consolidation of their understanding of the reality of Christ, and to strengthen the challenge to fidelity in discipleship. And finally, the parallelism provides the possibility of a local church helping to expand the history of Christian reflection that makes up the tradition. The two latter points are the subjects of areas 7 and 8 on the chart.

THE IMPACT OF THE TRADITION ON LOCAL THEOLOGY (AREA 7, SEE P. 25)

For a local theology to become a Christian local theology, it must have a genuine encounter with the Christian tradition. Any theological formulation can be subject to human failing, to a less than complete fidelity to the message of Jesus. For this reason it needs to be tested against the experience of other Christian communities, both present and past.

The encounter can result in an affirmation of what is happening in the local church. It may be another manifestation, in slightly different form, of a recurring experience of the reality of Christ in a local community.

At the same time, the circumstances and experience of two communities are never exactly alike. These differences can serve as a spur and a challenge to the local church to think beyond the similarities to the differences. Sometimes a local church will find its closest parallel in Christian history with ambivalent or even heterodox movements. The response to poverty in the sprawling urban centers of many countries today can lead one close to the responses characteristic of Western medieval movements concerning poverty, both heterodox and orthodox. Elaine Pagels has pointed out that contemporary feminist experience can find parallels among some early heterodox Gnostic communities.[10] The results of these encounters may lead to a chastening of the response of the local community, or perhaps to a rethinking of the nature of the heterodoxy of those earlier communities.

The tradition has more than this monitoring effect upon the development of a local theology, however. It can make genuine contributions by urging the local community into reflecting on issues that had not occurred to the people or by pointing to implications that had not yet clearly arisen. The ministry of Jesus ended at the cross, a clear sign of failure in the human sphere. What will that say about the spirituality undergirding our present struggle against injustice? Religious communities, both Christian and non-Christian, have had to deal with the dilemma of purity of doctrine in a community of the elect versus more inclusive community that offers at least some measure of salvation to all. As a local community finds itself opting more for one or for the other of these possibilities, how shall it complement its activity?

THE IMPACT OF LOCAL THEOLOGY ON THE TRADITION (AREA 8, SEE P. 25)

Just as the tradition is necessary for the development of a local theology, so too local theologies are vital for the development of the tradition. By raising the questions they do, local theologies can remind us of parts of the tradition we have forgotten or have chosen to ignore. The struggles of contemporary poor Christians have helped to remind us all that the issues of rich and poor are the most commonly raised moral problems in the Gospels. The theme of justice has been resurrected by the experience of these communities into the awareness of many other communities. The reflection of feminist communities is making the larger church aware of how parts of the tradition were forgotten, skewed, and even suppressed, and need to be reconstructed or rehabilitated.

The experience of local communities can also remind us of the fallibility of parts of the tradition. Black communities in the United States and in South Africa remind us of long-prevailing church attitudes toward slavery, even from the most official instances. Reformation communities in the sixteenth century reminded the larger medieval church how far it had strayed from what could be called Christian practice.

Local communities can also aid the tradition in its development by their reflections. They can contribute to the resolution of dilemmas that other local churches may be feeling. African senses of divinity and grace may contribute to Western struggle with theism. The sense of extended family in the Philippines and the Orient may aid the United States and northern Europe in their problems with the nuclear family. Some of these contributions are only now beginning to take shape, but they bode well for the development of the tradition of the larger church.

THE IMPACT OF LOCAL THEOLOGY ON THE CULTURAL SITUATION (AREA 9, SEE P. 25)

Local theology, while most likely intended in the first instance for the community in which it develops, ultimately will have some impact on the cultural situation in which it was born. Unless there is a strong bifurcation between church and culture that makes the gap unbridgeable, the theology is bound to have an effect on the culture and on the questions that the culture will raise in the future.

As an example, the civil religion that binds Americans together despite the plurality of voluntary church associations could not have taken the form it has without the reflections of the New England divines in the prerevolutionary period. Their experience of deliverance in coming to the American colonies they interpreted as parallel to the deliverance of Moses out of Egypt. By extension, then, the American colonies became the Promised Land. How this fed the wounded self-esteem of persecuted immigrant populations as they, too, became Americans needs no documentation. How it also fed national policies of Manifest Destiny, Big Brother, and America's own colonial practices, unfortunately, needs no further documentation either. A powerful local theology had an impact of tremendous proportion on the culture.

In another way the covenant theology put forth by the Nederduitse Gereformeerde Kerk in South Africa also had a powerful impact on the peoples of that land, giving theological justification to apartheid.

The reason for making the point about how a local theology feeds back into the cultural setting is to show how the issues in area 9 help to continue the dialectical cycle of the developing of local theologies. If looked at in a linear fashion, this marks the beginning of the cycle again as the process of discerning the response to the present of Spirit and gospel in the community again takes on urgency.

OTHER ISSUES IN READING THE CHART

In any map or chart certain templates imposed upon it will give the familiar contours different relationships. Certain issues give different shapes to the relationships just discussed. Some issues of this kind in local theology need at least mention here, although they will come up again in subsequent chapters.

THE AUDIENCE OF LOCAL THEOLOGY

For whom is local theology intended? Who makes up its audience? A simple question, perhaps, but one which, unheeded, can create great difficulties. The question of audience affects the choice of themes, the procedures for development, and the criteria for judging its adequacy.

American theologian David Tracy has made a valuable contribution in distinguishing three "publics" for theology: academy, church, and society.[11] Theology, as it is intended for each of these groups, will take on different contours and will need to be subjected to different criteria of adequacy. Often debates about what is theology are confused by not carefully distinguishing the public for whom the theology is intended. In the local theologies under discussion here, failure to make these distinctions can also affect how the theology itself is developed.

One could say that perhaps most of the theology that gets written down and published is directed to the academy, either to professional theologians or to scholars in allied fields. This is not surprising, inasmuch as those who are professional, full-time theologians are generally the ones who have the time or can take the time to write a book. This is a legitimate and important form of theology. One cannot imagine, for example, Vatican Council II as having taken place without the historical research or the theological reflection of the academy. In facing issues of secularization, religion and science, and Christianity and global social problems, the work of the professional theologian is essential. For local theologies, the work done by professional theologians in helping better to understand local theologies of the past or in interpreting what is happening in the present is of inestimable value.

Much of what might be considered local theology today, however, probably would not be addressed to the academy. The criteria for intelligibility and cohesiveness are not always the same as they would be for the academy. The alliance between theologian and community is different, since a primary focus of the academic theologian is the community of professional theologians. This is not to disdain the contribution of theologians, but again merely to try to situate their contribution for the sake of avoiding confusion.

Local theologies are more often addressed to the local church and the larger church. Those emphasizing the consolidation of the identity of a Christian community would fall into this category particularly. One of the criteria for intelligibility here is certainly the correspondence between what is said and what is experienced. The clarity sought is especially one that will illumine the experience of the community.

Often local theologies will be intended for society as well, particularly when it is a matter of dealing with issues of social ill and the need for change. Part of that address to the world is an attempt of a community to explain its own stance to itself; it can also be an appeal to all people of goodwill to join in the pursuit of justice.

These categories of academy, church, and society are not mutually exclusive. The theology of the academy is most often also intended to aid the church in some way. What happens in a local community can become important for the deliberations in the academy. Both academy and church can and do address society's problems and issues. But there is a primary focus, and that focus will shape what counts for clarity, intelligibility, and good argument. When constructing a local theology, an awareness of who is the intended audience is of the utmost importance.

LOCAL THEOLOGY IN A UNIVERSAL CHURCH

Local theology is certainly not anything new to Christianity. But a direct awareness and pursuit of it is relatively recent for most Christian churches. For Roman Catholics, the stress on universality has been such that it makes it difficult to think about how locality and universality are to be related. Vatican Council II in its Dogmatic Constitution on the Church (*Lumen Gentium*) revived ancient thought on the local church without giving all the contours it would now take. But even the reflections there were not intended to diminish the importance of the universality and unity of the church of Christ.

The first question that would arise to anyone concerned about maintaining the oneness of the church and confronted with the bewildering array of human societies and cultures is: How local should theology become? For example, there are seven hundred language families in Papua New Guinea alone. Should each have a local theology? Or should each village in each language family have one? Or should there be more effort put into a theology that will bind the Melanesian church together? "Local church" in Melanesia will mean for Roman Catholics something different from its meaning for Baptists. How are we to make our way through this muddle?

No simple answer can be given to this question. Energies and resources will probably limit theologies being fully constructed on the level of a small community. Even posing the question in this way assumes that two communities, side by side, will have vastly different theologies.

The concern for local theology is not only about the distinctiveness that may arise, but also about the engagement of a larger number of Christians in the enterprise of theological reflection. Such engagement contributes much to what makes a theology local, even if the results look similar to what is happening elsewhere.

Part of the resolution of this question has to do with the age-old problem of the relation of the particular to the universal. As this affects the discussions here in terms of cultural particulars and universals, it will be touched upon again in the next chapter. In reflecting on this problem, it may be good to remember that figuring out what is universal can be as problematic as figuring out what is local.

FURTHER THINKING IN ECCLESIOLOGY

What is happening in local communities and being expressed in their local theologies will raise questions on how to think about the concept of church itself. This affects not only the relating of the various structural components of small Christian communities to bishops and to the total church. It also affects what we think theologically, what become important symbols, images, and metaphors for expressing the reality of the church. In gatherings of the World Council of Churches, it has been noted that unity will not come about simply through doctrinal agreement, but when an ecclesiology can be found in which the three hundred or so member churches can all find a home. The same issue is present for the development of local theologies.

How these new developments will shape our sense of ecclesiology remains to be seen. But already the point is raised that ecclesiology is going to be one of the major issues in the developing of local theologies—prominent as hermeneutics, modes of cultural analysis, and christology.

Many other issues could be taken up at this point. These, however, are ones looming largely in the minds of many involved in constructing local theologies. These issues, and others, will be addressed again in subsequent chapters.

3

The Study of Culture

start w/ culture

LISTENING TO A CULTURE

In ideal circumstances the process of constructing local theologies begins with a study of the culture, rather than with possible translations of the larger church tradition into the local circumstance. This method grows out of two considerations. The first is to avoid the continuance of paternalistic history in which outsiders, barely familiar with a culture, would make decisions about adaptation and what would be "best" for a local culture. While many would accept this assumption today, the actual practice of it, as we shall see, is nonetheless difficult. This paternalistic attitude prevailed (often unconsciously) not only among those who invaded the culture, but often also in the "indigenous leadership" left behind to govern. Hence situations arise where leaders from within the culture have become so alienated from the roots of their own culture, and so socialized into the invading culture, that the situation is often much worse than it was under expatriate leadership. Many local churches are recognizing that a leadership educated in universities outside the country does not always bring a cross-fertilization of new ideas, but sometimes results in a suppression of local ones. The alienating influence can often go further and reach absurd proportions. The image of Third World seminarians being taught from neo-scholastic manuals long abandoned by the Euramerican cultures for which they were originally intended is one of the most poignant and distressing of these situations.

The second consideration is more theological. To maintain the desired openness and sensitivity to a local situation, it was suggested that the prevailing mode of evangelization and church development should be one of finding Christ in the situation rather than concentrating on bringing Christ into the situation. Without such an attitude, based on the theology of the incarnation, one consistently runs the risk of introducing and maintaining Christianity as an alien body in a culture. The word of God never receives the opportunity to take root and bear fruit. What results in many instances are dual systems of belief, wherein the older system continues alongside Christianity, with each being selectively used by the people as needs arise. This is the case in many parts of Latin America and Africa today. The issue of dual systems is a complicated one, and will be taken up again in chapter 7.

Nor can one be satisfied with having listened once to a culture and then presuming that the contextualization of the church has been achieved. This would presume that the culture is an unchanging and static reality. In some parts of the world that have been part of Christian history for centuries, Christianity has come close to dying out because its theological expressions and symbolic performances have not continued to listen to cultural change. The situation of Christianity in France, once heralded as the "eldest daughter of the church," is a case in point.

Rather, there must be a clear commitment to listening as a point of departure for constructing local theologies, and a commitment to continue to listen; indeed, to develop what Raymond Facélina has called a "listening heart."[1] While we can affirm a principle of listening to a culture before trying to speak to it, those who have tried this process know how difficult it can be. A whole range of questions and problems present themselves almost immediately: (1) How does one listen in such a way as to hear Christ already present? (2) How, as a foreigner, does one grow in understanding a culture on its own terms, rather than forcing cultural realities into the foreigner's categories? (3) How, for a native of the culture, does one come to that kind of reflexive thought about one's own culture, particularly if one has never experienced the contrast of another culture? (4) How does a community bring its experience to expression in such a way that it can indeed become the fertile ground out of which a local theology grows?

These questions indicate some of the problems underlying a study of culture. The *first question,* hearing Christ in a culture, tells us something of the perspective with which we approach the enterprise. It is clear that any study of culture has a perspective and particular interest. The local theologian will not be concerned, at least in the first instance, with any and every conceivable factor of a culture that can be studied. Although many aspects come into the purview needed for local theology, some will predominate. Among those are the values of the culture, its sources of identity, the ills that consistently befall the culture, the modes of behavior and codes of conduct in the culture, the cultural ideals, and the sources of power in the culture. Thus those cultural realities that cluster around the theological concepts of creation, redemption, and community are of paramount importance for a theologian wishing to listen to a culture: (a) *Creation:* How does a culture see its organization and how are the organizing factors expressed in behavior? (b) *Redemption:* What are the ills from which the culture suffers and what remedies are proposed? (c) *Community:* What is the quality of life together and how is that way of life developed? This somewhat simple framework, on which we shall elaborate below, should indicate that some things will be of greater importance to a local theology than other things.

The *second question,* how does one grow in understanding of a foreign culture, arises from the role of the expatriate in comprehending the local culture. It is part of the larger problem of one's own ethnocentricity, namely, to what extent can a person ever fully understand someone else's culture? The turns of language, the infrequently invoked custom, the full freight of a metaphor—all of these can confound a foreigner, even one who has spent many years in a culture. In trying to analyze a culture, we tend to bring categories from our own culture and apply them to this situation, whether they fit or not. Sometimes when the situations are similar there is no great problem. Other times the result can be ludicrous or disastrous. Even the best intentioned person can misinterpret a cultural situation because of unconscious categories at work. This is heightened by the growing consensus among cultural anthropologists that there may not be as many cultural universals as we had once hoped, that perhaps more of the cultural universals are in processes and modes of relationship than in content.[2] In that case, what constitutes a fair reading of another culture? A lot of debate is still going on around the question of cross-cultural categories. Perhaps, for our purposes here, the simplest answer would be this: if the cultural description can be affirmed as true by a significant segment of the culture itself, and can be understood by a significant number of persons from other cultures, then the description can be considered valid.

The *third question*, how can one reflect fruitfully on one's own culture, raises yet another problem, namely, the extent to which members of a culture can adequately describe their own cultural processes. In cultural anthropology, this is known as the problem of native exegesis or emic analysis.[3] Put simply, the problem is twofold: Do members of a culture have enough perspective to describe their own culture objectively and analytically? And is a native description of a culture necessarily a true description of a culture? Thus few of us may be in a position to set forth the grammar of our own language, know why we cannot marry our third cousins, or be able to explain why we are sure that immigrant laborers seem lazy and inefficient. In our description of ourselves we overlook things that outsiders might consider important (they may consider it odd; we may consider it natural), or misunderstand relationships because of an inherited "common sense." Structuralists such as Claude Lévi-Strauss will go so far as to discount the value of native exegesis, particularly when it relates to the deep, unconscious structures that govern change and identity in a culture. Most anthropologists will balk at such an assumption, but may concede that outsiders can often have insights into a culture which natives cannot have.

Much debate continues to swirl about the question of native exegesis. For the purposes of local theology, the following might be said: native exegesis is important to listening to a culture and plays the leading role in the analysis of a culture. Yet for it to come to its full realization, it needs a dialectical relationship with the categories of more formal analysis within the culture and from other cultures. This will be necessary to help bring to the surface unconscious relationships between empirical realities, and to help expose ideological arrangements that obscure the genuine meanings in the culture.

The *fourth question*, how does a community become fertile ground for a local theology, presents yet another problem to the task of listening to a culture: the move from analysis to communication. It is one thing to propose a model whereby the dynamics of a culture can be analyzed; it is another to make the results available for development into a local theology by a community of believers. This is more than a question of what might be termed applied research. It has to do with the shift of semantics (the study of meaning) to pragmatics (the study of communication processes) in culture. A concern for local theology has to embrace both of these realities. Some semantic systems can become so formal (as in structuralism) as to be nearly unintelligible to all but initiates in the method. On the other hand, effective patterns of communication do not guarantee truth, as any student of advertising knows. A semantic analysis that cannot be opened to communication is of little use to local theology; a communication system which has no semantic boundaries or rules becomes open to misuse.

These four questions, then, raise four issues that have to be taken into consideration in any attempt to listen to a culture. They provide certain boundary stones on the terrain that we hope to map here. The next matter for consideration is the nature of the tools that we are to use in learning to listen to culture.

TOOLS FOR LISTENING TO CULTURE

When one begins to consider the variety of ways in which to listen to a culture, one is confronted with a number of different approaches to the study of culture. Indeed, the concept of culture itself is often a controverted one. As Kroeber and Kluckhohn pointed out as far back as 1952, there are many, many ways to define culture.[4] In the time since then, it seems that approaches to the field have only multiplied.

Many of the debates about the meaning of "culture" will not concern us directly here, although they will be present in oblique ways. The breadth or the specificity of the concept of culture, the relation of the concept of culture to the concept of society, and similar questions are germane to our search for ways of listening to human life in the constructing of local theologies. Before trying to define "culture," let us, first, consider some general characteristics that any cultural theory should have and second, review some cultural theories that could be appropriate for our task.

Hence what follows is not intended to be a complete overview of contemporary theories about culture or methods for investigating individual cultures. The reading of the contemporary scene in cultural anthropology will be selective and eclectic.

CULTURAL ANALYSIS FOR THEOLOGY: SOME GENERAL CHARACTERISTICS

Before looking at some of the theories and methods proposed for the study of culture, let us consider three characteristics desirable in any cultural analysis used for local theologies.

1.   First, any approach to a culture must be *holistic.* This means that it cannot concentrate solely on one part of a culture and exclude other parts from consideration. It cannot too quickly evaluate some parts of the culture as more important and others of no importance. It cannot be reductionist in such a way as to see one part of the culture as nothing but another manifestation of some more important part of the culture. Some examples and specific points may be of help here.

A common differentiation made in listening to a culture is one between "high" culture (explicit religious beliefs, art, oral and written literary expressions) and "popular" culture (folk traditions and practices). While such a differentiation is possible and may be in some instances useful, it is a dangerous one for someone interested in local theology to make. The high culture sometimes does not come close to including the phenomena and experience people would want to call religious. The history of liberation theology comes to mind here. In a second period of its development, it became evident that the exclusion of folk religion (*religiosidad popular*) from consideration in the building up of liberation theology was a mistake. Without understanding the folk religion of the peoples of Latin America, one did not know how the people coped with oppression over a period of centuries. One did not know what resources the people, who were after all the subjects of the liberation process, had for liberation. The first written and published attempts at liberation theology showed some of the elitism that they were engaged in fighting in theology.

Connected with this is a realization that religion is not an exclusively high-culture concept. Religion is as much a way of life as it is a view of life. Distinctions between theology, magic, and superstition may be valid in theology, but are questionable in anthropology. In the latter's perspective they all become differing manifestations of a single domain. Thus to discover religious experience in a culture, one cannot confine the investigation to stated religious beliefs and practices. There may be many other phenomena going on hidden from view, or not even considered religious. The latter fact is particularly important in secularized and antireligious cultures. The domed sports stadium is a site for much religious activity in the United States, as in China is the Great Hall of the People in Beijing. In some cultures, such as that of Confucian China, what we would call religion may be more difficult to locate; yet the phenomena of creation, integration, and sustaining of meaning continue.

Whatever approach to culture is used must keep this in mind as it seeks out the religious roots. If an approach does not consider religion at all, or sees it only as an epiphenomenon to be reduced to some other cultural pattern, or investigates only what the expatriate would consider to be religious, then it will not be particularly useful for developing local theologies.

2.   Second, any approach to culture must be able to address the forces that shape *identity* in a culture. As was noted earlier, two principal tasks of theology are to express the identity of a believing community and to help it deal with the social change that comes upon the community.

What makes us who we are, and how do we get that way? These two ques-

Identity

tions lie at the heart of the concern here. What gives distinctiveness to a group, what are the bonds of commonality, and what are the processes by which they are sustained constitute key categories to listen for in a culture. These categories often center around two considerations: group-boundary formation and world-view formation. In the first instance, identity is formed by marking the boundaries of the group (a "we" vs. a "they"). Transcultural psychologists have pointed out that this may be one of the most universally present categories in human cultures. Within those boundaries, once they have been set up, questions of differentiation begin (male/female, child/adult, initiated/uninitiated, married/unmarried, living/dead), which help to define the status and roles of individuals. Some cultures have highly differentiated group-boundary formations (small agriculture societies); others leave them quite vague (urban-industrial cultures). World-view formation may also be more or less complex, depending upon the amount of phenomena for which a culture needs to account, the variety of situations it must continually confront, and the extent to which the world-view must be a shared one. The extent of division of labor, which allows for world-view specialists (poets, priests, adepts) can also be a factor.

In the concerns for a local theology, the approach to a culture must be able to attend to these twin dimensions of identity formation: group-boundary and world-view.[5] They relate to one another and influence one another in a variety of ways, which can have important consequences for the style, the interests, and the content of local theologies.

Third, any approach to culture must be able to address the problem of *social change*. Many approaches to the study of culture have been criticized because they can account for stable situations, but find themselves unable to deal with the dynamics of change.[6] Some critics have even suggested that commitments to the status quo and the maintenance of current class relations is the main reason for this.[7] Whatever the case, it is clear that many approaches deal better with the question of identity than with that of social change.

Social change is often the reason why local theologies need developing in the first place. Received notions of what it means to be a Christian, accepted modes of Christian behavior, formulations about the relation of the Christian to God may all be called into question by the emergence of new circumstances or by awareness of social relationships not previously understood. The growth of liberation theology is perhaps the best example of this. The growing realization of the nature of oppressive conditions prompted new reflection on the gospel in the light of that realization. Certain questions took on new urgency, such as those about relations of Christians to political activity, to violence, to being poor.

Moreover, the shrinking of the world through telecommunications and an interdependent economy, the continuing urbanization of much of the world's population, and the restructuring of existence that comes with these facts make for a period of continuing rapid social change. How is one to live the Christian life in light of these realities? How is one to live when accepted forms of identity become less viable, are rejected by whole groups in the culture, or become of no use to the majority? In listening to a culture, especially to the ills that befall a culture, one has to be able to deal with social change—not as an aberration but as part of the dynamic of a world such as ours. Change sometimes brings improvement, not just deviation from the mean.

And so listening to a culture in the interests of local theology means being able to listen also for the dissonances that mark the advent or progression of change. These cannot be arbitrarily tuned out. There is often a tendency to do so out of concern for the stability of the community. Yet this very concern for stability may mask other, less worthy concerns, such as the stability of the listener's position in the community rather than the long-range well-being of the community itself.

Any theory used, then, must be able to take up these three concerns as part of its attempt to understand a given culture. These three—holism, identity, and social change—are of key importance to local theology because of the very tasks that local theology has most often to undertake in its service to the local community: integration, maintenance of stability, and transformation.

In the sections that follow, we shall outline what proved to be (for this writer, at least) some of the more useful approaches to listening to a culture. The presentations here will emphasize the incompleteness of any one approach as a total approach to culture. Some approaches work better for certain problems than for others. Within anthropology today, it is clearly recognized that no single theory commands the adherence of all. Human situations seem to be too diverse to permit such parsimony. At the same time, the presentations will try to indicate the areas of usefulness of these different theories for local theology. In so doing, it is hoped that it will be of service to those engaged in local communities in developing theology.

In some ways we are perhaps fortunate that no single approach has such overwhelming theoretical and descriptive power. Our task is, after all, one of listening to a culture; and listening entails a certain discipline. On the one hand, it is not merely a passive undertaking; listening is an involvement in an exchange. But at the same time listeners must not forget that they do not control the direction of the exchange. Listeners are called to follow the direction of the speaker, and to move more deeply into the speaker's reality. Listeners must be aware of the structures that inform their listening, and be able to recognize when those structures no longer adequately give form to what they are hearing. To grow in the understanding of a culture is to learn the ascesis of listening and to stand open to the transformations that can ensue from it.

FUNCTIONALIST APPROACHES TO CULTURE

Functionalist approaches to culture are probably the most common in the English-speaking world. The term "functionalist" covers a broad spectrum of approaches, which includes the structuralist-functionalism and social anthropology of British anthropologists, the sociology of Talcott Parsons in the United States, and followers of Emile Durkheim and Max Weber. Certainly it has been the principal approach taken in missiology and in much of the more ethnographic contextual theology that has been published.[8]

It is difficult to give a characterization of the theory that might bind such diverse areas together. Basically, functionalist approaches are concerned with how the various aspects of society are constituted and interrelate to form a cultural whole. They study the mechanisms whereby new data can be introduced into a society, and how society resolves the tensions these data create and how equilibrium is restored. Functionalist approaches share something of the pragmatic sense of the cultures of the Anglo-Saxon world where they have most flourished. These approaches emphasize common-sense explanations and see the task of the cultural whole as one that mediates difficulties which arise and provides means for getting things done.

It has been said that, in many ways, functionalism is more a method than a theory. Certainly no other anthropological approach so emphasizes careful field method and close empirical description. This is indeed one of functionalism's principal strengths: its attention to empirical detail in any cultural explanation. Yet this lack of clear theory does create problems. The common-sense explanations based upon empirical observation often turn out to be Anglo-Saxon common-sense, which may or may not be shared by the culture under investigation. The question has been raised whether Malinowski's Trobrianders were as pragmatic as he made them out to be, or whether this was simply what an Englishman was bound to see. Anglo-Saxon commitment to practical reason as the principal organizing factor in a culture can skew the reading of a culture where more symbolically oriented considerations direct most action. Complex relationships not found in Anglo-Saxon cultures (such as extended kinship systems) often will escape functionalist description. The antimetaphysical bias of much of functionalism also hampers its ability to deal with nonempirical phenomena. Thus much symbolic and mental behavior will be dealt with in Durkheimian fashion, that is, as mental reflections of social arrangements. In the same manner ostensibly nonpurposive behavior, such as ritual and magic, will also not be explained well.

A final difficulty often raised about a functionalist approach is its inability to deal with the phenomenon of change.[9] While it can excel in the elaboration of the aspects of identity of culture, it cannot deal as effectively with transformations in a culture.

Where and when are functionalist approaches most useful in constructing local theologies? Certainly the holistic concerns, the attention to context, and the concern for rich empirical detail are all things that local theologies should contain. To understand, one must learn to attend to detail. At the same time, we have noted that the functionalist approach does not deal as well with the symbolic materials and behavior, a decided interest also of local theologies.

Functionalist approaches are well suited to translation approaches in local theology. They have formed the basis for developing "functional substitutes," namely, the replacing of one ritual or myth or magical practice with an empirical correlate from the Christian tradition. As was noted in chapter 1, translation approaches are often the point where local theologies begin. But as time goes on, more contextual approaches need to replace these. Empirical correlates do not guarantee the same correlation on the nonempirical level, as many church leaders have found out. One could say that the use of functionalist approaches shares the strengths and weaknesses of translation models of local theology. What they gain in immediate application they lose in long-term depth. They have the advantage of practicality and a methodology that can be used rather easily by a large number of people. And indeed, practitioners of other approaches will employ some of the functionalist methodologies. Local theologies will no doubt have to share some of the same eclecticism.

ECOLOGICAL AND MATERIALIST APPROACHES TO CULTURE

Ecological and materialist approaches center their investigations on the relationship between society and its physical environment. Ecological approaches, such as that of Roy Rappaport, stress how certain cultural activities serve as homeostatic mechanisms to keep society in balance with its physical environment. Rappaport has investigated how ritual in particular is often related to this process.[10]

Materialist approaches, such as that of Marvin Harris, are more concerned with showing how the realities of the physical environment (climate, nutrition, production) shape and direct the cognitive dimensions of culture.[11] Materialist approaches overlap in many areas with Marxist approaches, which see the relationships of economic production as determinative of world-view and thought.

Certainly one of the main values of these kinds of approaches is to remind us that the configuration of world-view or of social relationship may not be arising solely from the nonmaterial dimension of culture. They are also helpful in explaining some choices that cultures make and some practices in which people engage that cannot be accounted for by more ideational approaches. Harris uses materialist methods to explain the role of cows in Hindu cultures, and his explanation is perhaps one of the more persuasive that have been offered.[12]

These approaches are also particularly helpful in dealing with sudden or major shifts in a culture. Often these shifts have to do with major changes in the relationships of economic production. Indeed shifts in these areas often attend shifts in world-view by populations. Of all the approaches presented here, ecological and materialist approaches are among the better of those dealing with issues of social change.

What these approaches gain in focus they tend to lose in expanse, however. Centering upon the relation of physical environment and the ideational dimension can make for much more rigorous methods of investigation, but at the same time it offers a great temptation to reductionism. Even a determinism, which sees ideational dimensions of culture as merely reflexes of the configuration of the physical environment, can develop.

When and where are ecological and materialist approaches helpful in constructing local theologies? When major social changes are taking place and people seem more susceptible to major shifts in world-view and social organization, then these approaches can be helpful in locating some of the reasons for these changes. They can uncover some of the unconscious processes at work, which may not be discoverable by other means. Generally it is advisable to use them in conjunction with other approaches. When used alone, these approaches can easily lead into a determinism and a monocular vision of a culture. As methods, they call for more training than is the case with the functionalism approaches, and so are not quite as accessible to larger segments of a local community.

STRUCTURALIST APPROACHES TO CULTURE

The name of Claude Lévi-Strauss is most closely identified with the structuralist approach to the study of culture.[13] While others have contributed much to its methods (particularly some of the early Russian formalists,[14] the Swiss psychologist Jean Piaget, and the linguistic scholar Roman Jakobson), Lévi-Strauss stands out among exponents of structuralism.

Structuralist study of culture is concerned with uncovering the unconscious structures that generate the patterns of culture, and control their transformations and permutations. Drawing particularly on concepts from linguistics, structuralists see these structures expressed in a series of binary oppositions, which generate a network of systems that classify the data found in a society, and set out the rules whereby transformations take place. Many of the results of culture (kinship systems, systems of economic exchange) are in fact ways of trying to resolve basic oppositions in a society (nature vs. culture, male vs. female) according to sets of rules. Lévi-Strauss's work has been particularly helpful in our understanding of how a people shape their identity by systems of classification[15] of families, of animals, and of plants. His work in the study of myth has brought more advance in our understanding of how myths are constructed and how they function than any other approach.[16]

Structuralist approaches have a number of decided strengths. By uncovering the binary opposition at work in culture, they are able to show how diverse realms relate to one another, and especially how myths and rituals relate to other sectors of a culture. They help us, perhaps more than any other approach, to understand native metaphors and systems of classification. They give us a special insight into the identity structures and cohesiveness of a society. By setting out rules for transformation, they give us some idea of the possible trajectories of change that are open to a given society.

There are some difficulties as well. Principal among these is method. The methods are complicated and to an outsider seem arbitrary. The question has often been raised whether the binary oppositions identified and the rules discovered are based more on intuitive hunch and sensitive insight of the investigator than on a publicly replicable method. The method is not particularly empirical, since the empirical is seen as a manifestation of more important underlying rules. Whereas materialist approaches can be reductionist in terms of physical environment, structuralism has an almost Cartesian reliance on the structures of mind as generative of culture.

When and where are structuralist approaches helpful in constructing local theologies? They are most helpful in getting at the sources that shape, direct, and transform the bases of identity in a community. They also help to point out directions of change. They are particularly helpful in deciphering myths and symbolic dimensions of a culture and help to locate and describe peculiar patterns of thought and metaphor in a culture.

Structuralist approaches are also easily used methods, and are not easily accessible to larger segments of a local community. They seem to rely, as methods, as much on the aesthetic sensitivity of the investigator as upon any replicable procedures of operation. Hence two investigators looking at the same phenomenon may come up with two quite different interpretations.

There are, of course, a number of other approaches to culture that have not been explored here. The four considered here in differing ways contribute important dimensions to a study of culture as part of the development of local theology. A new approach, which may hold the most promise for developing local theologies, is what we may call the semiotic study of culture. Potentially, many approaches may be grouped under this heading, and so we shall explore it at some length.

THE SEMIOTIC STUDY OF CULTURE

Semiotics is the study of signs (from the Greek *semeion* = sign). It sees a culture as a vast communication network, whereby both verbal and nonverbal messages are circulated along elaborate, interconnected pathways, which, together, create the systems of meaning. Central to this process are the bearers of the message. How these bearers are identified will depend upon the semiotic approach followed. They are called "symbols," "signs," or "signifiers," depending upon nuances desired by different authors. Perhaps the most generic term is "sign," so that the bearer of the message is seen to stand for the message. The movement of the messages through the pathways of the system is determined by a number of codes or sets of rules, which are important to the intelligibility of the message to the receivers of the message. The sharing of sets of rules makes it possible for the signs to be understood correctly, since the same sign in the same system may carry different meanings (e.g., fire as warmth and as destruction), or, when translated into another cultural system, the same sign may have radically different meanings (as many people who have crossed cultural boundaries have found out in trying to communicate with their hands). Some signs carry only a single meaning (such as a numeral). Other signs (such as water) can be polysemic, that is, bearers of many messages.

While signs can have natural, or iconic, relationships to the messages they bear (such as smoke from a fire bearing a message of danger), most signs have an artificial, or assigned, meaning (thus, to place one's hand in front of one's mouth can mean surprise, awe, embarrassment, refusal to speak, or mourning, depending upon the culture in which it takes place). Because signs often have such a relationship to their message, a number of factors are needed to determine the message. Contrast and contiguity are one set of factors. Thus, left makes sense only in terms of right, high in terms of low, lighter in terms of darker. Context is another important factor that helps us to read the meaning carried by the sign. Knowing the codes or sets of rules that govern the use of the sign can also help us to elicit the message that is borne by the sign.

The codes or sets of rules are seen to center around three areas: syntactics (the defined sets of relationships between signs, which govern their movement through the cultural system—something like the way in which a grammar governs the movement of words through a language), semantics (the content or meaning of the message), and pragmatics (the rules that govern the communication and ranges of intelligibility of the messages). Knowing these rules, or codes, is essential to understanding the signs and how they carry messages in a system of culture. Cultures are able to formalize these rules to some extent (as in codes of behavior and marriage), but many of them remain implicit; only an extended period of life in the culture will reveal them to the observer. Take, for example, the experience of Roman Catholic converts. While they may be more conversant with the doctrines of Roman Catholicism than many who have been Roman Catholic from birth, there is something of an ethos of nonformalized rules that still govern Roman Catholic behavior, and which any experienced Roman Catholic can recognize. But most Roman Catholics would not be able to give an explicit account of what these rules are.

The interaction of signs, groups of signs that mutually define each other, and these three kinds of rules are a creative collaboration that produces a culture. They span more than the verbal dimensions of culture and more even than the visible dimensions of culture. The task of semiotics is to describe and explain the signs, their interaction, the rules that govern them, and the complex that we call culture which emerges from all of this.

It is clear that metaphors drawn from language and linguistics seem to predominate in this model for studying culture. Indeed, much research into the semiotics of culture, seeing language as the culture product par excellence, uses linguistic methodologies to study a wide variety of phenomena in the culture. There has been considerable debate about the extent to which one can use linguistic models in defining all aspects of cultural systems, and there seems to be growing consensus that, while the linguistic model is a powerful and widely applicable one, not all cultural systems are amenable to this kind of description and explanation. Semiotics owes much of its development to experts in linguistics and those trained in linguistic methods; the names of Ferdinand de Saussure, Roman Jakobson, and the Prague Linguistic Circle figure prominently in the genealogy of semiotics.[17] Some of the best work in semiotics has been done in the area of language in culture.

When speaking of genealogy, certainly the structuralism of Claude Lévi-Strauss also needs to be mentioned. The concern for underlying structures, often unconscious, which give shape to empirical reality; the concern for binary opposites as generating meaning; the role of mediation and transformations in the development of meaning—these are all surely structuralist ideas, and many semioticians have acknowledged their debts to Lévi-Strauss. Structuralism has been called the "godparent" of semiotics, and rightfully so.[18] Yet there are important distinctions, especially in method and in assumptions about the ultimate nature of the creative processes of society. Semiotics generally does not share the passion for formal explanation as strongly as does structuralism. Its methods are more replicable. Semiotics concerns itself more with a study of the sign than with the interest in uncovering the ultimate structures of mind, which in turn generate society.

Semiotics has concerned itself with a wide variety of cultural manifestations, from animal communication, to art, folklore, religion, economics, and attempts at description of larger cultural systems.[19] It is envisioned as an interdisciplinary undertaking, already now drawing upon genetics, cybernetics and computer science, literary criticism, linguistics, sociology and social theory, psychoanalysis, philosophy, anthropology, and formal logic and mathematics. Since the formation of the International Association for the Study of Semiotics in 1969, hopes have been raised that the study of signs might make possible the old dream of a unified concept of scientific investigation and discovery, not seen in the West since the Middle Ages.[20] Whether such a unification of scientific endeavor is possible, or even desirable, remains to be seen. Semiotics, while having many precedents, is relatively young as a conscious and systematic discipline. Most of the research relevant to our undertaking here has been published since 1960. That brief length of time points out also that, as a young science, many of semiotics' concepts are still in flux, and a consensus still has to be formed. But the potential that it represents could lead us into what Thomas Kuhn would call a "paradigm shift" in the study of culture, namely, a new investigative framework, which could resolve problems that have been consistently insoluble in other systems. Irene Portis Winner, a leading cultural semiotician in the United States, summed up elements that might be resolved in this paradigm shift in this way:

> . . . the unsolved problems which cultural semiotics attacks are the reconciliation of the static and synchronic with the dynamic and diachronic within cultural systems, the relation of meaning and content to form and structure, and the question of how cultural systems are in-

ternally organized, how such systems change, how they are related to each other, and finally what is the significant unit of culture.[21]

While no one would maintain that cultural semiotics has actually resolved these problems, the insights provided do open up new possibilities for investigation, some of which will be followed here.

Why, and in what ways, is a semiotic study of culture suited for constructing local theologies? There are a number of reasons. First, its interdisciplinary approach and its concern for all dimensions of culture, both verbal and nonverbal, both empirical and nonempirical, represent the kind of holism that is important when it comes to listening to a culture. It allows study of the so-called high cultural elements (art, poetry, music, religious belief) and the so-called popular elements (customs, superstitions), and other elements of the cultural systems (social organization, economic and political organization) in a way that allows them to be seen as interlocking and interdependent. In so doing, it lessens the risk of reductionism and determinism.

Second, its concern for observation of the various sign systems in a culture, and their configuration, allows for a closer look at how the identity of the culture and the identity of members of the culture are constituted. By studying not only the sign systems (which functionalism also does in one kind of way), but the relations among the signs given in the syntactic, semantic, and pragmatic rules, the culture is allowed to emerge in its own configuration, and still be reasonably comprehensible to the outsider. While there has been some argument that semiotics still represents a Western mode of explanation,[22] it is fair to say that the risk of Western ethnocentrism is significantly reduced below the level of other competing explanatory and descriptive possibilities. For this reason, using methods of cultural semiotics seems to provide a better possibility for local communities to describe their own cultural uniqueness, and at the same time to put it into a form that may have a better chance of being intelligible to others.

Third, the concern for patterns of change is very strong in semiotics. Trying to define trajectories of change, the limits of such trajectories in relation to the problems of identity, and the mechanisms whereby cultures cope with chaos and change are all of central importance in the investigation. In view of the importance of these areas for local theology, an investigative method which sees change as more than deviance from identity is of importance.

What are the limits of semiotics in its use for local theology? The models and modes of investigation still have not been worked out in the detail that the methods promise. It starts with a clear assumption about the central role of the sign in human culture; and closer study shows how ambiguous that category of sign can be. Deconstructionists in France and the United States have challenged the representational assumptions underlying the primacy given the sign.[23] And those who would be willing to come in under the umbrella of semiotics often work from vastly different assumptions, as the following section will show. Yet the risk seems worthwhile. The primacy given sign and symbol, themselves so central to understanding religious language and behavior, makes semiotics seem a good wager in understanding culture better so as to allow for a more integral and lively response to the gospel within it.

While the name "semiotics" is generally taking hold, some variations on it continue to occur. Sometimes semiotics is referred to as semiology, a designation often preferred on the European continent. In cultural anthropology the area of cultural semiotics is sometimes referred to as "symbolic anthropology," especially among Anglo-Saxon anthropologists.[24] The British anthropologist Victor Turner spoke of "symbology" or another variant, "symbolic studies." This points out that, while investigators are connected in their concerns, their terminology and investigative methods may vary. For the sake of uniformity, and what seems to be somewhat of a consensus growing among these investigators, we shall stay with "semiotics."

Contributions to the semiotics of culture can be grouped roughly into three areas, following somewhat linguistic and national lines: French, Anglo-American, and Russian. The central figure in French semiotics has been Roland Barthes, who, following the work of de Saussure, applied semiotic principles to the study of popular culture (fashion in clothing, athletic events, posters) and to literary texts.[25] His work overlapped particularly with others in Paris concerned with understanding the structure of narrative and how literary texts are produced (A. J. Greimas, Julia Kristeva). The semiotics coming from France shows not only the strong and direct influence of de Saussure, but also Lévi-Strauss and Marxism. In the presentation following, we shall make least use of this area of semiotic endeavor.

In the Anglo-American area, the name of the American anthropologist Clifford Geertz stands out. To quote Geertz on this matter:

> The concept of culture I espouse . . . is essentially a semiotic one. Believing, with Max Weber, that man is an animal suspended in webs of significance he himself has spun, I take culture to be those webs, and the analysis of it to be therefore not an experimental science in search of law but an interpretive one in search of meaning.[26]

Geertz represents a major direction in semiotic study. Drawing upon the tradition of Max Weber and Talcott Parsons, concerned with the careful observation of detail championed by functionalists, and sharing the somewhat antimetaphysical stance of Anglo-American social science, Geertz wants to concentrate on the richness and complexity of the sign systems as seen in action. He is interested in what he calls (borrowing from the British philosopher Gilbert Ryle) a "thick description" of culture. This thick description shows the wealth and the randomness of human behavior. "Whatever, or wherever, symbol systems 'in their own terms' may be, we gain empirical access to them by inspecting events, not by arranging abstracted entities into unified patterns."[27] Geertz follows his own directive and gives us close readings of events within cultures: Balinese cockfights, Moroccan sheep thefts, a Javanese funeral. In these analyses he shows that his primary interest in the semiotics of culture has to do with interpretation or explanation of meaning: the messages and the signs (he call them symbols) that bear them. He is not so interested in elaborating the codes or sets of rules. He is interested in how the messages are understood rather than the structures that make intelligibility possible. He is not looking for a unified theory of semiotics; he is concerned more with the interpretation of the prolixity of human life in its concrete settings.

But Geertz is certainly no antinomian. He has addressed the more theoretical questions as well. The concept of "cultural systems" has been an intriguing one for him, and he has sketched out several: religion, ideology, commonsense.[28] He has provided one of the most thoughtful essays on the prospect of cultural universals (he agrees with other researchers that no "human nature" as such can be defined; we have only individuals in cultures), and on how world-views affect human life.

Geertz's concern for metaphor, that device whereby two distinct worlds of meaning are linked together, will be an important element of the following section. His concern with keeping close to the cultural flow, and his reluctance to develop a semiotics reduced to "intuitionism and alchemy,"[29] making it yet another hermetic science, are also shared by the presentation that follows.

Other Anglo-American researchers important for the discussion that follows include Victor Turner, especially in his definitions of "liminality," which describes a mediating device between two sign systems; Mary Douglas, whose concepts of grid and group, of "in place and out of place" are important for discussions of identity; and the psychologist Kurt Lewin, whose field-systems approach to psychological identity, done some forty years ago, complements the mathematical topological theory used in semiotics today.[30]

The third group is often known as the Moscow-Tartu school, given their locations at the Institute of Slavic Study in Moscow and the University of Tartu. Jurij Lotman would be considered the preeminent theoretician, but others, such as Boris Uspenskij, Vladimir Ivanov, Ivan Toporov, and Andrei Pijatigorskij, also figure prominently. Among the many works coming from this group now available in translation, certainly their 1973 "Theses on the Semiotic Study of Culture" are the most significant.[31] These have received a great deal of commentary[32] and form the quickest entry into their semiotics of culture.

The Moscow-Tartu school's roots go back to the Prague Linguistic Circle of the 1920s and 1930s (of which Roman Jakobson and Jan Mukařovský are the most prominent names), and the Russian formalists Vladimir Propp and Viktor Shklovskij.[33] Lévi-Strauss has also exercised a great deal of influence upon them more recently.

Members of the Moscow-Tartu school have their background in Slavic studies, literary criticism, and linguistics. These give direction to their methods. Whereas Geertz was concerned primarily with the interpretation of meaning and the prolixity of sign systems, the Russian group, while doing a great deal of study of cultural detail, is concerned about developing the theory of semiotics and the elaboration of the cultural codes. In this it has had its strongest influence there.

This group defines culture in three different ways: as the hierarchy of sign systems; as the sum of culture texts; as the means of generating culture texts.[34] The first definition, as a hierarchy of sign systems, emphasizes the group's concern for the interconnected nature of sign systems; and how some systems come to dominate and direct other systems. While the Russians have presented one formal model for how this hierarchy might be construed, they have not worked out this idea yet in much detail. The concept is significant, however, since we know that sometimes particular signs and their systems (Victor Turner's "root metaphors") can and do shape other parts of the systems. This is an important idea to which we shall return below.

The second definition, as the sum of culture texts, introduces the important concept of "text," first elaborated by Pijatigorskij in 1962.[35] The text is seen as the basic cultural unit for investigation, containing a single sign or series of signs, bearing a message. Texts may be nondiscrete (having an inner unity in their sign-power, which does not allow easy dissection, such as a picture), or discrete (made up of multiple, separable signs, such as literary composition or a musical score). While the word "text" comes from linguistics, texts are both verbal and nonverbal phenomena, which can bear a message and thus serve as the basic unit of investigation. Paul Ricoeur, in a different context, has elaborated something of the same idea.[36] Thus a text can be a set of words, an event, or even a person. Culture then becomes the total sum of these texts shared by a given people. This will be an important concept in what is developed below.

The third definition sees culture as those mechanisms that generate texts. This refers to two distinct areas of interest: the codes or sets of rules, and memory. The generative structures will give something of the typology of the culture (something with which the Moscow-Tartu group is much concerned); much of their energy has gone into typing different kinds of cultures from archaic to modern.[37] While those not working from strong evolutionary or Marxist models might place less emphasis on the discrete character of cultural typologies, it is one way of trying to get at the distinctiveness of each culture.

Culture is also memory, the stored and retrievable information that guides the selection and exclusion of new information in the cultural system, and provides the information for the development of identity. The concept of memory will be an important one for our understanding of tradition.

The Moscow-Tartu school has studied a wide variety of phenomena. It has studied literary texts, art, folk customs and costumes, cinema, and the Orthodox church.[38] Its interest in and development of theory for cultural semiotics will be of great help to our work in constructing local theologies, particularly its concept of the culture text, Lotman's work on world-views, and Ivanov and Toporov's work on transformations.[39]

TOWARD A SEMIOTIC ANALYSIS OF CULTURE

Clifford Geertz tells us that cultural analysis has to do with "sorting out the structures of significance . . . and determining their social ground and import."[40] This sums up the analytic enterprise, but does not give much clue as to how to go about it. Sorting out the structures of signification of locating and describing the culture texts as signs (or sets of signs) bearing messages is often a complicated exercise. Models and examples exist showing how to go about it,[41] but none pretends to be comprehensive. There is no one kind of recipe for field investigation, no single template that we can drop on our data to "score" its meaning. This fact can seem particularly frustrating, since we can be presented with a culture text that seems surely to be a discrete one, that is, not susceptible to our sorting out into any more detail than that which we were given in the first place.

But does that reduce our activity to intuition and alchemy, as Geertz warns us against? Geertz also reminds us that the process of interpreting cultures requires us to ask lots of questions. We can be led astray, but a continuing flow of the right kinds of questions can allow patterns to emerge. It must be remembered that a semiotic analysis of culture allows cultural structures to emerge in a way different from how they emerge in day-to-day life. In some ways analysis can be called a "decoding" of the codes, or a "recoding" of them into a metalanguage in different texts at once. Thus the results may, in the first instance, not be immediately familiar to those most at home in the culture. The reason for this is that they try to explain things that may not ordinarily call for explanation when one is at home in the culture. They are simply "commonsense," "natural law," "the way things are." But to make the symbolic interaction between a culture and the larger church tradition possible, this recoding needs to take place. When interconnections between sign systems are made, they should, at some point, make sense to those who live with them. Ordinarily this would come as a new insight into behavior and identity, which reinforces the individual's or the community's sense of what they are about, who they are, and where they are located in the world.

What kind of guidelines can be given to the "listening heart"? Guidelines for a semiotic analysis of culture may be grouped under four headings. In each there will be examples from different cultures. For a number of reasons this method seems more appropriate than drawing them all from a single culture. First, because some of the principles are based on alternatives, not all such sign systems are present in a single culture. Second, to give the impression of describing somewhat fully a single culture goes against something we are finding to be quite important to local theologies, namely, that theology may be returning to its status as an occasional enterprise. A full semiotic analysis of a culture cries out for a systematic theology, and while the great themes of the Christian heritage need to be addressed in the fullness of a Christian life, any attempt to develop a systematic theology at this level is rather quickly prey to becoming a translation of someone else's. Better perhaps to move slowly and piecemeal to preserve the concreteness than to try to exercise the control of the systematic presentation too rapidly.

Under each of these four headings, then, come considerations that, more often than not, will need to be raised. The list is not exhaustive, but does highlight important areas.

DESCRIPTION AND PERSPECTIVE IN CULTURE

In a semiotic study of culture, the variability within the various sign systems—both in the polysemy of the signs themselves and in the codes and their interlinkage—means that a culture can be described in different ways. Within certain limits, all these descriptions can have their own validity. The reason for such a variety of different, and sometimes opposing, descriptions of culture has to do with the matter of perspective.

The question of perspective was raised at the beginning of this chapter, in terms of the perspectives of natives and foreigners. Anthropology has long recognized the difference in perspectives, in such distinctions as "emic" (view from the inside out) and "etic" (view from the outside) descriptions of culture. Different kinds of participant-observer models proposed by functionalist approaches have also yielded different descriptions. And we know that such shifts in perspectives can often be important in attaining new insights into culture. The programs of conscientization growing out of the cultural pedagogy of Paulo Freire are essentially such shifts in perspective.[42]

We shall consider here briefly two sets of perspectives—inner and outer, speaker and hearer—and some questions that surround each. The inner-outer distinction is based primarily upon the position of the person describing the culture: Does one stand inside, as a member of the culture, or outside, looking in, during the process of description? The significance of the distinction works at two levels: the style of the description and the criteria for adequate description.

From an inner perspective, the description will often be characterized by narrative. Explanation (stepping out of the narrative) may occur, but usually to support the narrative rather than to translate it into another mode of discourse. Thus, in describing marriage patterns, someone from the inside might begin by talking about who has married whom, about situations where someone has married someone whom he or she should not have (and how it has not worked out). Explanations will remain internal to the system ("Poles shouldn't marry Irish"; "Catholics shouldn't marry Protestants"; "Bear people shouldn't marry Owl people"); hence, if the questioner does not already understand the system, the explanations are not of much help—they are not really translations into another mode, but variations within the same range of discourse. This points out an important dimension of description from the inside: it is meant to reaffirm realities rather than dissect them. Hence people will describe their families by relating stories about significant family members living and dead. In so doing it becomes clear that their family is always meant to be leaders, strong, intelligent, brave, or whatever, and members of the family listening are reminded of the standards that should govern their behavior. Outsiders listening to the narrative are given clues on how to recognize a genuine member of this family.

Style of description from the inside, then, is marked by narrative. Good description from the inside is judged by how well it reinforces the identity of those on the inside. To use a religious example: a good United States black preacher is one who can "tell the story" (as it is often described by black American listeners). And telling the story has to do with weaving together biblical narrative with the narrative of the community.

Outer description uses narrative also, but more as a means of exemplification. It uses it to set up a case study to which analytic principles are then applied. Thus an outer description may be phenomenological in its approach, but the concern is always setting the stage for explanation. And the criterion for explanation is not increasing a sense of identity to those who live in the situation, but translating the reality into another mode of discourse or into another sign system.

What is the purpose of such translation? It can have both internal and external purposes. The most common internal one (i.e., reflecting the interests of members of the culture), is to deal with social change. Internal forms of description as just described no longer are forging the same bonds of identity; the culture is being called upon to change in some fashion. Thus in a rural Latin American situation, traditional self-descriptions in a peonage system may change into Marxian-style class analysis. From an inner perspective, such a translation is the transition point to a new sense of identity. In Western systems of psychotherapy, a sick person's traditional means of talking about personal identity have to be described in new language (Oedipus complex, obsessive-compulsive, overachiever) in order for that person to shift from a self-image no longer adequate to a new, more satisfying one.

A second reason for such translation is to allow a culture to absorb new relations into its pattern of identity. Much identity in human existence is built up by contrast. At a given point, a simple two-part contrast (us vs. not-us) may no longer be adequate, and a more textured one is necessary. In that case translations can be helpful. For example, the name by which many cultural groups call themselves means simply, in their own language, "the people." The implication is that those who are not part of this cultural group are not human. As living situations become more complex, more differentiations between groups who are outsiders but friendly, and outsiders and unfriendly, need to be made. Or consider the situation where Roman Catholics divide the world into Catholics and non-Catholics. When that non-Catholic group has to be divided into Protestants of varying kinds, into Jews, Muslims, and other groups, each progressive differentiation changes the meaning of what it is to be Catholic.

Hence, outer descriptions can be of great importance to a culture and should not be written off as imperialist intrusions immediately. They often serve important purposes to the inner life of a culture.

But there are also outer descriptions that serve those on the outside more than those on the inside. The purpose of these descriptions is to translate the sign systems of the culture into the sign systems of the outsider. They run the risk of mistranslation when the sign systems are not parallel. They can serve a variety of purposes, both noble (nation building in a tribally divided area), and less noble (to provide means for better control of outside forces). Always key questions to ask in outer description are: What is the purpose of the translation of the sign system? Who is being served by this translation? And how is the translation being authenticated?

In a pluralist world where some sense of unity needs to emerge, outer description is necessary to allow some basis for intercommunication and eventual cohesion. In situations of rapid social change, translations of sign systems provided by outer description may be as important to the inner life of the culture as are traditional inner descriptions. In describing a culture for the sake of developing a local theology, both inner and outer descriptions are necessary. Inner descriptions provide the sign systems that make up the identity of a people; outer descriptions help with social change, and with linkage to the larger reality of the Christian church.

A second pair of perspectives is that of speaker-hearer. This pair, familiar from communications theory, is a central analytic tool for any description, be it inner or outer.

The perspective of the speaker is one in which concern centers upon clear transmission of messages in the culture. Criteria for such clear transmission center upon the content of the message. There must be a minimum loss of information in the transmission. The information must reach the hearer in the same form as that given by the speaker. There must be no adulteration in transmitting the message. In speaker-oriented description, the hearer must be conformed to the message both in its content and in its structure; the speaker controls the sign system and serves as the judge of the adequacy or inadequacy of any change in the sign system.

When a description is hearer-oriented, concern centers on the ability of the hearer to relate the message to his or her world. A good transmission of the message means that the hearer has been able to do this. In order to achieve maximum success, the speaker will vary the structure of the message (use variants in the sign system) in order to achieve maximum integration into the sign system of the hearer, even if some peripheral aspects of the content are not totally transmitted. The speaker's concern for control is less important than the speaker's ability to communicate adequately.

Some examples might be of help here. In theories of pedagogy one finds both speaker- and hearer-oriented methods. In the former, good pedagogy is marked by the ability of the hearer to repeat the message in the same form as it was transmitted by the speaker. In such systems the role of memory and mnemonic devices is important (as in traditional Qur'anic schools). In hearer-oriented pedagogy, the transformation of the world of the hearer by the message, the ability of the hearer to reformulate the message in a sign system coherent with the hearer's world becomes more important. In theology, what were called translation models in the first chapter would conform to speaker-oriented models; contextualization models would be examples of hearer-oriented pedagogy. In transmitting a tradition within a culture, those responsible for guarding the integrity of that tradition will tend to prefer speaker-oriented models. Those concerned with maintaining the cohesion of the group will tend to prefer hearer-oriented models (if their own identity as leaders is not at stake). One sees this pattern recurring in the Roman Catholic Church since the changes wrought by Vatican Council II. Leadership in Rome and in parts of the episcopal magisterium will often stress speaker-oriented models for transmitting the gospel message, even to the point of preferring neo-scholastic formulations. They will be concerned about uniformity of teaching and practice (minimal loss of information in transmission) in discussions of pluralism. Leadership in the theological magisterium, in parts of the episcopal magisterium, and local pastors will often stress hearer-oriented models for transmitting the gospel message. They will be concerned about whether traditional formulations are intelligible, or even alienating to a people. The discussions in this book have a preference for hearer-oriented models; the very concept of local theology is based on this assumption.

In cultural description, there is another dimension to differences between speaker- and hearer-oriented descriptions. This is the older distinction between *esoteric* (meant for a few initiated elite) and *exoteric* (meant for the general populace) descriptions. In a way these correspond to speaker- and hearer-oriented descriptions, respectively. The usual purpose of esoteric descriptions is one of elaborating the message in a more complex sign system, which, if transmitted to hearers unfamiliar with the complexity of the system, would lead to radical loss of information in the message or even a misunderstanding of the message. The exoteric description of a phenomenon in a culture is then intended to be either a simplified description or a translation into a less complex sign system. In manuals of Indian meditation, the remark is often found that at one point, the person meditating must come to realize that the god worshiped is actually oneself. This is an esoteric meaning of the principles of meditation and contemplation of images of the godhead. Until one has reached a sophisticated sense of self-identity, the sign system in which this statement is made is not accessible. "God" as a sign in larger systems of the culture means something different from what is meant by "god" in this sign system. Or to take another example, religious authorities are often concerned about theologians' publications of their "opinions," since these can "confuse the faithful." What is meant is that the general populace, uninitiated into the more complex sign systems of the theologians, may misconstrue the theologians' message by mistranslating it into a different sign system. Take, for instance, Augustine's dictum "Love God, and do what you will."

Without understanding the sign system in which Augustine is working, and the codes that regulate the sign "love," this could be taken as license for any kind of behavior.

Even in a hearer-oriented approach, as local theology tends to be, there is room for esoteric and exoteric differentiations in descriptions of culture. One of the tasks of esoteric description is careful and complete storage of information within a skein of a delicate sign system. Only certain people in the culture need to be concerned with the maintenance of some of these kinds of information. This is simply a matter of differentiation of roles within a culture. Hence not every Christian need have the grasp of the tradition that would be expected of a professional theologian. At the same time, if the gap between the esoteric and exoteric descriptions grows (as happens in the case when esoteric information and sign systems are used to segregate a certain class or to enhance its power), then such descriptions can be harmful to the Christian community.

In the matter of perspectives in cultural description, then, those involved in developing local theologies need to ask themselves which perspective is guiding their descriptions: inner or outer? speaker or hearer? All of these perspectives have a role in local theology. Inner descriptions help a community to find its authentic voice. Outer descriptions help it to deal with change and with cross-cultural communication. Speaker-oriented descriptions help it to preserve the integrity of its traditions; hearer-oriented descriptions are necessary to ensure continued intelligibility and liveliness of those traditions. Keeping in mind the perspective and the purposes of the perspective will help in developing the kind of richly textured theology needed to respond fully to the gospel in a concrete situation.

THE SEMIOTIC DESCRIPTION OF CULTURE TEXTS

When one has made some determination on perspectives, the next step in the semiotic description of culture is to locate the culture texts. The culture text is the basic unit of analysis. It can consist of a single sign, but more commonly it is a series of interlocking signs, held together by a set of codes and/or by a common message. One culture text can serve as a subset of a larger culture text as well (e.g., the gestures that are part of a ritual; the gestures can be understood as a separate sign system).

The task of description and analysis is to "read" the text, that is, locate its signs, the codes that place the signs in dynamic interaction, and the messages that are conveyed. Some culture texts can be hard to analyze because each seems to consist of a single sign or because there seem to be no clear points of division in the text (as in a dance). Other culture texts are more easily analyzed (such as stories, where one can distinguish different roles and actors). This is the distinction between discrete and nondiscrete texts, between texts that break down easily into more manageable units and those that do not. Texts that do not break down easily into their signs and codes are often the more important texts in a culture, defying both inner and outer description.

It should be remembered that texts can be verbal and nonverbal, visual, auditory, and tactile, simple and highly complex. A culture can also be viewed as a hierarchy of such texts, where one text incorporates another. Large texts that incorporate a whole series of other texts will be called here "semiotic domains." Thus the sum of the culture texts about economic production would be the economic domain, the texts about politics the political domain, and so on.

If any sign or system of signs is a text, where does one begin in locating culture texts? In view of the interests of local theologies, we would want to concentrate on culture texts that "speak" of identity (group-boundary formation and world-view) and of social change.

Common culture texts that speak of identity can often be found in communal celebrations. Celebrations frequently serve to reaffirm identity both in terms of who belongs to the group and in terms of how the world is to be perceived. Annual celebrations often have these kinds of concerns. Rites of passage (surrounding birth, puberty, marriage, change of leadership, death) are rich culture texts in this regard. Part of these rituals is usually devoted to reviewing what it means to be a member of this culture, what one's duties and responsibilities are within the culture, and how one is to perceive the world (values and ideals) if one wishes to remain a member of this culture. Dominant signs, which serve as metaphors bearing rich messages about culture, often emerge as part of these rituals. One such set of signs has to do with the names given in the naming rituals of birth and puberty, the change of names coming in marriage. The signs of ornament for such ritual (wedding bands, special clothing or body painting, ritual instruments) also communicate what a culture thinks these various states in the culture (childhood, sexual maturity, marriage, leadership, ancestorhood) mean, and what codes of behavior are to govern them.

Celebrations are also held to incorporate new elements into the identity of the community. New year's festivals are examples of this. Rites of adoption are others.

Other culture texts speak more strongly about how a culture deals with social change and with threats to identity. Culture texts that deal with adjudication would be examples of the first, namely, those situations where decisions have to be made between two competing persons or events. How is this done? Who does it? What is the process of such adjudication? The sign systems used in divination, in courts of law, in settling arguments, in dealing with strangers all give some idea of the codes that govern social change. Rituals surrounding healing are good culture texts for learning how a culture sees and deals with threats to its identity. Such sign systems will indicate what can be considered a threat (e.g., what nonhuman element enters a human body to make it ill: an animal, a ghost, a mineral, a plant?) and what codes must be followed to restore identity (reachieving balance, homeopathic methods, contrasting methods, excision or exorcism, etc.).

Perhaps the richest of culture texts that give evidence of how a people build up and maintain themselves can be found in art (music, poetry, plastic arts). These are also among the most difficult to analyze, especially from an outer perspective. Much consideration has been given to artistic culture texts, and they do provide an important resource. This is the case because the aesthetic sense seems to be the point where the forces of a culture converge to make a statement about itself.

Depending upon situations, certain texts can become very important to analyze. Economic texts need to be addressed in situations of oppression and rapid social change. Kinship texts need to be addressed when traditional group-boundary situations are called into question.

But what of more specifically "religious" texts? These are often, along with art texts, the most difficult to analyze and the most easily misconstrued by outsiders especially. Religious texts depend upon signs that have complex metaphoric capacity, and the understanding of a myth, a ritual, or other religious text depends upon them. While there is often some urgency in beginning with these texts, it may be more useful to begin with the other kinds suggested here. This is the case because of some of the holistic concerns of local theology listed at the beginning of this chapter: what to an outsider seems religious (or non-religious) may not be perceived in the same way by an insider. And even insiders can be misled on these. Moreover, since religious texts are most often tied up with the central traditions of a culture, they are more susceptible to having both esoteric and exoteric readings. Outsiders can ordinarily count on receiving the exoteric readings only.[43] And many insiders may not have access to the full range of meanings or messages that the signs in the religious texts are carrying.

To understand better the roles of culture texts, it might be helpful to turn now to more specific considerations of identity and social change as concerns in culture texts. This should allow a little clearer picture of semiotic analysis.

IDENTITY IN SEMIOTIC DESCRIPTION

As was indicated above, there are two principal components in identity upon which we wish to concentrate: the formation of group boundaries and the structures of world-view.

In his research into these areas, Jurij Lotman has found, in conjunction with the findings of transcultural psychologists, that the basic group boundary is one that distinguishes ourselves from others: the us vs. not-us boundary.[44] Lotman refers to this as the internal (I) vs. external (E). This is a fundamental distinction from which others grow, and can be diagramed as Figure 1 on page 64.

In its simplest form, those who inhabit I (namely, ourselves) are "the people," the civilized; those who inhabit E are the nonpeople, barbarians. Our society is seen as organized; theirs as chaotic, bordering upon the animal. The nonorganized, chaotic functions assigned to E often carry with them negative overtones: those in E have malevolent designs upon us, and would destroy us if the opportunity arose. Their only level of human organization is that of conspiracy to undo us.

Figure 1

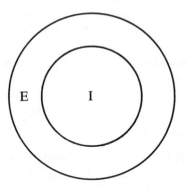

This pattern is familiar to societies in times of war, where the enemy, inhabiting E and threatening the boundaries of I, is often portrayed as barbaric or subhuman. The same is also chronicled in history in the case of invaders (Europeans into Japan or China, Asians into Dark-Age Europe), who are considered inferior to the invaded society.

Part of the message carried by this pattern of signification is that chaos and entropy lie beyond the boundaries of one's own group. Even E's most refined actions of meaning, such as religious ones, are marked by subhuman practice. (Christian allegations of infant sacrifice among the Jews in the European medieval period is a case in point.) Hence there is a need to reinforce I's boundaries against the onslaught of inhabitants of E.

The internal-external boundary also works in the nonvisible area. In this instance the invisible world is seen as E: outside our control and often malevolent, the world of ghosts, demons, and witches. Patterns of organization are either beyond the ken of those in I, or represent a reversal of human values. In many cultures the nonvisible world of E is divided into two zones: one positively disposed toward I (heaven), and one negatively disposed (hell), with appropriate signs bearing both positive and negative meaning (angels and devils, benevolent and malevolent ancestors).

The internal-external boundary works not only in matters of group formation, but also in the structuring of the world-view. In the case of the world-view structured along the lines of Figure 1, I represents the real world, and E some inferior situation less acceptable than that of I. Thus when someone in I dies, the afterlife state is considered inferior; it is "going down into Sheol," or living in the world of the shades.

But the internal-external boundary can be reversed, with this world becoming E, and the afterlife becoming I. In this kind of model (Figure 2, page 65), a different set of values is recognized.

Figure 2

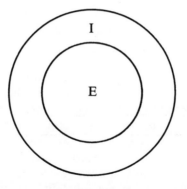

This, the visible world, is seen as but a pale and imperfect copy of the world to come. It is indeed a place of exile and illusion. All that is in this world can be understood only in relation to the more perfect world of the afterlife. One can recognize in this model medieval Christianity and models of liberation in Indian and Buddhist religious systems.

This way of describing world-views bears some further comment. What Westerners call "modernity" is characterized by a situation where this model in Figure 2 is reversed back to Figure 1.[45] Thus the real world against which everything should be measured is structured in the same way as the Figure 1 model, but with an important difference. In societies in a more traditional mode, the world of E may be unknown and malevolent, but it is also significant, having a clear bearing upon the realities of I. In the world of modernity, however, the world of E is seen as a projection, a skewed projection, of I. It is the world of illusion, and indeed is trivial.

Thus in the world of modernity, the prospects for transcendence are greatly reduced. The world of E has little to say to the world of I. There is no dialectic to continue to reinforce the boundaries between the two; there are no outside forces of meaning, no systems of signification to aid in the transformation of I or to serve as a critique upon its own systems of signification. This would seem to be one of the reasons why identity can often be such a problem in societies marked by modernity.

Besides the issue of levels of organization in I and E, there is a second consideration of importance for establishing identity, namely, the nature of the boundaries and boundary markers between I and E. In some ways the nature of the boundaries is the most interesting part of the problem of the identity. Following the insights of topology in mathematics, the nature of the boundaries determines what is internal to their bounding function. The boundaries are the areas of ambiguity between two states, the "no-man's-land" where the codes of neither I nor E obtain. They are perilous areas in human existence. To restructure boundaries is to restructure identity. To use a political example, the restructuring of territorial boundaries in Africa by

European powers, without reference to traditional tribal boundaries, created in the new states whole series of tensions, which would not have been the case otherwise. In psychology the restructuring of a person's identity after therapy or after a life crisis will mean new boundaries between the "I" and the "not-I."

The boundaries are dangerous precisely because of their ambiguity. They represent power that has not been marshaled into the signs and codes of the systems of I or E. They can therefore become the significant sources of transformation. They correspond to what Victor Turner has called "liminal states"; they serve as thresholds between two worlds.[46] Boundaries are often supervised by specialists who know the territory and have experience of crossing over them and being able to return safely. Priests, shamans, seers of different varieties, healers, and magicians all fit into this category. In times of stress within society, artists will also explore these boundaries to receive new insight into the tensions that these boundaries are sending back into society.

Change in society most often comes when certain boundaries are transgressed. Thus, when Jesus rearranged the boundaries concerning who would have a place in the kingdom of God, who would have the first place and the last, a distinctively different image of what it meant to be a part of the chosen people arose. When the Buddha declared that all could reach enlightenment, not just those in the brahmanic caste, he rearranged the boundaries of caste in the eyes of his followers. Vladimir Propp and other folklorists have shown that action in folktales takes place when the hero transgresses boundaries—leaves home, travels into a foreign country, visits the underworld.[47]

The purpose of these references is to give some indication of how identity becomes structured, in terms both of group membership and of world-view. In engaging in the semiotic description of a culture, one can get at the question of identity in both of these areas by trying to identify the boundaries and the signs that form the boundary markers. For Roman Catholics, special uniforms and special codes of behavior marked the boundary keepers of the religious world-view for many years. These are becoming obscured in many places as priests, nuns, and brothers doff habits and question the rule of celibacy and other forms of discipline. Such changes in the boundaries portend larger transformations taking place in identity in a people. The removal of the communion railing in many churches marked a restructuring of the boundaries between God and humankind. The boundary has now become the perimeter of the church building rather than one transecting its interior.

In the semiotic description of culture, then, questions need to be asked about boundaries. Codes of behavior in the sign system help to locate the boundaries and the boundary markers. Who may marry whom, boundaries in economic relations (what constitutes honesty and fraud), what is considered wrongdoing (e.g., killing an enemy is virtue, killing someone from the clan is a crime)—all these help to give a picture of the elements that, in turn, help to constitute identity. Certain actions may mark the boundary (e.g., whatever constitutes incest, eating the wrong kind of food, becoming friendly with the wrong kind of people); certain persons may mark boundaries (persons considered eccentrics) by their being able to live in both worlds. These kinds of questions deliver up not only a mapping of the boundaries, but also the signs that bear messages about the nature of what it means to be part of this society. What professions are considered honorable, which necessary, which suspect all say something about the messages of what constitutes value and nonvalue in a culture. Persons engaging in the arts are often boundary markers, since their free play with structures both threatens and renews the structure of society. Thus in many cultures people connected with theater, with the circus and carnivals are considered marginal people in the society.[48] They play with the structures of reality too easily for most people's taste.

When one begins an internal examination of the territory marked off by the boundaries of identity, the questions of the signs, the codes, and the messages of society become more clearly focused.

The *signs*, as was indicated above, are the bearers of the messages, which inform, on a conceptual level, the identity of a given culture. The signs stand for part or all of the message. The eucharistic bread and wine are signs of the presence of Christ in a Christian community. The priest as sign has been read as Christ, as representative of the Christian people, as mediator of the boundary between the two. While some signs have only one possible message (as in the case of numbers or letters of the alphabet used in English), the more important signs of a culture carry many meanings. Signs such as water, fire, dirt, trees, houses, clothing can carry a variety of different messages, depending upon the codes in which they are working, and the other signs to which they are juxtaposed. The sign "fire" in some Christian culture texts can stand for the power of the Holy Spirit, the love of God, the punishment of hell, or illicit passion, depending upon its context.

In the semiotic description of culture, signs need to be identified in culture texts. To discern the messages involved will depend upon the codes in which the signs are embedded and the other signs with which they are juxtaposed.

A simple way of describing *codes* in a culture is to envision them as answering the questions: How are things done? How is this to be understood? Codes provide the basic rules for the exercise of the sign function. They are, so to speak, the "grammar" of culture texts. They encompass the rules of action of a culture, of what is done and what is not to be done. In so doing, they not only define the range of activity of the sign, but can also tell us something of basic messages. Consider, for example, the change in code for relations to the Eucharist sign. When the Eucharist began to be celebrated by Roman Catholics with the priest facing the people, the sign function of the Eucharist underwent change. The sacrificial element of the Eucharist was weakened in favor of the meal aspect. The altar as sign was shifted in the code from being the point where God and humanity met in sacrificial communication to the table of the eucharistic meal. This change in code led to other repercussions in the code. Now that the meal message was predominating over the sacrifice message, the code for reception of the sign (the bread) changed. It became permissible to receive in the hand rather than only on the tongue. Nonordained persons could touch the sign and even distribute it.

In this changing of the code (how the Eucharist is to be celebrated), relations to the sign thus changed. The eucharistic bread began carrying its messages about the presence of Christ in the community in a different arrangement.

Just as general identity can be discerned from seeking out the boundary markers, the edges of codes give good ideas about their working, the effect they have on the signs embedded in them, and the range of messages that they can carry. High divorce rates in urban areas and other emerging patterns of human relationships may help us to find out more about our marriage codes than investigation of "successful" marriages. The contrasts one finds on the edges are of particular interest. How does one differentiate the polygamy of some African and Muslim societies from the serial polygamy of Western industrial-urban centers? In the one instance, one may have many spouses simultaneously; in the other, one may have many spouses, but only one at a time. What does "indissolubility" mean in the code of marriage when the exceptions are so extensive?

The *messages* form the third unit for investigation. They emerge through a study of the signs and the codes. The messages, as indicated above, comprise the basic meanings conveyed by a culture.

In semantic study, "meaning" is often defined in a contrastive or decisionist fashion. The meaning that forms a message in a culture is a matter of choosing one approach and not another. In so doing, the meanings define the values and ideals in a culture. What does it mean to be good? What does it mean to be successful? How does one become an outcast? The positive questions give an outline of what can be considered patterns for identity; the negative questions suggest the patterns of threat to identity.

Messages in and of themselves often sound like truisms to the outsider: "life is to be increased"; "harmony is of utmost importance"; "life is an illusion to be overcome"; "conflict is at the heart of all things." But when carried by a variety of symbols and encoded in a number of ways, they take on astonishing concreteness. Think how a sign, such as a boundary keeper, is encoded differently with the four messages just presented. Take the priest as mediator of the boundary. In the case of the first message, the priest is responsible for the good fortune and prosperity of a culture; in the second, the priest functions as a mediator; in the third, the priest serves as a sign of contradiction; in the fourth, the priest exercises a primarily prophetic function in the culture. The same sign is encoded differently in order to bear different messages. In the first instance, the priest should marry; in the third, the priest should not. Codes of temperance and wisdom characterize the priest in the second instance; passion and critique in the fourth.

Cultures have more than one message. In times of change, differing messages will compete with one another. By investigating the signs and the codes in a culture text, one can start to move toward discerning the messages.

One final area in the semiotic study of identity needs to be taken up: the linkages that create sign systems. To do this, we need to address two notions: metaphor and semiotic domains.

Metaphors are keys to how signs can be linked together and how sign systems are created. A metaphor results when two discrete signs are identified with each other. In this activity not only are the obvious and immediate linkages made, but all the other associations surrounding the signs are brought into new and creative contact. When we say Jesus is the Son of God, bread consecrated is Jesus Christ, or the emperor is the Son of Heaven, two signs, each bearing different messages, are brought together and considered one. The less than exact homeomorphism set up between the two signs makes it possible for each sign to carry more meanings than was the case before. Metaphors are central to the functioning of culture texts, especially those culture texts that express in a special way the structures of identity.[49]

One of the reasons for the power of the metaphor is the metonymic process, whereby part of the sign stands for the whole (the crown for the king, the cross for Christ). The metonym can create new linkages with other metaphors and so create a network of possibilities for communicating messages within a culture.[50]

When this complex sign, code, message, and metaphoric process spreads itself over an area of culture and brings it together as a constellation of meaning, we have a *semiotic domain*. A semiotic domain could be considered an assemblage of culture texts relating to one set of activities in culture (economic, political, familiar), which are organized together by a single set of messages and metaphoric signs. Often the semiotic domain is governed by what Turner has called a root metaphor, which gives direction to the signs to be included and the codes to be developed. For example, a root metaphor for the economic domain in capitalist societies is the marketplace. The exchange of relations of production in a culture is a marketplace, a capitalist economist would say. The metaphor of the marketplace then governs the codes of behavior (competition, maximization of profit, use of labor).

A culture can be seen as a series of linking (sometimes hierarchically organized) semiotic domains: religious, economic, political, social, sexual, and so on. Often one or other of the domains will be given priority over another. Thus in precommunist Tibet or in medieval Europe, the religious semiotic domain would predominate. Only those activities that mirrored the afterlife or an enlightened state were good; others were merely tolerated. One reached the cultural ideal by becoming a monk. The religious calendar marked time— when one could fight, make love, plant and reap. In Western urban societies, the economic domain predominates. Life is seen as a race, a struggle in the marketplace. Success is the result of success in the marketplace (whereas wealth gained in the marketplace in a medieval European situation was considered tainted, even unnatural). Economic codes of efficiency, maximal utilization of capital, and progress influence other domains besides the economic in such a society.

The root metaphor of the dominant semiotic domain often provides the major linkage between the sign systems of a culture. They become the language "which everyone understands." They reflect the cultural ideal. In investigating a culture, one needs to try to seek out those metaphors governing semiotic domains, and especially those that aid in linking the domains together to create a cultural whole.

These, then, are some basic guidelines for engaging in a semiotic description of a culture in terms of its identity. With this we turn to identity's correlate, social change.

SOCIAL CHANGE IN SEMIOTIC DESCRIPTION

It was noted in the discussion of functionalist approaches to culture that cultural description is often better at dealing with identity than with social change. There are a number of ways of envisioning social change in semiotic descriptions. The choice of these will depend to a great extent upon the perspective taken: whether inner or outer, speaker or hearer. Also, the anticipated outcome of the change will reflect the attitude toward the change. If change threatens one's security, it will no doubt be seen as an evil or an aberration from the norm. If change will improve one's situation, it is seen as a positive value or even a necessity.

Being able to address social change in a semiotic description of culture is very important for local theology. Social change is a social fact in many of the world's cultures today, and in some instances the change is so rapid and thoroughgoing that not to address it is not to describe the culture. The impact of urbanization on rural peoples, the growth of technology and communications, the shifts in economic resources are all having an impact on virtually everyone.

There is another reason for concern about describing social change in cultures in developing local theologies. Central to the Christian experience of God is the experience of salvation. And salvation means a deep and powerful change involving a rescue from evil and ill and deliverance into a new reality. To describe adequately experiences of salvation in a culture, to be able to locate culture texts relating to ill, evil, and salvation, one needs to have ways of describing the process of transformative change.

In its more general form, the semiotic description of change deals with the transformation of sign systems. This can happen through a transformation of the relations of signs to their messages, or through changes in the codes that govern the interaction of the signs. Within this framework, one needs to allow the rules of transformation to interact with the messages of a culture. In other words, is change seen primarily as a process of incorporation whereby new signs, messages, and codes are included in a system, or is it primarily a conflictual process whereby one set of signs, codes, and messages is eliminated and another takes its place? It is obvious here that perspective will play a large role.

In the first, incorporative approach, the culture's image of itself is that of one which is forever incomplete. New options presented become new opportunities to enrich the semiotic domains by incorporating new elements. Classic processes of religious syncretism are examples of this approach to change. New deities introduced become identified as manifestations of already known deities. Or compromises get worked out in other fashions. Thus in medieval India a newly introduced deity could be seen as yet another incarnation, or avatar, of the principal deity, be that Vishnu, Siva, Brahma, depending upon the region. Sixteenth-century Mexicans could identify the Virgin of Guadalupe with an older, already known goddess whose temple had been on the same site as Guadalupe's apparition. Christianity's development in Europe involved incorporating many religious practices from the older European peoples. And as times changed, occupations previously considered alien (soldiering, theater, money management) could be incorporated into Christian life.

The key to the incorporative approach as a way of describing how a sign system in a culture can take in new realities is whether or not the receiving culture has sufficient strength of identity and resources of survival to incorporate the new elements. When the basic sign systems of the culture can remain in control, then this process can take place. The receiving culture can absorb new information along these lines. But if the pace of confrontation is too rapid, the new information too cohesive and powerful, then the receiving culture may have to adopt a different stance.

This brings us to the second process, a conflictual one. In this situation two sign systems enter into competition, with one of them finally prevailing. While both may be transformed in the process, one will come to predominate. In colonializing patterns, the invading sign systems will attempt to supplant the receiving culture. In situations within an established culture, the inadequacy of the identity boundaries may force a similar conflictual pattern between competing sign systems within the same culture. In the first instance, that of colonialization, the colonizing power will enter an area and bring with it its "superior" semiotic system. Such would describe the Aryan invasion of India, the Incan rise to power in the Andes, the nineteenth-century adventures of Europe in Africa. The colonizing power's systems of government, education, and religion are imposed upon the invaded culture. In the second instance, that of inner conflict, one group no longer accepts the designations given it by other members of the culture and rejects the sign systems that heretofore have dominated the culture. The French Revolution, the Russian Revolution, the situations described in liberation theology—all are examples of this second process. In this instance a new sign system (republicanism in France, communism in Russia, Sandinista rule in Nicaragua) prevails over the previous sign system. In conflictual change, either the two sign systems are incompatible or the old situation has become so intolerable that it becomes well-nigh unredeemable in the eyes of a majority of the members of the culture. The old sign system can no longer account for the problems with which the culture has to deal, or the loyalties it demands and the codes it prescribes are no longer acceptable to the members of the culture.

Within the general framework of these two ways of describing change, let us address a number of items. First, metaphors used in the culture for tension, resolution of tension, and change. If one looks to areas of manifest tension in a culture, what metaphors are used to describe them? Is it the result of covert invasion of outsiders (communists, a virus, outside agitators), is it the result of a failure to maintain standards (violation of a taboo, decadence, breaking of codes of honesty or cooperation), is it the result of direct malevolence from within (witchcraft)? And how is the ill or tension resolved? By expulsion or excision? By counteracting with a more powerful agent? By a restoration of standards? By homeopathic means, representing a superior semiotic domain (healing suffering with a Christian cross)? And what metaphors are used for change? Do these see change as an aberration, as an opportunity (New Deal, New Frontier, in the history of United States politics), as a necessity (a new supply to create a new demand in a consumerist economy)? Is change envisioned as new enslavement or as deliverance and vindication? These are all important questions that need to be asked about the processes of change in a culture.

A second consideration here is understanding change as the reorganization of boundaries in semiotic domains. Boundaries are usually changed by their transgression. When slaves no longer act as slaves, when the mute begin to speak, when lower classes no longer "know their place," boundaries have to change within a culture. Consciousness of boundaries is tied up with consciousness of identity. They interact, causing the one to bring about change in the other. Certainly the reorganization of physical boundaries in the celebration of the Eucharist, as noted above, has had a profound effect on laypeople's consciousness of their own position and role within the Christian community. Conversely, the consciousness created by the experience of secularization caused an increasing disparity between the sense of identity in religious semiotic domains as opposed to the rest of the semiotic domains in society, resulting in the need to convoke an ecumenical council for the sake of aggiornamento.

A question that certainly comes to mind in considering reorganization of boundaries in local theologies is: How will reorganization in the religious domain interact with the sense of identity growing out of the other semiotic domains? If the disparity is too great, or if the changes are forced, there is a reasonably good chance that a dual religious system will be the result.

Another related question on the matter of identity, change, and boundaries has to do with urban-industrialized societies where continuing rapid social change is considered the norm rather than the exception. In these kinds of societies, where boundaries of group identity are not well defined (e.g., one may marry whom one wills, or not marry at all), and where world-view is marked by a great deal of pluralism, then constant change is seen as a way of preventing entropy rather than causing it. Continually new sign systems need to be generated to cope with a flood of new information and possibilities. We do not have enough experience to know how long these kinds of societies can continue at this rate. The need to set up boundaries of identity, in these situations, becomes internalized. These boundaries become a psychological rather than a cultural or sociological problem. A metaphor of progress, drawing upon eschatological imagery from the Jewish and Christian Scriptures, has been one way of organizing this approach.[51] But this was developed in a culture where the economic domain dominated the semiotic systems of the culture. When economic resources became scarce, the metaphor of progress lost its power to organize boundaries in this fashion. One wonders if eschatological imagery will be able to continue to deal with this reality of rapid change without lapsing into the darker side of apocalyptic metaphors.

A final consideration has to do with the rules of transformation that may govern patterns of change. Marx tried to formulate some of these on an economic level in the nineteenth century. Economic realities have become increasingly complex in the century since his time. Based upon analysis of folklore and mythology, various semioticians have tried to identify and formulate basic rules of transformation.[52] Among these basic observations are the following:

1. Change is initiated when a boundary is transgressed. The transgression of a boundary calls for a reorganization of the semiotic domain.

2. Because of the binary nature of many signs, depending upon contrastive elements, it is not unusual for a sign to reverse itself in a situation of change. What was good becomes bad, what was dominant becomes recessive.

3. Structuralism has taught us that two irreconcilable signs can be mediated by a third sign that somehow incorporates the first two. This has also been a common principle in dialectics.

4. Change can be expressed in the semiotic system by changing either the spatial metaphors or the temporal metaphors.

CULTURAL ANALYSIS AND LOCAL THEOLOGY

We have covered a wide range of concepts and principles in this chapter, all meant in one way or another to help us with listening to a culture. In concluding, it must be stressed again that no culture is ever so simple that a comprehensive explanation and description can be given. Nor is it ever so static that all is entirely cohesive and consistent. Yet by concentrating on culture texts and various semiotic domains, an understanding of the culture can emerge, which can give new voice to the members of the culture from an inner perspective, and capacities for dealing with change and intercultural communication from the outer perspective. It can provide a way for coming to understand the sign system of a culture, and something of the metaphors that collect and guide the signs in a cultural system.

Once this has been done, where does one go in a local theology? The next step is selection: selection of culture texts that will become the focus of theological reflection. Criteria for selection can vary, but certainly those points where tension and ill are most strongly felt, those areas where identity can be enhanced, those problems that need correlation with practice in the larger church would seem to take some precedence. Theology for many centuries in Christianity was primarily an occasional enterprise, developed to meet certain needs as they arose. Certainly the concern in many countries with initiatory rites into Christianity to deal with problems of Christian identity is one good place to start. Another is an investigation of what metaphors will characterize the reality of the Christian community or the experience of the saving reality of Christ. The need for a restructuring of ministries provides another area for reflection.[53]

But these are primarily internal concerns. Relating the religious domain to the other semiotic domains of society is equally pressing. Liberation theologies have taken leadership in this regard. How is one to follow Jesus Christ in all aspects of one's life? How does one discern the reality of the kingdom in the sign systems of a culture? What messages (justice, harmony, love, hope) will predominate in the incarnate religious domain of our community?

Once the issue for theological reflection has been located within the sign system of the culture, one is ready to begin the gospel dialogue with the larger church tradition. The local situation takes the leadership in defining the problem. The community is now in a position to turn to other local churches for dialogue.

From the point of view of local theologies, there are two dimensions to this dialogue. The first is determining the proper mode of discourse. What kind of theological result will make the most sense for dealing with the situation at hand? This will be the subject of the next chapter, where different forms of theology and how they relate to local circumstance will be explored. The second dimension has to do with the quality of the theological result. By what criteria do we determine whether the result of our reflection is faithful to the gospel of Jesus Christ? This raises the question of variance and invariance in tradition, the subject of chapter 5.

4

Theology and Its Context: Church Tradition as Local Theologies

THEOLOGY AND ITS CONTEXT

The previous chapter explored ways of listening to a culture so as to allow its configurations to emerge. Special attention was given to a semiotic model of understanding culture, concentrating on the sign systems in culture texts. This model provides a way of allowing the symbolic potential of a culture to become more evident.

A careful investigation of the sign systems of a culture can make us all the more sensitive to how much theology itself is embedded in culture and takes on cultural forms. Awareness of this is, of course, not something new. But the dramatic increase in the number of cultures now making up the church, all seeking a Christian identity, compounded by their struggles to be freed from socioeconomic and political oppression, gives a particular urgency to developing a greater sensitivity to theology and its context.

Theology has often been defined as faith seeking understanding, *fides quaerens intellectum.* Local theologies make us keenly aware that "understanding" itself is deeply colored by cultural context. Indeed, even the epistemological forms for understanding can have a strong cultural tint, reminding us that to start with a "universal" anthropology means starting with a local anthropology extended beyond its cultural boundaries. How human knowledge is experienced, although communicable across cultural boundaries, is nonetheless largely shaped by local circumstances.

The experience of the cultural rootedness of theology rebounds again on a local community when it engages the church tradition, entering into that dialogue to test, affirm, and challenge its own understanding of the gospel. We now know that what had often been called the Christianization of a people was in fact their Westernization, depriving them of their own past. When encounter reminds these churches of their enmeshments with that colonial past, the situation becomes even more difficult. Instead of being nourishing, the encounter becomes alienating, and tradition is held at arm's length. What often results is that the tradition comes to be understood positivistically (a surface reading of its culture texts, based on assumptions from the culture of the reader), or it is read selectively (only those texts from the tradition that affirm the identity of the local church), or it is not read at all.

How does one go about overcoming these difficulties raised in the encounter of culture and church tradition? The answers usually focus on ways of seeing the tradition less positivistically or monolithically. Three ways are commonly followed.

In the first way, one reconstructs the witnesses of the New Testament to form an ideal type, the New Testament church. This approach is found most often in Reformed Protestant Christianity. This ideal type is then used as a guide for the development of the local theology, often providing the models for proper contextualization.[1] This kind of approach has the advantage of a continuing encounter with the New Testament, and so gives an aura of authenticity to the results of the encounter between the ideal type and the local community. There are, however, a number of significant difficulties: (1) There is a strong consensus among New Testament exegetes that one has to speak of New Testament churches, rather than a single New Testament church.[2] A harmonization of first-century realities does violence to the data and reflects a homogenization that came much later in history. (2) When one creates the ideal type, one must ask who does the harmonization and what principles are at play, emphasizing some aspects and playing down others. Any reading of a series of texts as diverse as those of the New Testament will have to call for principles of selection. Those principles usually have more to do with the contemporary situation than with first-century circumstances. (3) The New Testament churches themselves represent different cultural and social circumstances. Why would those circumstances be read differently from the way in which we try to read our own? One major reason would be the normativeness that all Christians accord to the New Testament. But how normativeness and cultural analysis come together still needs to be asked.

The second way of pursuing the encounter between the tradition and a local situation is by dealing with the great recurring themes in theology from a local perspective. Sometimes this amounts to translation of great theological concepts into local terminology. At other times a more elaborate form of interpretation is used. The advantage of this approach is that it makes possible a dialogue between older and younger churches, since the same issues are being discussed. It gives the younger church a status not inferior to the older church, since the younger church has the possibility of making a contribution to a traditional question. Often forgotten, however, is that the younger church is accorded a certain theological maturity on the older churches' terms; in other words, a subtle paternalism is again at play. This becomes obvious when the traditional question has no obvious roots in the culture. One example of this has been the attempt to develop an African theology of original sin in sub-Saharan regions. When there is no myth of the Fall in the local culture, it becomes hard to build a local correlate of an ancient doctrine. A similar problem, shared by many cultures of the world, is to translate Chalcedonian terminology of person and nature, or the translation of hylomorphic categories long favored for explaining the Real Presence in the Eucharist. A large number of cultures do not have such categories. These all manifest a common problem. The church tradition's form and its formulation are considered as being somehow supracultural. But forms and formulations are always born in some cultural context. The Western doctrine of original sin does not take on the same form or the same significance in Orthodox theology,[3] and the terminology of Chalcedon or of medieval eucharistic theology likewise bespeaks a certain cultural context. To forget this does the tradition a disfavor by disincarnating it.

The third way of pursuing the encounter addresses this problem of terminology more directly. It realizes that the great theologies of East and West have drawn upon philosophical systems elaborated in their respective cultures to frame their questions and their answers. Therefore, what needs to be done is to find the philosophical correlate in other cultures, or to construct one if it is lacking. Placide Tempels' pioneering work in Bantu philosophy, utilizing Neo-Thomist categories, was mentioned in chapter 1, as was the later project of Charles Nyamiti. The same kind of work has been carried on elsewhere, at the level of comparative philosophies (the work of Alexis Kagame comes to mind[4]), or through the use of contemporary linguistic philosophies (e.g., O. Bimwenyi-Kweshi's work on critical foundations in a fundamental theology[5]). This approach recognizes the importance of organizing concepts in framing a theology, and can offer great insight into local understandings. The difficulty posed by this approach is that it assumes only one kind of relationship between cultural forms and theological expression, namely, the model of theology as sure knowledge (*scientia*), which has been the principal form in the West since the thirteenth century. It assumes one set of cultural relations for the expression of knowledge to be valid for all cultures at all times.

To summarize: the approach to the church tradition in the development of local theologies means understanding not only how the questions and the content that are in the tradition receive their shape, but also the cultural conditioning of the very paradigms of thought themselves. These paradigms of thought have to be considered in constituting an adequate local theology, and one must be sensitive to relations of paradigms to their culture. In the previous chapter it was noted how important root metaphors can be to the organization of a semiotic domain and how codes can shape signs differently. So perhaps theology in African villages could best be expressed in proverbs rather than in Bantu philosophy. Perhaps theology could be done in poetry in

Japan; or in the form of sutra and commentary in South Asia. Melanesian theology might be done in songs and oratory, and United States black theology in the dialogue of gospel preaching. We need to locate those paradigms of thought in a culture which shape meaning and affirm it in the culture. Until that is done, the tradition is used naively or even paternalistically.

Carrying out this project is an enormous task. On the one hand, one must engage in a semiotic study of culture, reading the culture texts to discern the signs, codes, and messages in the sign systems. On the other hand, one must reappropriate the church tradition in such a way as to make it available for the dialectic with the culture, which will give birth to a genuinely local theology.

The purpose of this chapter is to pursue that second part of the problem, finding a way to reappropriate the church tradition. As indicated by the critique developed so far, this reappropriation will have to involve (1) examining within the tradition the relation of theological forms to their cultural contexts, identifying what makes them bearers of the concerns and the responses to those concerns in a given situation, thereby allowing (2) the church tradition to emerge as a series of local theologies for the sake of the encounter with the culture in order (3) to lay the foundation for a more comprehensive theory of tradition and issues of change within the tradition.

THEOLOGY AND THE SOCIOLOGY OF KNOWLEDGE

There are a number of ways to undertake study of the relation of theological forms to cultural contexts. The one that suggests itself most readily is the sociology of knowledge, which is concerned with how ideas and systems of thought relate to their social contexts. The sociology of knowledge tries to answer the questions: Why is it that certain ideas or ways of thinking become prevalent at a particular point in time? How does an idea become outmoded? What do we mean when we say that an idea appears prematurely or ahead of its time? What is the nature of that "time" in each of these instances?

There were indications of efforts to answer these questions systematically from the time of Francis Bacon onward, especially in France.[6] But it would be fair to say that with Karl Marx the sociology of knowledge first came into a complete form. Marx explored how systems of thought were related to class interests and values. Class interests and values were in turn expressions of the relations of production in a society. Thus systems of thought were determined by the economic and social conditions of a society. These systems of thought either gave an accurate mirroring of social relationships or perpetrated a false consciousness (which he called ideology) to protect the interests of the ruling class. Marx used this model to analyze a variety of societies in human history.

Later thinkers have built upon Marx, but have often rejected what they saw as a unilateral determination of ideas by social conditions. It was evident that ideas could also be shaped by other ideas, and that in some instances ideas reshaped social conditions (as in the case of some revolutionary situations). Karl Mannheim did some of the most thorough work in the sociology of knowledge in the early part of the twentieth century.[7] By pressing the argument of the sociology of knowledge to its extreme, seeing a relation between every idea and every social relation, he ended up in a relativist conundrum: Was the sociology of knowledge itself the product of certain social conditions? Confronted with this kind of bind, the sociology of knowledge found itself chastened. It became less confident about finding a link between every idea and every social condition and considerably more cautious about describing the nature of the relation.

As used today, the sociology of knowledge is prone to point more modestly to those relationships of ideas and society and to hedge considerably on the question of causation. But it continues to be helpful in suggesting answers to the questions stated above about the relations between ideas and their environments.

What value would the sociology of knowledge have for the study of the church tradition, particularly for the task of seeing the tradition as a series of local theologies? Its principal contribution would be to help to identify different forms of theological expression and suggest links between these and social conditions. This not only has the advantage of providing a way of classifying the various local theologies in the church tradition, but also might offer newer churches some suggestions about what forms of theological expression have been found useful in the past in situations similar to their own.

The sociology of knowledge works from a variety of different assumptions about procedure and the phenomena it studies. It is important to be explicit about which of those assumptions inform this investigation, especially when dealing with a subject as important as the Christian tradition. Here are some of the most important assumptions shaping the presentation that follows: (1) Forms of thought are embedded in social conditions, but are not unilaterally determined by them. Ideas can shape culture as much as culture shapes ideas. (2) Religion has an exceedingly complex set of relations to a culture, involving legitimation, socialization, conservation, and innovation. No single one of these functions will be given dominance over the others here. (3) Religion is more than a set of doctrines or ideas. It is also a way of living in the world. Put simply, religion is both a view of life and a way of life. (4) The approach taken here follows especially the concerns of Clifford Geertz, who feels that the sociology of knowledge cannot restrict its concerns to seeking out how social interests are legitimated or social strains mitigated. The sociology of knowledge should also concern itself with a sociology of meaning and of symbolic forms.[8] (5) It is assumed that, although one form of thought may predominate in a culture at some point in time, it can and will live side by side with other forms. (6) The relations between forms of thought and social conditions are such that they rarely allow for exhaustive description. This presentation concentrates only on those relations instructive for developing local theologies.

While the sociology of knowledge has often been applied to religion itself, it has been less often applied to theology as such. Such a rereading of the church tradition, however, can be useful in developing a theory of tradition as well as opening up the dialogue necessary for the development of local theology.

A SOCIOLOGY OF THEOLOGY

A sociology of theology, then, tries to see how particular forms of thought might be related to particular cultural conditions. The purpose of such an investigation is to come to a better understanding about the special strengths and also the limitations of any particular style of theology, to see under which cultural conditions it might best be utilized, and to broaden our awareness of the range of possible forms of theological expression available to local theologies. The latter point is especially important, since one group often judges another group's theology as not being "real" theology, or as being more or less unsophisticated. We shall see that often such comparisons are indeed odious and based upon comparison of qualitatively different entities.

A sociology of theology should not be confused with a history of dogma, which tries to trace the historical development of Christian belief and doctrine, using some set of unifying principles. The concern here is not so much the ideas as the forms the ideas take: what counts for a good formulation, and what does not. Moreover, there is no necessary progression in the forms of thought as there is in the development of an idea. The forms can exist side by side; they can flourish and then decline. But a sociology of theology can throw some light on usual distinctions made in the history of dogma, such as the distinctions between the patristic and scholastic periods,[9] or between theology as wisdom (*sapientia*) and theology as sure knowledge (*scientia*).[10]

Four forms of theological expression will be dealt with here. The first is not an approach in the same way as the others, yet it brings together in a useful way a number of forms important for developing local theologies. The four approaches are: (1) theology as variations on a sacred text; (2) theology as wisdom; (3) theology as sure knowledge; (4) theology as praxis.

THEOLOGY AS VARIATIONS ON A SACRED TEXT

In a way all theology can be considered a variation on a sacred text. Put into the language of semiotics, the culture text of theology communicates a message by varying the signs originally employed, yet maintains the same codes. Through this expansion of the sign system, the message is invested with a wider semantic capacity than was originally the case.

As was indicated in the previous chapter, the linkage that brings signs together is called "metaphor," and metaphor is basic to the possibility of creating variations on a sacred text. By the bringing together of different signs in the metaphor, messages are related and thereby expanded, since the metaphor posits a similarity between the two signs (as in "God is Father" or in

"God is light"). Along with metaphor, the use of metonymy permits an expansion of meaning by positing contiguity within a metaphoric domain (for example, "Jesus is the Lamb of God" is expanded to include "the Lamb of God who takes away the sin of the world"). Metaphors create new semantic space, and metonyms fill up that space. If a metaphor is a discovery, then metonyms are the implications of the discovery. By drawing out those implications, metonyms create the possibility for the emergence of new metaphors. Metonymy can be seen as a logic of development within metaphor.

A number of different researchers have located the metaphor-metonym structure at the basis of religious thought. Claude Lévi-Strauss sees it as fundamental for understanding how mythic thought incorporates experience.[11] Roy Wagner has shown how metaphor works in magic and ritual among a New Guinea people.[12] James Fernandez has shown its role in creating the religious semiotic domain among a West African people.[13]

While these considerations can be extended to virtually all forms of theological thought, they apply in a special way to those forms that concentrate on units within a culture text and the possibilities those units possess apart from the larger structure of the sign system itself. In other words, these forms work especially with variations on elements within a text and take the overall structure of the text for granted. Three of those forms deserve closer examination: the commentary, the narrative, and the anthology.

The *commentary* concentrates on the transformation of one part of a text by bringing it into contact with another sign system. This forms the basic kind of theology in many, if not most literate religious traditions. Rather than producing new sacred texts, commentaries are produced that extend the sacred text into new semantic domains. One thinks of the role of the Midrash and the great talmudic commentaries in Judaism, or the *hadith* literature in Islam; the Vendanta literature in Hinduism even in its name implies this relation of variation to the sacred Vedas. The innumerable commentaries on sutras in Mahayana Buddhism, and the commentaries on the Christian Scriptures in the patristic period are further representatives of this form. Indeed, up until the time of Abelard, the most common term for what we now call theology was *sacra pagina* (sacred page), referring to the fact that theology was but a commentary on Scripture. This was the form of the magister's lecture in the early medieval university: a portion of the Scriptures would be taken, the commentaries of the great authorities (*auctoritates*) of the past would be noted, and the magister would then add his own commentary.

In many religious traditions, one gained one's theological credentials by memorizing the commentaries (in Judaism, Islam, and early medieval Christianity) or by writing a commentary oneself (the writing of a commentary on Peter Lombard's *Sententiae* being the doctoral dissertation of the early medieval Christian theologian). While the commentary could include critical grammatical details, it generally allowed a greater semantic freedom than would be permitted in Western hermeneutics today. One thinks of the allegorizations at Alexandria, the play on letters of a word in Jewish Cabala, the classic four senses of the Scriptures in medieval Christianity, the *sensus plenior* later developed, and, in the twentieth century, what Karl Barth was to achieve with his commentary on the Epistle to the Romans. All of these approaches in commentary presuppose working with units within a larger text, and without regard for the structure of that larger text. The interest is in expanding those units into new semantic domains.

Commentaries were often done in a more scholarly and academic sphere. Perhaps the one form of commentary most frequently practiced outside the academic sphere has been the sermon. The sermon, a form of oral address found in all the great literate traditions, is an extension of one particular text into different semantic spaces, usually the spaces of an audience. In so doing the text comes to inhabit a world different from that of its origins or even different from its place among other texts in a sacred canon. The importance of sermons as theology can be seen from the collections of homilies made in patristic times and down to the published collections in our own day.

A second important form of variation on a sacred text is the *narrative,* or story. The narrative differs from the commentary in that signs within a text are extended through a series of transformations, which not only extend the meaning of the original text, but engage the hearer by getting him or her to identify with some of the agents in the narrative. The first few Christian centuries used stories to develop in further detail meanings seen in the New Testament canon; we call these stories today the Apocrypha or Pseudoepigrapha. Later the stories of the martyrs, the desert dwellers, and other saints developed reflection on the Christian message through the medium of the life of one unusually dedicated to God. The stories of the Hasidim in Judaism or those about the Sufis in Islam are similar expressions of faith and its extension. Stories have exercised the imagination of most believers in religious traditions more than has the scholarly commentary. In contemporary Western Christianity, especially in the United States, the use of the story form has successfully helped individuals to find their own place in Christian meaning by examination of their personal histories. Retelling of the biblical stories subtly weaves together biblical and contemporary narrative to open the semantic possibilities of the biblical text. John Shea's *Stories of God* is a good example of this.

A third form of variation on the sacred text often employed is the *anthology*. Anthologies were particularly popular in the first millennium of Christianity in the West and have continued their popularity in the East to the present time. The *florilegium* (compilation of short texts from the Fathers and other authorities), the *catena* (a chronological chain of commentaries on a single biblical text), the *philokalia* (collection of texts of a single author)—all bring together discrete units of text from authors for a stated purpose. The florilegia were often considered a degenerate form of theology by contemporary twentieth-century historians, since they do not respect context or the integrity of the text itself. But through that period known in the West as the Dark Ages, theology survived because of the florilegia, and these became the backbone of the medieval commentary and gloss and survive today in their modern counterpart, the footnote.

Can the cultural conditions that seem to foster theologies built upon commentary, narrative, and anthology be isolated? Let us consider two such sets of cultural conditions that seem to be especially conducive to these kinds of theology.

The first set of conditions supports oral over literate forms of culture. Even though the idea of variations on a sacred text presupposes a written text, the memorization process of those texts in all the literate religious traditions suggests that the written character of the text itself played a secondary role. Even though commentaries came to be written down, they were in the first instance part of an oral tradition. The sermon as variation on the text is a prime oral exercise, which can expand or contract based upon the response of the audience. Even the writing down of texts in the florilegia was meant, first, to preserve texts and, second, to serve as an aide mémoire.

We cannot go into all the specifics of oral versus literary culture here. Only a few comments may be in order. The kind of commentary or hermeneutic that has developed since the eighteenth century, which hews much closer to the written text than previously, has to be seen as the result of the fact that each scholar can own a copy of a text. While almost all cultures now have some measure of literacy, the impact of literacy itself on how people organize their experience waxes and wanes. Among the highly literate peoples in the industrialized West, literacy seems to be losing ground to aural and visual media such as radio and television. Whether the computer will reimpose literacy remains to be seen.

Folklorists have studied oral patterns for a long time. More recently exegetes have been investigating some of the differences between orality and literacy; the synthesizing work of American literary theorist Walter Ong should also be mentioned.[14] Orality has to do with the expansion of texts in nonlinear fashion. The linear patterns to which we have become accustomed result from a habit of following a line of print. But other arrangements are possible in a progression. Art work from nonliterate cultures often exhibits some of these other patterns.

A second set of cultural conditions is suggested by the fact that so many variations on a sacred text deal only with units within a text rather than with the text as a whole. The best example of that is certainly the florilegium. How is it possible to move about that freely with units in a text without destroying the text itself? It seems possible only when the culture itself protects the text from outside threat; in other words, when a text can live in a fairly self-enclosed society. The relative security of cultural boundaries (such as the monastery walls of the Dark Ages) allows room for that free play with the text. The texts have lost their original contexts, and the new cultural setting becomes the context, allowing the units in the text to be recombined freely. Lévi-Strauss has pointed out that this process is close to that found in the death of myths, which may be related to why historians see the florilegium as a degenerate form of theology.[15] But it does point out how much variations depend upon a secure boundary. This seems to be the case because then the speaker can share an assumed context with hearers. Elements can be moved around freely since everyone present knows the framework, even though it might be puzzling to the outsider. To use a secular analogue: jokes seldom travel well across cultural boundaries because the play with the units of the text presumes knowledge of the single context. What is amusing or pleasant may depend to a great deal on that context.

What do these two sets of cultural conditions suggest about developing local theologies? What do they say about matching forms of expression with cultural conditions? We may summarize some of what they suggest as follows.

1. In cultures that still have a strong oral focus, commentaries, narratives, and anthologies may be the most likely forms of theology. Instead of trying to write systematic treatises, many of the cultures of Africa, Latin America, and Oceania should be trying to write Bible commentaries, as indeed some of them are. It was noted in an earlier chapter that much of the theology of liberation that is being developed is never published. A reflection on what has been presented here should help to explain why people may not even want to consider doing so.

2. The natural forms of handing on the central messages of the culture—proverbs, old stories, and the like—are therefore legitimate vehicles for the developing of local theologies. There is ample precedent for this in the Christian tradition as well as in other traditions.

3. Given the analysis of the oral cultures, it might be easier to understand why preaching is so unsuccessful in many industrialized cultures. In those cultures that do not have the same access to written texts, people are more able to listen to a single speaker for greater lengths of time, and those speakers know how to keep their listeners engaged over longer periods. At the same time one is struck by the success of evangelistic styles of Christianity in oral cultures. Would this explain the success of certain styles of preaching among the poor (United States black storefront preaching, the preaching in the chapels of early Methodism)?

4. Understanding the dynamics of transmitting messages in oral cultures (especially their nonlinearity) helps to situate the kind of theology emerging as commentary, story, and anthology. When judged against the academic treatise and its standards, it is quite different and can look deficient. But the patterns of expanding the semantic domain are different in oral cultures from that of literate academe. This will become more evident after we have looked at theology as sure knowledge. Nonetheless there are criteria of adequacy in this method of developing local theologies, based upon quality of engagement of the culture. Some of the criteria have been grouped under what would ordinarily be considered aesthetics. Perhaps it is there that we should look to find the criteria for these kinds of theology.

5. While enclosed cultures are rapidly disappearing on the planet, poverty and isolation can still create those enclosed worlds, even though the territory is densely populated. In these situations, collections of sayings, reminiscent of the *fioretti* of Francis of Assisi, will continue to flourish.

THEOLOGY AS WISDOM

One of the predominant forms of theology in Christianity, as well as in other great literate traditions, has been theology as wisdom, or *sapientia*. In Christianity it is identified especially with the patristic period, with the theological tradition in the East down to the present, with the Augustinian heritage in the West, and with the theology growing out of the spiritual and mystical traditions.

Wisdom theology shares much with the theologies discussed in the previous section. Like some of those theologies, wisdom theology is concerned with the meaning of texts and with experience. Wisdom theology's differences lie principally in its intended scope, its preoccupations, and its logic. It differs through its continuing effort to extend those meanings to encompass the cosmos. It shows a strong interest in integrating all parts of the world by faith into a single, meaningful whole, to include realms both seen and unseen. All of those different aspects of the whole are interrelated, often in images of ascent and descent. The work of Pseudo-Dionysius and Johannes Scotus Erigena come to mind here, with their constructed worlds ordering the various levels of meaning and life. So the scope of wisdom theology is, quite literally, cosmic.

The preoccupations of wisdom theology often center on psychology, that is, on the interiority of human experience. The human subject is seen as the prism through which one is to contemplate God and the universe. An intimate knowledge of human subjectivity, gained through a disciplined examination of one's own inner life, leads to knowledge of divinity. One is reminded of the admonition of one of the great theologians of the wisdom tradition, Augustine, in this matter: "People are wont to set a high value on the knowledge of earthly and celestial things. But they are certainly better who prefer knowledge of themselves to this knowledge."[16] These preoccupations with the human subject are not ends in themselves. Through this knowledge one gains access to the all-embracing knowledge of the universe and the universe's creator. Human life represents the highest form of this creation in the visible sphere knowable to us; hence a study of human life is the surest way to wisdom.

The logic of this form of theological expression is determined by those preoccupations with the human prism. Knowledge of the human is seen as a vehicle to divine knowledge. Thus, whereas laws of association and contiguity (the laws of metonymic expansion of the metaphor) ruled theology as variations on a sacred text, laws of analogy become important in wisdom theology. Interest in type and antitype configurations, in seeing patterns in the world as traces of the creating godhead (*vestigia Dei*) left in creation, in any speculation that reveals the ordered character of the universe (numerological and astrological speculations), development of hierarchical orders, controlled allegory, relating the visible to the hidden—all of these analogical forms are seen as logics with an anagogical function: leading us upward to *theologia*, the contemplation of God. An example of a work embracing virtually all of these logics is Augustine's *De trinitate*, which leads the reader to a contemplation of God in the Trinity by examination of triadic manifestations of nature and especially in the human subject.

An image or metaphor that recurs in many of these logics is the *path* or *journey*. Beginning with the Ways of Life and Death in the first-century Didache, and moving through the treatises on the True Gnosis of Clement of Alexandria, the catechetical treatises of Ambrose of Milan and Cyril of Jerusalem, the *Mystagogia* of Maximus Confessor, the *Itinerarium mentis in Deum* of Bonaventure, to the *Ascent of Mount Carmel* of John of the Cross and the *Interior Mansions* of Teresa of Ávila, the idea of faith as an experience of a pathway and a gradual initiation recurs over and over again. The progression along the way leads to wisdom, which is the knowledge of God, genuine *theologia*. In Orthodox Christianity, the title "theologian" has been reserved for those mystics who go most deeply into the wisdom of God.

Can cultural conditions be indicated for a wisdom theology? It is not an easy task, since wisdom theology has flourished in so many different times and places. But there are some recurring factors that deserve our attention.

First, wisdom theology seems to predominate in those places where human life is seen as a unified cycle, marked by progressive development. True human, faith-filled existence is characterized by an initiation into, and growth within, the frame of Christian life and mystery. One moves through stages and patterns as one matures in faith and knowledge of God through a deepened sense of self. Perhaps this is why wisdom theology has been maintained in many Christian groups through a monastic tradition, where the rhythms of the horarium allow for such a perception of reality. Wisdom theology seems to be in the intellectual framework for virtually all Christian (and perhaps all non-Christian) traditions of mysticism.

Second, wisdom theology places great stock on being able to see the world, both the visible and the invisible, as a unified whole. The quest for wisdom carries with it a sense of being able to relate all the parts to the whole. While this could characterize any religious endeavor, it holds in a special way for wisdom theology. It is a pathway where learning, though important and indeed essential, is subordinated to devotion. Cultures configured in this fashion will find wisdom theology a congenial way of expressing their own belief.

Third, in cultures where human growth is not seen as personal achievement, but as discovering the underlying and unchanging patterns of the universe and coming into conformance with them, wisdom theology will find a ready home. The ideal of a fulfilled human life becomes one where a conformity to these archetypes of existence is carried out. One thinks of the Greek concept of *paideia*, the quest of the alchemist, and the discovery of the unity of the atman and the Brahman in Indian religion, in this regard.

Fourth, wisdom theology tends to prevail in cultures marked by a strong sense of interiority, by the pursuit of the psychological as the path to perfection. The inner way leads to the outer reality.

Fifth, cultures that adopt a two-level approach to ultimate reality, an exoteric and an esoteric one, are likely to follow the patterns of a wisdom theology.

What implications do these cultural conditions suggest for the development of local theologies? First, a wisdom theology will be a likely development in those cultures that have maintained their important rites of passage. It provides a way to bring together the wisdom of the ancestors with the wisdom of Christ, the first ancestor in faith.

Second, only gradually have Westerners discovered the deep interiority of many so-called primitive peoples, who often have an elaborate wisdom theology developed in their own tradition but keep it hidden from Westerners. The experience of Marcel Griaule among the Dogon in Mali is a graphic example of this.[17] Where people prize wisdom above learning and wealth, wisdom theology becomes the natural vehicle for their expression in faith.

Third, cultures placing great prize on a unified view of the world, often sacrificing many other things to maintain it, seek the way of wisdom. This kind of approach still characterizes many peoples of the world. For this reason it is not surprising that wisdom theologies are among the most common forms of theology coming out of the newer churches in the Pacific, in Africa, and in southern Asia. When one recalls that wisdom theologies have always been the predominant kind of theology in Orthodox Christianity, and held the upper hand in the West for the first twelve hundred years, one should not be surprised by this fact. In quests for new spiritualities in the West, this kind of theology is reasserting itself: the quest for unity in self and society as the way to God, the source of all unity.

Fourth, wisdom-theology models have remained the most fruitful for catechesis. The development of the rite of Christian initiation for adults has utilized this form once again, and quite successfully.

Fifth, wisdom theology functions best where a unity in world-view is possible. In strongly pluralistic societies, where world-views compete, it is less successful. Where values of individual achievement and assertion are prized, wisdom theology makes way for formulas and recipes for getting ahead. Perhaps this points to why, in secularized and urban cultures, wisdom theologies tend to be absent, yet many of their values continue to be sought out.

THEOLOGY AS SURE KNOWLEDGE

Theology as sure knowledge, or *scientia*, is probably the most common form of theology in Roman Catholicism and mainline Protestantism in the

West today. When people there think of theology, they think of this kind of theology. Theology as sure knowledge tries to give a critical, relational account of faith, using the tools of a discipline that can offer the most exact form of knowledge known to the culture. This has often meant the use of human reason, but also now includes disciplines in the social sciences and to some extent in the natural sciences. The knowledge gained in this kind of theological reflection is, first and foremost, sure.

This kind of theology has its precedents in Christianity among the Greek apologists. However, its more immediate roots are with Boethius and the Carolingian schools, where rhetoric and dialectic began to be applied to the stuff of theology to create a more ordered expression of faith. The rediscovery of important texts of Aristotle allowed for a greater refinement of theology, based upon his logic. This culminated in the great theological syntheses of the high Middle Ages, of which Thomas Aquinas's *Summa Theologiae* is the best known. It was in this period that theology as sure knowledge was to become the preeminent form for theological reflection, allowing for ever more subtle distinctions, and eventually for the development of new subdisciplines in theology. These new disciplines were pursued in the subsequent centuries, leading finally to the work of the Encyclopedists and the Manualists. The Enlightenment had introduced a more acute questioning of the theological enterprise and resulted in some change of form, but the basic thrust remained the same: to give the most exacting account possible of Christian faith as it relates to reality.

Throughout the centuries where theology as sure knowledge has dominated the scene—from the twelfth into the twentieth century—a number of concerns have given shape to this kind of theology. First, there has been a constant concern to relate theology to other, and often competing, forms of knowledge. The quality of theological knowledge and how it measures up to other forms of knowledge has been a continuing preoccupation. Aquinas's *Summa* opens with this very question,[18] and twentieth-century studies in method continue that tradition.[19] This kind of theology is aware that there are many ways to know in the world and so tries to establish in what ways religious knowledge is at least equal, if not superior, to other ways of knowing values in the culture.

Second, theology as sure knowledge is concerned about giving a rigorous internal account of the experience of faith and sets for itself the task of studying exhaustively different aspects of faith and the sacred texts. Analysis is the key word here: the ever more subtle distinction, the ever better-defined relation, which allows the fullness of the faith-experience to unfold and so be extended. In the early period this was achieved through the *quaestio* and the *disputatio*; in later periods this was done through the development of the subdisciplines (dogmatic theology, moral theology, fundamental theology, and so on).

Third, this interest in a rigorous internal account of faith gave a continuing impulse to the building of a system. Whereas wisdom theology tries to discern the unity of the world, theology as sure knowledge constructs a system to explain it. Any account of Christian belief, for theology as sure knowledge, cannot be considered complete until it is an interrelated account of the whole experience of faith. System has been the sign of a complete theology from the *Summae* of the Middle Ages, through the *Institutes* of Calvin, to the *Church Dogmatics* of Karl Barth.

Fourth, as the different kinds of knowledge became more distinctive and refined their own methods for gaining knowledge, a greater, less reconcilable pluralism emerged. As a result of this, method became as much the subject of discussion as did the content of each of the disciplines. The same has been the case in theology. The nineteenth and twentieth centuries have found theologies unusually preoccupied with the question of method.

What are the cultural conditions that support this kind of theology? Theology as sure knowledge looms so large in the West, and is so often held up as the theological ideal elsewhere, that it is hard to think of it as one form of theology alongside others. Yet this form, too, owes its beginnings and its maintenance to certain kinds of cultural configurations. Much has been written about the origin of this kind of theology; a summary of some of the important points here might be helpful to understand better its own situated character.[20]

The first important aspect to play into the origins of theology as sure knowledge was the rediscovery of Roman law in the West and its spread in the eleventh century. Without a code of law, society could not have been reorganized sufficiently to allow for the reemergence of cities and urban economies. The bureaucracy needed to sustain city culture was made up of clerics, trained in cathedral and abbey schools. Law came to have a profound impact on the church through the clergy. A more unified church law had repercussions on the study of theology. Thus Anselm's great work on the redemption borrowed its metaphors from the law and the law's concept of the *ordo* as a societal ideal. Law's concern with relationships and with precision played an important formative role in making analysis, precision, clarity, and the making of distinctions important criteria in developing an adequate theology.

A second factor was the rise of the towns and cities in what had been a predominantly rural economy. In the towns and cities a greater division of labor came about, and the guilds grew out of that division of labor. A proto-capitalist economy was born, with money and banking systems replacing exchange economies. The training and teaching of persons for this more complex society moved away from rural monasteries to new centers in towns and cities. Those teachers were organized into guilds, as was the case in other occupations. The university was born.

The development of the Western university is perhaps the most significant factor for theology as sure knowledge. It provided a new environment and offered the protection of the guild to the magistri. For the first time a larger numbers of persons reflecting on faith came together on a full-time basis. The city and the university offered not only an environment but some measure of protection to the guild of theologians from the rural bishops and from the hierarchy in general. Abelard could still be condemned effectively by a synod of rural bishops but, a century later, the bishop of Paris could not make a condemnation of Thomas Aquinas stick. The flow of communication in theology was no longer between monasteries and episcopal palaces so much as it was among the universities of Paris, Oxford, Cologne, and Bologna. Aristotle's philosophy provided the analytic tools and even the framework for the reconstruction of the experience of faith. These tools were shared with other faculties in the university, initiating new dialogue partners for theology.

All of this had some important influence on what theology was to become: (1) Theological reflection came to be understood as the work of full-time, trained professionals. They were teachers who engaged in theology, rather than persons who taught because they had reflected theologically (such as bishops and novice masters). (2) Training in theology emphasized more strongly intellectual discipline, sometimes at the expense of the spirituality so central to wisdom theology. (3) Since theologians were primarily teachers, theology came to be seen as a school enterprise. This led to an important shift in audience. While theology was still intended for the illumination of the experience of the Christian community, its language was directed more and more to students, to other professors of theology, and to other disciplines of the school.

This was perhaps the greatest revolution in the symbolic forms for reflection and extension of the experience of faith. Without it, it is hard to imagine how religious knowledge could have continued to hold its place alongside other forms of knowledge that developed in the cities. At the same time the advances made by this kind of theology created problems for the church. The sophistication of theology as sure knowledge led this kind of theology to overshadow other forms, to the point where those other forms came to be judged by sure-knowledge standards. Needless to say, those other forms would be found wanting. It led to the situation today where it is now a struggle to relearn how a community engages in theological reflection.

What are some of the implications of these reflections for the role of theology as sure knowledge in developing local theologies? First, theology as sure knowledge functions best in two environments: the highly specialized and differentiated situations in urban economies, and wherever there is a plurality of competing world-views. When either of these situations prevails, theology as sure knowledge is the best tool for theological reflection and articulation of Christian experience.

Second, because of its emphasis on precision and clarity, theology as sure knowledge has special capacities for cross-cultural communication. It can develop categories that can be translated across cultural boundaries with a minimum of information loss.

Third, analysis and explanation are the great strengths of theology as sure knowledge from a methodological point of view. Where this needs to be done (as in taking an etic, or outer, view of a culture), theology as sure knowledge is the best tool.

Fourth, it should be remembered at the same time that theology as sure knowledge has limitations, as does any other form of human reflection. Having a system can be helpful, but it is not always necessary. System may even be impossible in situations of high pluralism. Too often attempts have been made to impose the methods and results of theology as sure knowledge in cultural contexts where they do not fit: among the poor, the uneducated, the rural. Many local communities feel that they do not have "real" theology until they have theology as sure knowledge. There needs to be greater awareness that theology as sure knowledge is but one form of theology, alongside wisdom theology, theology as praxis, and theology as more occasional variations on sacred texts.

THEOLOGY AS PRAXIS

Theology as praxis has come to the fore more recently as a major form of theological reflection. Although Origen remarked in the third century that all theology was praxis, the word has taken on a different meaning since that time. For a good amount of Western history, *praxis* was contrasted with *theoria* and *poiesis*. Hegel begins the more modern usage, and he and Karl Marx have shaped the understanding of praxis prevalent in contemporary theology.[21]

As understood today, praxis is the ensemble of social relationships that include and determine the structures of social consciousness. Thus thought and theory are considered sets of relations within the larger network of social relationships. Theory represents a dialectical moment within practice, as does action. Theory's task is to illumine the exact nature of those social relationships. By so doing, theory can point to false and oppressive relationships within the social fabric. This pointing to false and oppressive relationships brings them to awareness, which is the first step toward transforming them.

Since oppressive relationships occur in every society, and in many societies characterize the larger part of social life, praxis can come to be defined as a revolutionary or transformative praxis, aimed at the changing of those patterns.

In many parts of the world, especially in oppressive societies, a Christian praxis of faith has emerged. Like all praxis, it has a theoretical and a practical moment, both of which are considered essential to the theological process. In the theoretical moment an analysis of the social structure is undertaken, revealing the relationships of power, oppression, and freedom. The theoretical moment includes reflection on how God is active in human history, bringing judgment and a transformative moment to history. Such analysis and correlation with the perceived activity of God lead to transformative action on the part of the community of believers. In turn that action is reflected upon to reveal God's activity, leading to yet further action. The dialectical process of reflection and action are both essential to the theological process. Theology cannot remain only with reflection; nor can it be reduced to practice. Good reflection leads to action, and action is not completed until it has been reflected upon.

Understanding theology in this fashion has become widespread in oppressed societies around the world. It has come to be known as liberation theology.[22] The Latin American liberation theologies have become the best known, although liberation theology is not all of the same type. The nature of social oppression will reshape the focus from place to place. In some instances an analysis along the lines of class is the most enlightening. This has been the case in much of Latin America. In other areas the issue is race. Reflections of minority populations in Latin America, North America, and parts of Asia fall into this category. In South Africa liberation theology gives voice to an oppressed majority. In yet other instances, other categories are more to the point. Praxis arising from reflection along lines of sex is found among women on several continents. Or again, the factor can be religion, language, or caste. It can also serve the purposes of seeking political independence.

What are the tasks of a theology as praxis? Three can be mentioned specifically: (1) Theology as praxis is to help disentangle true consciousness from false consciousness. False consciousness arises out of accepting the oppressive relations within society as normative, either as an oppressor or as an oppressed person or group. Technically this task is known as ideology critique, "ideology" being a Marxist term for false consciousness. In theology the biblical-language style of prophecy is commonly used as a medium for carrying out this task. (2) Theology as praxis has to be concerned with the ongoing reflection upon action. What is the significance of the transformative praxis of a community? (3) Theology as praxis is concerned with the motivation to sustain the transformative praxis. In this it is especially distinguished from many other kinds of theological reflection that are devoted solely to clarification and amplification of experience. The adequacy of theology as praxis is measured in good part by the quality of action that emerges in its practical moment.

What are the cultural conditions correlative to theology as praxis? The most obvious ones are those that gave birth to it in the 1960s: situations in deep need of social change due to the oppressive relationships in society. Theology as praxis develops in those areas among the people who are oppressed. The same methods are not pursued in those societies by the oppressors. As a form of reflection, it is geared toward transformation and remains the most powerful approach to social transformation available to theology at this time.

The method of praxis has been extended to other cultural settings less clearly marked by oppression, often through the small-Christian-community movement. There it has been found useful in helping a community shape its identity and respond to its environment. Whether or not liberation theology, as the prime form of theology as praxis, can be sustained as a mode of theological reflection once liberation has been achieved is still an unanswered question. It remains unanswered because of the long and difficult road to liberation. It does, however, seem to be able to sustain communities engaged in liberative struggle over long periods of time.

What implications and possibilities does this form of theological reflection have for developing local theologies? Its emphasis on social analysis and its emphasis on social transformation have already made this kind of theology widely used in communities struggling in the midst of oppression. In those communities, its utility is obvious. As a method, it has been more of a conundrum to the older churches than to the newer ones. It is particularly helpful as a way of recovering a world-view or way of life that has been blocked by false consciousness on a large scale. This has been the experience in many feminist circles.

Its concern for salvation and wholeness, caught in the word "liberation," makes this method of praxis a close relative of the wisdom theologies. One could argue that liberation theologies are wisdom theologies turned outward. What wisdom theologies try to achieve through reflection and action via the interior path, liberation theologies do via the outer path. This could account for why the development of a spirituality for liberation was so high on the agenda of communities in the mid- and late-1970s after a decade's experience of action in liberation movements. This form of theological reflection works best when acute social transformation is needed. It has been less successful as a means for sustaining identity. It still exhibits difficulty in dealing with the complexities of popular religion.

THE TRADITION AS A SERIES OF LOCAL THEOLOGIES

The purpose of this chapter has been to open church tradition in a different way, by seeing it as a series of local theologies, closely wedded to and responding to different cultural conditions. To this end four theological forms were investigated and located in various parts of the church tradition. The relations between these forms and cultural conditions were looked at, and implications for the development of local theologies were drawn out. In summary, such an investigation was meant:

1. To attune our ears to the different kinds of theology being undertaken today. This is meant to encourage reading any attempt at local theology in a concrete way: What is the relation of the form to the local cultural conditions? This can help to prevent the imposition of the wrong forms in a situation, which promotes false consciousness—to use the language of theology as praxis.

2. To free us from thinking that theology as sure knowledge is the sole, legitimate form of "real" theology. It is a very important form, but still one form among several, and in many instances unsuited to the task at hand.

3. To allow local cultural and religious forms to dialogue more easily with the church tradition, thereby offering a better chance of maintaining a genuine catholicity in a local church's expression of its faith.

With the work of a sociology of knowledge applied to theology in mind, we are now ready to move more directly into the question of a theory of tradition and ways of ascertaining what constitutes Christian identity.

5

Tradition and Christian Identity

The previous chapter examined a way of looking at the Christian tradition so as to make easier the encounter between local theology and the Christian tradition. But making that encounter more possible only makes the questions about the nature of that encounter more pressing. This chapter looks at that encounter, and what it implies for local theology and the larger Christian tradition.

LOCAL THEOLOGY ENCOUNTERS CHRISTIAN TRADITION: SEVEN PROBLEMS

Any local theology that is truly Christian has to be engaged with the tradition, however a church might understand that tradition: the Scriptures, great conciliar and confessional statements, the magisterium. Without that engagement, there is no guarantee of being part of the Christian heritage.

That encounter with the tradition can raise many problems for the churches as they develop their local theologies. They are not trying to dilute or avoid aspects of the tradition; there is a deep desire to remain truly faithful to the apostolic tradition and to be themselves faithful witnesses to the gospel in their own circumstances. The problems arise instead from wondering whether or not the encounter with the tradition actually takes place at all, whether or not there is sufficient dialogue taking place to allow for mutual understanding between tradition and cultural situation. A heightened sensitivity to culture has made local churches only more keenly aware of the difficulties in communication. How can the tradition be truly received if the very grounds for dialogue are not first achieved?

Of the many different kinds of problems regarding the tradition with which the local church finds itself faced, seven deserve special attention here. These will help to form the context for a discussion of an understanding of tradition adequate to the problems being faced in local churches today. The first four have grown out of the kinds of concrete problems that have arisen in the dialogue between local theology and tradition. The last three are more reflexive in nature and result from dealing with the concrete problems.

1. How can a local church incorporate a received church doctrine when it is given in a form for which there is no cultural analogue in the local situation?

An example of this problem would be the difficulties many African cultures face in trying to incorporate the Roman Catholic tradition on original sin. The doctrine, which presents the belief in the universal need for redemption, draws heavily in its Roman Catholic form on the stories in Genesis 2–3 for its expression. The Western Christian development of this belief was shaped especially by Augustine in his debates with Pelagianism. His reading of Romans 5:12 led him to concentrate especially on the garden story in Genesis 2–3 and to derive from that text the framework for the theology of original sin. The Council of Trent reaffirmed the teaching in that form for Roman Catholics. Pius XII drew upon the same framework for addressing the discussions surrounding the origins of the human race in his *Humani Generis* in 1950.

When this tradition of talking about universal sinfulness and the need for redemption is brought into non-Western cultures, questions have to be raised about the close alliance between this doctrine and its Augustinian form. Many African cultures do not have a story of the Fall (as Christians have come to designate the garden story in Genesis 2–3) in their own origin stories. This need not mean that there is no sense of universal sinfulness; it can find expression in other ways. But the problem runs deeper than this. The Augustinian reading of that text has brought with it more than an equation of that story with the origins of universal sinfulness. It has brought with it an entire understanding of human anthropology that may have more to do with Augustine's own history and culture than with the Bible's: his understanding of human sexuality is perhaps the most commented upon in this matter. Must non-Western Christian cultures take Augustine's reading as normative, imbued as it is with his own history and culture?[1] This equation has become problematic even in Western cultures, as Western Christians tried to adjust their understanding of the garden story in light of their own developing understandings of human evolution. *Humani Generis* continued to try to respond to the evolution question out of the Augustinian framework, leaving the basic problem largely unresolved.

Even more interesting is the fact that, when the garden story was read to peoples who did not know the Augustinian tradition, they came up with quite different readings. When the story was read to some Ipili elders in the New Guinea highlands, they thought it must be a Christian initiation-rite story, describing what it is like to grow from childhood to adulthood.[2] Among the Sherenti in Brazil, local people changed the man-wife relationship to brother-sister in the story; for why should man and wife be ashamed of appearing naked before one another?[3] When the story was told to a people in East Africa, they missed the point of the Fall altogether. They were fascinated with how God walked with the couple in the cool of the evening.[4]

These variant readings should not surprise us, since exegetical evidence points to the fact that our Augustinian reading of the garden story is only one among several possibilities. Perhaps the story was first codified to act as a polemic against Canaanite cults. When analyzed from a structuralist perspective, the story does indeed look as though it might first have been told as part of an initiation rite at puberty.[5]

The question posed here is not whether Christians need hold a doctrine of the universal need for redemption or not. The question is, rather, how much that doctrine has to be tied to one long-standing reading of one biblical text, guided as it was by what was most likely a misreading of the Greek in Romans 5:12ff.[6] Western exegetes and theologians have struggled with this problem in light of their own changed world-view, which is now equally dissonant with a surface text reading of Genesis 2–3. Should this now be imposed as such upon the newer churches? If it is not, what are the guidelines for properly articulating this sense of universal need for redemption?

2. How does a local church resolve its question when the tradition's only experience with its concern was under quite different circumstances?

An example of this kind of problem occurs in dealing with polygamous marriage in rural Africa. More specifically, must a man (the examples in Africa are all of polygyny) send away all of his wives but the first in order to receive baptism? When such is required, long-standing and faithful relationships are sometimes severed. And worse, a grave injustice is done to those women sent away, since they are now excluded from the only social-welfare system the society has. They are condemned to a life without social relationship in a society where such is the equivalent of death.

All the dimensions of this thorny problem cannot be set out here. Eugene Hillman provided an exposition on this subject in his *Polygamy Reconsidered,*[7] and a number of the important elements need to be brought out here. Many Westerners think that polygyny arises from male lust and the exploitation of women. While this sometimes happens, the roots of the practice in rural Africa are primarily in the economic domain. In most of these societies there are more women than men, due to the fact that female infants are hardier and survive infancy in greater numbers than do males. Polygamous marriage provides those for whom there are no husbands a chance to be part of a family and have employment and a social security for which there is no alternative in a rural society. In urban settings this has changed, since the economic bond is no longer the primary one. Marriage is more than an economic relationship, to be sure; but to ignore the importance of the economic is also foolhardy.

When the question of polygamy came up in the past in Christian tradition, those economic relationships were not always clearly recognized. In instances where royal polygyny was forbidden,[8] one could argue that women should not be used as tokens or counters to weld relationships in political games. But was the economic aspect of marriage recognized in other instances? The problem is made more difficult when polygamous catechumens point to the patriarchs or the early kings of Israel, who were not only accepted but sometimes even especially chosen by God.

At the same time the long-standing and much cherished image of the relation of marriage as the relationship between Christ and the church cannot be forgotten. Monogamy has been the dominant tradition, with some churches allowing in some instances serial polygamy (i.e., multiple spouses, but only one at a time). Those ideals also should not be easily set aside. How is one to go about resolving this problem satisfactorily?

3. What is one to do when the traditional resolution of a question serves to block development in a local church?

An example of this is the question of celibacy for the Roman Catholic clergy in many cultures where the church is taking root. According to Roman Catholic statements, the celibacy of the clergy serves a number of purposes, but especially that of being a sign of the impending kingdom of God. As far as the present writer knows, no semiotic study has been done of this sign system, though it might be worthwhile to do so. Many members of local churches, including bishops, have communicated to central Roman Catholic authority their doubts about the relative value of this sign system in their culture, particularly when it seems to be a principal cause of the shortage of applicants for the priesthood, on the one hand, and a scandal to the church, on the other, because of the practice of concubinage.[9] Hence a sign system long part of the discipline of the Western church is not only not communicating the messages for which it was intended, but has become a countersign to the detriment of the local church. How might this problem be resolved in such a way as to respect the tradition and stop communicating contrary messages?

4. In view of all the problems that are present in the encounter between tradition and local theology, can one ascertain criteria for what constitutes a genuinely Christian identity?

The language for this concern is various; one hears questions about the limits of contextualization, how far is one to go, the dangers of syncretism, and so on.[10] One can make all kinds of decisions for what seem to be eminently plausible pastoral reasons. These can be taken with what seems to be clear biblical, traditional warrant. But how is one to judge whether or not the results are Christian, especially when the decision leads to practice or belief without clear precedent in the tradition, or even offering a countersign (at least in a surface reading of the culture text)?

Many churches are now facing this question in the area of exorcism and healing. Both exorcism and healing have long traditions in Christianity, but probably have never had the importance they now exhibit in many African cultures. The problem is not only admitting healing and exorcism rites into Christian liturgy, even on a small scale. One has to face the world-view that has made healing and exorcism a necessity; often this world-view involves sorcery, witchcraft, and trafficking with demons. If one pursues a path of large-scale inclusion of exorcism and healing rites into liturgy, how is one relating to those traditions and world-views?[11]

The further the results of a decision vary from what has clear warrant in the tradition, the more the question of criteria for Christian identity becomes an urgent one. Is there some way of measuring or testing a situation to gain some sense of what is genuinely Christian and what is not? This may be the single most urgent question facing local theologies today. And the question arises not only in the new churches, but in the older ones as well. Here is one example, discussed widely now in the Western churches: Can one maintain a just-war theory in light of nuclear armaments? What is the Christian response to the prospect of participating in a war where the warring parties have access to such armaments?

The question of criteria for Christian identity will be taken up explicitly later in this chapter. This question also provides a transition to the three questions that follow, which local churches are raising. They arise not so much out of specific problems to be solved as out of some underlying concerns that recur in the background of any question raised about relations with the tradition.

5. *Many churches feel themselves misunderstood or insufficiently listened to by other churches as they struggle to find a faithful response to the gospel. Is paternalism the reason why communication breaks down?*

Many churches of more recent origin have this feeling of being misunderstood or unheard. Given the fact that colonialism has often been part of their national history, they are keenly sensitive to what amounts to a paternalism in church relationships. They feel that the tradition is enacted in a paternalist fashion in their situations. This means, basically, that it is assumed that the younger churches are not in a position to understand their own questions or that their questions are really not as they might believe. The older churches impose a solution to their questions, knowing much better what the younger church needs or would ask for if it could properly speak.

Often this is done in a cavalier fashion, with the older churches not bothering to learn many of the details surrounding the younger church's question. The abrupt character of the answer often given doubles the sense of offense.

At other times, paternalism is exercised in a different and more subtle fashion, often unbeknownst to a well-meaning older church. Three varieties of this kind of paternalism recur often, and may be called the fallacies of the primitive, of evolution, and of maturity.

In the *primitivist* fallacy, the older church tries to recreate the "New Testament church" in the local situation. Not only, of course, is there no such ideal type of the church in the New Testament (there are only New Testament churches), but also two other messages are being communicated. First, it is the older church's idea of what constitutes the New Testament church that almost always provides the criterion for encounter with the tradition. Some of the problems with that were explored earlier. Second, always using the criterion of the New Testament church can be a subtle way of telling the new church that it will have to repeat twenty centuries of history before it can be considered an equal of the older church.

The second fallacy, a variant upon the primitivist one, is the *evolutionist* fallacy. While it does not insist upon a New Testament church model in the culture, it does maintain that somehow the new church will have to repeat the doctrinal development of the older church before it is allowed to vary from it in any form. Thus Africa will have to adjust its optimistic anthropologies to accommodate an Augustinian one, so as to have the proper doctrine of original sin, even though the Orthodox church has got along without such an anthropology through the centuries. The message beneath the evolutionist fallacy can be starkly paternalist. It can presume a reading of church history as a constant movement from strength to strength, guided by a nineteenth-century view of progress. Some of the younger churches have called this optimistic view of church history into question. Black churches in North America wonder about how to read this growth in strength when that same history condoned their enslavement and even permitted church leaders to own slaves.

The third fallacy is the *maturity* fallacy. This appears in the discussions of when a newer church is to be considered mature enough to function independently of the older church. Many of these discussions, it should be noted, take place among members of the older churches to the exclusion of the younger churches. Once again the older church makes decisions on behalf of the younger church. "Maturity" comes to mean that the older church can feel comfortable with an autonomous younger church, the younger church can comfortably speak the older church's language, and the younger church can be counted upon to listen to and follow the advice of the older church.

Even in well-meant discussions, these problems can creep into the fabric of the decision-making process. Ways have to be found to avoid them as much as possible.

6. *Given all the obstacles that a local church may face in developing a genuine encounter with the tradition and the frustration and weariness engendered by such obstacles, is it even possible for a local church to make a genuine contribution to that tradition?*

If the same question (such as that of the necessity of celibacy for the clergy) is answered in the same fashion each time without apparent effort on the part of the older church to listen, why should one even make the attempt to engage in dialogue? As a result, solutions are now and then reached without the benefit of dialogue with the tradition, to the detriment of the entire body of Christ: the local church has lost the opportunity to have its response to the gospel tested, challenged, or affirmed; the larger church may have missed an important incarnation of Christ in culture. Human communication is always difficult. The complexities of cultural difference are often confused by relations of power. But there is a growing danger that more and more in the future there will be no dialogue with the tradition at all. More facile models of contextualization will be pursued, and blame will have to be placed on both sides of the erstwhile dialogue—on both older and younger churches.

7. *These six problems discussed so far point in different ways to a single question regarding cultural diversity and Christian tradition. In the midst of cultural diversity and the sensitivity needed to the presence of Christ already in the culture, how does one also respect the normative character of Christian tradition?*

While different parts of the church construe that normativeness differently, all agree that there is a normative tradition of some sort. The sheer plurality of situations encountered seems to dilute the clarity of the gospel message. As those involved become more aware of cultural diversity, many things that once seemed normative show their culturally conditioned character. How is one to ascertain the normative within the Scriptures, within conciliar and confessional documents, within magisterial pronouncements? And how is one to remain faithful to that which is indeed normative? Sometimes this question is answered in terms of allowing less cultural diversity. But that seems to be sidestepping the question rather than resolving it, since it leaves unanswered how some cultural diversities are acceptable and others are not. The problem is not one of the unfortunate spread of Christianity to so many different cultures. It is one of how to understand a heritage received, a treasure to be cherished: the gospel of Jesus Christ.

CHRISTIAN TRADITION ENCOUNTERS LOCAL THEOLOGY: FOUR PROBLEMS

The problems of encounter between local theology and church tradition is not only one for the local church or for the newer church. It is also a problem for the tradition and those charged with its preservation. The impression should not be given that those in church leadership entrusted with the maintaining of the integrity of the faith are inimical to newer local churches, seeking only to maintain a restrictive control. Leadership in the older churches can be, and quite often is, keenly sensitive to the problems of the gospel in new situations. They can share in that struggle for faithfulness going on in a local church, older or newer.

But they also see some additional problems of this encounter, more obvious to them perhaps than to those seeking solutions in the local church. Four such problems deserve special attention here.

1. *Cultural diversity among Christians is a fact. At the same time, however, Christians believe that unity is one of the signs of God's church. What unity means in the concrete is differently understood, but it does involve the Pauline "one Lord, one faith, one baptism, one God and Father of all" (Ephesians 4:5).*

A principal charge to those who lead the church on whatever level is maintaining its unity. Unity is not the same as uniformity. Yet unity and uniformity are not unrelated. To put it into the language of semiotics: How many different signs can carry the same message without alteration of the code? How many different ways can there be of celebrating the same Eucharist before the meaning of that Eucharist begins to come apart? How many varieties of church order can be had before the churches can no longer work together or communicate with one another? This kind of questioning has to be in the back of any church leader's mind as local theologies are developed.

2. *Closely related to the question of the range of diversity is the possibility of syncretism, that is, a dilution and loss of the Christian message in the local context.*

When one looks at the rise of the many Independent Churches in Africa, at the new religious movements in Japan, at some of the cargo movements in Melanesia, is one not inclined to ask: Are these the outcome of a contextualization played to its utmost? In these instances, local people interpret the Christian message as they understand it within their culture. Judging by the number of adherents gained by some of these churches and movements, they seem to be "successful" contextualizations. But the grasp on traditional Christianity seems to have been lost. True, some of them come back into the mainstream of Christianity (such as the Kimbanguist Church of Zaire), but most continue their development apart from any consideration of the rest of Christianity. Is this where conscious attempts at contextualization ultimately lead? If this is not the case, where does the point of demarcation ultimately lie?

3. *A step back from the possibility of syncretism leads one to deal with the discontinuities that arise in the local theology in a given culture. In this situation, the theology as it is developing in a local setting lays significantly different emphasis on the relationships between parts of the tradition, and may be missing some parts altogether.*

This problem has emerged in certain liberation-theology contexts (for example, United States black-theology contexts), where the figure of Moses and the story of the exodus become more important to the community than the story of Jesus. In sixteenth-century Spain the number of shrines to Mary outnumbered the shrines to Jesus by a ratio of two to one.[12] Are the Moses spirituality in the first instance and the Marian spirituality in the second to be considered genuine forms of Christianity? Or do they stand in need of some correction?

A similar problem is the Neo-Marcionite attitude taken by some communities, which would eliminate the Hebrew Scriptures from the Bible, calling them the cultural testament of the early Christians, and would replace them with the pre-Christian history of the local community. Variants on these call for elimination of part or all of a book of the Bible because it cannot be contextualized. While one does not want to fall into some of the paternalist fallacies outlined above, to what extent can one ignore parts of the tradition as it has been accepted by all Christian communities before? And what criteria would direct and legitimate such discontinuities with the tradition beyond personal whim or convenience?

4. *Finally, if one believes that the purpose of the encounter of local theology with the tradition is to test, affirm, and challenge the new expression of faith, when is it not only legitimate to challenge that expression, but necessary to do so?*

All would agree that it is important not to lapse into a cultural romanticism, whereby any cultural form is automatically accepted as a vehicle of Christ in culture. Therefore we ask: how and when does someone really make that challenge? What are the safeguards against cultural romanticism, on the one hand, and paternalism, on the other? This becomes an acute problem in churches with more centralized authority, such as the Roman Catholic Church, where such decisions have to be made. What kind of criteria can be brought into play?

The problems are as crucial to the success of a local theology in incarnating the gospel as were the first seven questions explored. And they too call for the two things that will preoccupy the rest of this chapter: the development of an adequate theory of tradition and the development of criteria for Christian identity. These eleven questions only highlight in different ways the problems both local theology and Christian tradition face in their mutual encounter and growth. The Christian tradition is too precious a heritage to be squandered carelessly or treated lightly. But without its continued incarnation in local communities it becomes like that treasure buried in the ground, producing no profit (Matthew 25:18).

Before moving directly into developing a proposal for an adequate theory of tradition, we need to step back and look at how traditions function in human communities. This is necessary, since the full range of these functions are rarely explored. Most often, only the oppressive, legitimating, and ideological functions of tradition in communities come under discussion. Without having some sense of the range of positive contributions of tradition to the life of a community, we shall be unable to judge whether or not any theory of tradition developed is adequate to the task before us, and whether or not any set of criteria for Christian identity developed covers the range of issues needed to secure both the tradition's and the local community's integrity.

THE FUNCTIONING OF TRADITION IN HUMAN COMMUNITIES

Pluralism and competing world-views are becoming more and more part of every cultural situation. This has prompted an increased interest in investigating what role tradition plays in human communities, after a period in which tradition was given little or no attention.[13] For a long time the forces of optimism and progress led some to feel that tradition was something that would disappear from society as a factor of any significance, once the critique begun in the Western Enlightenment had achieved its purposes. Tradition was something a culture might depend upon until the forces of reason were allowed their full play. In many consumerist societies, constant innovation seemed to have taken the place of tradition. Thus what was newest was best and provided the norm for living: the newest in medicine, technology, services, and ideas. Tradition became an ornament of private existence, an aesthetic preference of some who preferred to retain some linkage with the past. But to the extent that it could not be accounted for by human reason, to that extent it no longer played a significant role in human life. Societies that had been largely directed by tradition were rapidly being replaced by the urban cultures that were guided by practical reason.

One of the reasons for the disappearance of tradition was the logic that directed it. Its authority was exercised along nonrational (and therefore coercive) lines. The power that a tradition had to direct human life derived from a source other than the community itself. At any number of crucial junctures it could not account rationally for the direction it demanded. Societal critique demanded the gradual elimination of this kind of hegemony from human life.[14]

The twin principles of rationality and innovation have run into some serious obstacles in replacing the role of tradition in human communities, however. Perhaps the most serious has been the restriction of resources for innovation. If energy sources and raw materials are not in unlimited supply (as the 1973 oil embargo warned consumerist societies), is unlimited innovation possible? The answer was No. Innovation, as a replacement of the past and as a hedge against entropy, seemed to have met its limits. Political experience with the most industrially advanced countries raised questions about rationality as the sole principle for guidance also. If the most rationally run of societies could produce nuclear weapons and bring the planet to the brink of ruin, was reason all that it was made out to be? Because it was possible, did it

Innovation

have to be done? And was the scientific materialism of the Marxist state socialist societies really attractive as a form of human society? Tradition could be an oppressive and hindering force in society, but the solutions offered by reason and by innovation were not without fault either. As it became obvious that the continued success of those rational, advanced consumerist societies was tied up with keeping the rest of the world poor, the innovation and rational ideals no longer could be so easily squared with the most fundamental of Christian values.[15]

Thus a renewed interest in the questions of tradition and authority has been developing. Some of that research will be drawn upon here to analyze the functioning of tradition in human society as a prelude to a proposal on a theory of tradition adequate to the needs of local theologies in the church. Three aspects of tradition will be looked at: what it provides for a community, what are its essential aspects needed to function, and perspectives for interpreting it.

TRADITION'S CONTRIBUTION TO HUMAN COMMUNITY

Tradition contributes three things to the development of human community: it provides resources for identity; it is a communication system providing cohesion and continuity in the community; it provides resources for incorporating innovative aspects into a community.

Tradition, first of all, provides resources for identity in a community. Human life is the least instinct-directed of all the animal species, and culture develops to serve as a mediator between the physical exigencies of existence and the realities of time. Each culture chooses its pathways among the myriad possibilities open to it in the combinants of physical environment and inner realities. Those pathways chosen create the resources for identity.

Tradition can be seen as the articulation of those pathways chosen. When one concentrates on the question of identity in culture—that is, what makes us who we are—we can turn to some of the considerations given to identity in the discussion of the semiotic study of culture. Group boundary and world-view formation were the two axial categories presented there.

Group boundary gives one of the most basic forms of identification by dividing the world into "us" and "not-us." That boundary appears in roles, in status markers, and in the line between publicly discernible behavior and privately held truth. Such markers, of varying strength within a society, form a prime source of identity. They tell us who we are in ever greater progressions of definition. They are important for forming the human ego, that tenuous region of self between the unconscious and the physical world.

Paired with group boundary is world-view, the grid[16] whereby a society decided what needs to be explained and how to explain it. Those resources of explanation embody the values, the beliefs, and the classificatory categories of a culture. Like the group boundary, the world-view may be more or less tightly woven, depending upon the needs of the environment.

Group boundary and world-view together form a matrix within which both the society as a whole and the individuals within it find that selfhood called identity. Tradition is the repository of the lore about group boundary and about world-view, usually transmitted to the young of a society in preparation for full participation in the culture as adults. This transmission takes place through rites of initiation at puberty, through educational systems, and through the give and take of day-to-day living. Tradition provides this expressed repository, which can be referred to in order to maintain identity when threatened, and to reaffirm it when needed. Since identity is not a self-evident thing of nature, it needs that reaffirmation.

The latter point leads to the second contribution of tradition to identity, namely, a communication system providing cohesion and continuity in a human community. Tradition, as a body of lore, includes stories, activities, memories, and the rules governing group boundary and world-view formation. It provides a semiotic system, a set of codes within that system, whereby the basic messages of identity can circulate through a culture. What it means to be, act like, think like a member of culture *x* is the content of these codes. It helps to choose the signs and sign systems that will carry those messages through the circuitry of the culture. Tradition, because of its complex interrelating of stories, activities, memories, and rules, gives a sense of cohesion and continuity to a culture and the individuals who live within it. The "cohesion" means that it all fits together, it makes sense (common sense being the experienced logic of a tradition). To an outsider, such cohesion may not be obvious, but then it only needs to make sense to insiders who live with it. "Continuity" means that the solutions to problems can be counted upon to stay relatively stable over a period of time. When asked who I am or what I am supposed to do in a set of circumstances, I can count on the answer being pretty much the same in each instance. Identity is not given, nor is it self-evident; it is achieved and agreed upon. Without cohesion and continuity, identity becomes an arbitrary posture at any given moment. A total breakdown of identity, at either the individual or the societal level, means that the individual or the society ceases to be able to relate. It loses its cohesion or wholeness and disintegrates. Tradition serves as a guarantor of the resources for cohesion and continuity over stretches of time.

Finally, tradition provides resources for incorporating innovation into a society. No society lives in such secure circumstances in its environment that it is not confronted with new data. If the tradition is a workable communication system within the culture, it can relate new signs to the codes and messages of the culture, incorporating them into the meaning systems of the culture. The codes or rules of a society also modify over a period of time, as they try to bring the messages of a society and the environment more into harmony with one another. When a culture is confronted on a regular basis with new data that need to be dealt with, one of two things happens to the culture. Either it becomes invigorated by the expansion and transformation of its codes in accommodating the new signs; or the codes, unable to accommodate the signs and the basic messages to one another and to the tradition as a communication network, cease to provide cohesion and continuity to a culture, resulting in its breakdown. The latter is what has happened in many instances in the past century. The data being received in a culture either came too fast or were incapable of being interpreted in accordance with the basic codes of a society. And when a tradition breaks down, it loses the allegiance of its members.

A tradition presents a way of life, providing pathways on how to behave and how to think. That way of life can be analyzed semiotically, as a means of seeing how the culture functions. It provides basic messages (values) and codes (rules), which relate (signs) those messages to data in the environment. Together they create meaning. The proper interaction and working of these three dimensions makes for that fragile creation, identity; when circumstances prevent their interaction, the culture breaks down. Thus too many messages, or codes inadequate to the messages, make it impossible for the signs to bear the messages promoting cohesion and continuity.

ESSENTIAL ASPECTS OF TRADITION

The previous section explored something of how tradition functions in culture, that is, what it tries to do. We saw that it is bound up with matters of identity, maintaining that identity, and dealing with the need for change as it continues to arise. Those functions were related to a semiotic analysis of culture.

To fill out the picture on tradition, another kind of question must be asked: What things does the tradition itself need in order to be able to carry out its tasks in a culture? There are four essential things a tradition must have in order to function within a culture.

First, a tradition must have *credibility*. It must be accepted by its culture. It will be accepted if the manifest concerns of the tradition match the manifest problems of a culture. The tradition may not be able to solve all the problems of a culture, but it must be evident to the members of a culture that their concerns are the tradition's concern. There is a certain circularity in what happens here, inasmuch as a well-developed tradition takes leadership in defining what is a problem in a culture. As long as there is perceived congruence between the two sets of concerns, the tradition can be credible. If issues arise that the tradition cannot or will not face, that credibility will begin to weaken.

Second, a tradition must have *intelligibility* to the members of a culture. The sign system and codes in the tradition must be close enough to those in other semiotic domains in the culture (especially economic and familial domains) to be understood. In other words, the tradition must be a participant in the creation of the common sense, of the natural law in a culture. The forms of thinking and reasoning that are accorded high value in a culture must also be employed by the tradition. Thus one of the problems facing church tradition is that the logic by which it makes decisions is often perceived as different from the rationality of Enlightenment culture. When "religion'' and ''science'' are seen as irreconcilable, that logic which solves more problems in the environment has the greater chance for acceptance by the members of that culture.

Third, the tradition must have *authority*. Richard Sennett has defined authority as an unequal relationship of power, whereby certain centers or individuals receive more power in a society than others.[17] That power may be freely given, or it may be taken. Tradition must have authority; that is to say, its ability to mediate identity and environment in a culture must be lifted beyond the level of the merely arbitrary. It must not have to gain the right to make such mediations each time it does so.

Authority could also be equated with what was called above ''normativeness.'' It assumes a power to speak and act on behalf of the tradition. Because the source and action of authority is not always susceptible to rational explanation, its position can become problematic amid the relativities of cultural conditioning and cultural diversity. As a result, one of the difficulties in establishing the authority of tradition in many cultures today is that the tradition has lost its credibility, that is, its ability to deal with the problems that the society is facing. Yet no matter how patently nontraditional a society may become, groups within the society, and sometimes the whole society itself, will remain willing to turn over power to individuals or groups who can fulfill tradition's basic functions, especially in times of crisis. Max Weber called this lodging of the functions of authority in an individual or group its charisma. Investigating the phenomenon of charisma may be the most useful way to get at the functioning of authority in both traditional and nontraditional societies. It may provide the key to understanding how normativeness is established and functions in situations of pluralism.[18]

Fourth, tradition must have a means of *affirmation* and *renewal*. Societies are constantly faced with change, and a tradition continually needs to incorporate innovation and weave it into a culture's identity. By engaging in this process and running the risk of failure, it can find its credibility always at stake. Credibility can become strained, and with it the acceptance of the tradition as a means for dealing with the life of a culture. And so any tradition is in need of affirmation and renewal. The affirmation must come from its adherents; they must be renewed in their trust in this tradition. Successful experience with the tradition (i.e., experience of those situations when a tradition successfully mediates the problems of the culture) provides an important and ongoing source of affirmation and renewal. But a deeper level must also be reached, to sustain the members of a culture in their belief in the tradition in those times when belief and adherence are not easy things to give. This is accomplished by recounting the myths of the origin of the tradition, and by engaging in rituals that relate the individuals more deeply to the tradition.

Traditions have beginnings, but not manufactured ones. They begin in revelations, in unexpected insight, in the charisma of leaders. The stories of how the tradition came about, how it came to us, need to be retold and to be reaffirmed. Christians believe that Christianity is not just a set of ethical principles; it is based upon a long history of revelation by God, culminating in the revelation of Jesus Christ. These great myths need to be recounted, especially in ritual situations where they can be reaffirmed and invite the allegiance of the adherents once again. A tradition that is not celebrated is a tradition that is dying.

These four points say something about what a tradition needs in order to function as a tradition. They become important in terms of testing a theory of tradition and in ascertaining criteria for tradition's proper implementation. They are also helpful in diagnosing the ills of a failing tradition.

PERSPECTIVES ON TRADITION

Earlier in this chapter it was noted that although all Christians share the same concern about the preservation of the heritage of faith in the encounter of the tradition with local theology, different perspectives will lead to concentrating on certain kinds of questions. Those perspectives grow out of the distribution of responsibilities within the community, and also the problems that will be uppermost in each person's mind. Beyond those perspectives are perspectives on the functioning of tradition as a whole, which need to be taken into account in a theory of tradition. Without an awareness of them, one can mix up important questions and even find their answers contradicting one another. Four of those perspectives need to be examined briefly here. They fall into two pairs: inside and outside perspectives, and speaker and hearer perspectives.

From the insider's perspective, one is able to live totally inside a tradition. In such instances the concept of tradition as such does not need to be formulated; it is hard to imagine this tradition as simply one tradition among many. An awareness of how the insider's perspective functions is most familiar to persons in cross-cultural experiences. Until one moves out of one's home culture, it is difficult to imagine one's home culture as merely one way of doing things; it is quite simply the *only* way to do them. One does not theorize about the nature of one's tradition; one simply accepts it as it is. To play upon the etymology of the word: one does not have to think about the nature of the *traditio* (the process of handing on); one has only to be concerned with the *tradita* (the things handed on). Whatever organizes the *tradita* is not of immediate importance; it can be taken for granted. One has only to direct one's efforts to the observance and the preservation of the *tradita*. In the Roman Catholic tradition this received classic formulation in the idea of a *depositum fidei*, a storehouse of *tradita* to be safeguarded, and neither diminished nor extended. One did not have to ponder the nature of the *depositum*. In Protestant traditions a similar status was often accorded the Scriptures, seen as a storehouse of verses of revelation.

But there is theorizing going on from the insider's perspective, and its purpose is to emphasize the continuity and cohesiveness of the *tradita* as well as their antiquity or coeval status with the tradition itself. Vincent of Lerins in "quod ubique, quod semper, quod ab omnibus creditum est" (what has been believed everywhere, always, by everybody) captures this sentiment.[19] The validity of the tradition is above question; only its cohesiveness and continuity are capable of becoming problematic.

If this is the case, it is important to see how tradition as tradition is dealt with from the inside. What are the ongoing concerns about it?

This first concern is maintaining its authority. The maintenance of authority requires that the power accorded it be itself maintained, so that its credibility remain intact. An important way of maintaining that authority is the harmonization of any apparent contradictions that appear in the tradition. One is reminded of the theological energy expended through the centuries in the harmonization of the Gospels in particular and of the Scriptures in general. This harmonization helps to emphasize the cohesiveness and continuity in the tradition. To an outsider this can appear to be ideological manipulation, but to an insider it is but the clarification of apparent contradictions which, upon investigation, do not prove to be contradictions at all.

A second concern has to do with how to read the tradition. From an insider's perspective, the tradition can be read synchronically, that is, the diachronic or temporal sequence of the emergence of parts of the tradition need not be respected. One can freely juxtapose elements from different parts of the tradition in order to achieve a clearer understanding of the messages of the tradition. One finds this throughout the history of premodern biblical exegesis, and it is the justifying principle behind the anthology form of theology discussed in chapter 4. It continues today in charismatic and Pentecostal uses of the Scriptures. From an insider's perspective, a deeper reading of the tradition's text is not achieved by probing the origins of the texts, their development, or their philosophical properties. The medievals reminded us that this is the lowest form of exegetical knowledge. Rather, one finds the deeper meanings of the text by juxtaposing units of the texts, by allegorizing upon them, if one wants to reveal those hidden meanings. The medievals spoke of the four senses of the Scriptures, and attempts at esoteric readings of tradition's texts can be found in all the great literate religious traditions.

A third concern has to do with incorporating change into the tradition. In Christian theology this has been called the development of doctrine. A theory is developed to allow incorporation of new ideas into the tradition by showing that they were already implicit, albeit not evident, in the primal revelation. Roman Catholic theology has utilized this structure in explaining the emergence of later dogmas (such as the Marian dogmas) and devotional patterns (such as devotion to the Sacred Heart), which do not have clear scriptural warrant.

The insider's perspective is possible when a tradition is stable, credible, and not threatened effectively by competing traditions. While to an outsider the insider's perspective might seem myopic, self-serving, and even oppressive, one must remember that there is no full participation in a tradition or a culture without the insider's perspective, as anyone with cross-cultural experience knows. The insider's perspective, besides being necessary for full participation in a tradition, also serves as a constant check against a nonparticipatory relativism when approaching a tradition.

But the insider's perspective, necessary though it may be, is not the sole perspective possible. When a culture changes suddenly or rapidly, when members of a culture have a cross-cultural experience, or when competing world-views seriously threaten the received way of experiencing the world, the authority of a tradition can be called into question. In the West this certainly took place at the time of the Enlightenment, when the authority of reason provided a broad enough base to challenge the authority of religion. The *philosophes* and the rationalists saw themselves as liberating Western society from the hegemony of a religious tradition. That challenge, plus the experience of other cultures during the period of colonial expansion, profoundly altered approaches to tradition in Western cultures.

What happens in the outsider's perspective is that members of a culture can no longer live solely inside their tradition. To relate to the *tradita* is no longer enough; one must consider the *traditio*, the process of handing on itself. The architectonics of the tradition itself become the subject of investigation, since now the tradition must find a way of validating itself over against competing traditions if it is to maintain its credibility and authority.

Being an outsider does not mean the reader necessarily is inimically disposed to the tradition. It simply makes note of the fact that the reader is aware of the structure and situated character of the tradition itself among other traditions.

What are the concerns for the tradition from the outsider's perspective? The first concern is that a diachronic reading of the text is restored to a place of prominence alongside synchronic readings of the text. The more competitive the world-views, the more prominence the diachronic factors are given. The origin of the texts of the tradition, their development and transmission, their relation to other texts—all these become central concerns. A look at the history of Western hermeneutics shows this shift from insider to outsider perspectives in reading traditions. Allegorical, moral, and analogical readings of the Scriptures have moved into the background in favor of historico-literal forms of reading. Discerning the origin of scriptural texts, the intent of the human author, the precise lexicographical meanings of words, the social setting of the text—these have all become part of the royal road to the text's meaning.

The second major concern is judging the relative value of texts or traditions one to the other. To use the vocabulary developed here: the value and normativeness of the text itself is a concern of the outsider's perspective. What criteria are usually invoked to make such a judgment? While there is no consensus, we should consider two: adequacy and comprehensiveness.

Adequacy is used here in the sense of the medieval *adaequatio*. Adequacy is the measurement of a text or of a tradition's bringing together what needs to be brought together. This has both an internal and an external perspective. On the side of the internal, how well does one kind of reading of a text make sense of the internal features of a text? On the side of the external, how well does one kind of reading of a tradition account for its explanatory power and provide an actual explanation of its cultural setting? Such adequacy is essential for credibility, which in turn is a *sine qua non* for authority. The more one kind of reading reveals the meanings of a text, and thereby engages the reader more fully, the more normative that reading becomes. The more one kind of reading of a tradition opens up the explanatory power of that tradition in terms of the questions being raised in the environment for the reader, the more normative that tradition becomes.

Normativeness is also achieved by comprehensiveness, or the ability of a text or tradition to deal with the widest range of data possible and to interrelate them. Thus the more the Christian texts and tradition could deal with problems in its historic environments and also in new territories, the more normative those texts and traditions became. If a text or tradition finds tself helpless before a significant number of problems facing a population, it loses its comprehensive allure. Comprehensiveness is tied up with the cohesiveness and the continuity of a tradition.

This is not a complete answer to the question of normativity. It obviously itself reflects one perspective: that of the reader of the text or tradition. To fill out these perspectives, we must turn to the second pair of perspectives, those of speaker and hearer.

The speaker and hearer perspectives were discussed in chapter 3. At that time examples were used of the exercise of authority regarding tradition. These can now be elaborated upon.

The speaker's perspective regarding tradition is especially concerned with maintaining the integrity of the tradition and preventing information loss in transmission. The speaker perspective realizes that in the transmission of messages, either through transformations within a sign system or in the transfer to another sign system, loss of information is to some degree likely. "Loss" here is a relative concept. Often the information is not lost, but is deemphasized or placed in the background. Anytime a tradition decides to emphasize one thing, something else will have to recede into the background. Examples could be taken from eucharistic theology. If other matter is allowed for the eucharistic elements, the information in the Christian message about the Eucharist as a sign of unity will be lost to some extent. But the information about the Lord feeding us with the staple of the culture wondrously transformed could be better preserved. When the altar was turned to face the people in eucharistic liturgy in many restored liturgies, the "meal" message came out of the background and was restored to its older eminence. The "sacrifice" message has receded somewhat, or at least a different moment in sacrifice is now being emphasized.

The speaker perspective, in the engagement with tradition, is concerned about the integrity of the message and preserves that to a great extent through maintaining the integrity of the channels of transmission. Creeds, confessions, and fixed formulas of other types are a common vehicle for this. Intelligibility is an essential aspect of this concern. This is why, in cases of ambiguity, the fixed formulas are appealed to in order to assure no loss or adulteration of information. In so doing, authority is maintained.

The hearer's perspective shares the speaker's perspective about concern for loss of information. But that concern is expressed in a different way. The hearer approaches it from the perspective of how the message interacts with the environment. If the message successfully can account for the situation in the environment and provide a pathway for response to that environment, then it has maintained its authority. In other words, the hearer's perspective emphasizes the credibility of the message as the guarantor of its authority, while the speaker is concerned with intelligibility.

If one looks at the contemporary theological situation, one can see these forces at work. It is not accidental that the contextual theologies spend so much time analyzing their environment as part of the theological process. Such analysis is essential to the kind of encounter between tradition and local environment envisioned. Church authorities responsible for maintaining the tradition, on the other hand, spend less time worrying about the diversity of environment and more time about the integrity of the tradition as received. In conflicts between the two, this is why they can often talk past each other. Both are concerned about the transmittal of the tradition and maintaining its authority, but they concentrate on different ways of doing it: the speaker on intelligibility, the hearer on credibility. Because of the concern for maintaining the integrity of the tradition, the speaker is most at home with the insider's perspective on the tradition. Hearers are at home with the insider's perspective as well, but are preoccupied with the outsider's perspective—the problem of rhyming tradition and environment so as to maintain the tradition's credibility.

Having examined these perspectives, we are now in a position to turn toward proposing a theory of tradition.

TOWARD A THEORY OF TRADITION

Throughout this chapter we have been building up a matrix within which a theory of tradition can be developed. This activity began by looking at what tradition provides to human community: identity, a communication system with cohesion and continuity, and resources for dealing with innovation. This was followed by a discussion of essential aspects of tradition: a successful tradition must have credibility, intelligibility, authority, and the means for affirmation and renewal of itself. The discussion then turned to different perspectives, which affect how tradition is perceived: insider, outsider, speaker, and hearer perspectives. A theory of tradition needs to take these various aspects into mind in its development.

The theory that this writer would like to propose here is based on a linguistic model for communication. Since communication, maintenance, and management of information are central concerns of tradition, the model recommends itself as a possibility. The model grows out of a proposal of American linguistics scholar Noam Chomsky's model for language acquisition.[20]

The starting point is Chomsky's distinction between competence and performance in language systems. In trying to develop a model for describing natural languages (i.e., a language used by a people or culture, as opposed to a formal language in mathematics or computer science), Chomsky distinguished between competence and performance in language. Competence is something that we all have in our native language. Out of that competence we are able to generate a seemingly infinite variety of correct sentences, which are intelligible to other speakers of the language, even though we may not be able to articulate the grammar of our language (in other words, say *why* our sentence is correct and intelligible). Even a six-year-old can exhibit astonishing competence in a language, as is evident to someone from outside the culture trying to learn the six-year-old's language. Those actual sentences we generate Chomsky calls "performances." There are good, well-formed performances, and incorrect, ill-formed performances. Any native speaker can instinctively recognize the difference between the two kinds of performances, but may not be able to account for the difference perceived. How is this possible? And why is it that we rarely, if ever, can match the competence in an acquired language with the competence in our native one?

Chomsky set out to investigate this in his theory of grammar. The theory of grammar into the nineteenth century was that grammar was normative for language performances. In other words, the grammar determined what was a well-formed or ill-formed phrase; performance flowed from the grammar. But the difficulty with this approach was that no grammar has ever been produced that can give the rules for all the performances in a language. There are always "exceptions"—immediately understood by anyone who has language competence, but not explained in the grammar.

This led to a change in understanding of what grammar was, paralleling a similar move at that time in lexicography. Grammar does not create a language, it describes it. We know that as a language changes, older rules of grammar may no longer apply. Thus grammar could be understood better as describing a language rather than determining it.

Chomsky carried this a step further and suggested that grammar be seen as a series of rules mediating between performances and competence. These rules try to explain how well-formed performances are generated from language competence. This approach, called transformational grammar, gave a new insight into how languages are put together.

Chomsky set about trying to establish as many of these mediating rules as possible and achieved a good deal of success in doing so. His rules gave a more accurate account of language performances. But they were ultimately unable to account for competence itself. Rules could be seen emerging from competence, but the rules for competence itself remained hidden.

As long as competence's basic structure remained hidden, grammar remained ultimately a negative set of rules, accounting for any ill-formed phrase, but not for all well-formed phrases. In other words, the grammar could account for all grammatically correct usage, but fell short still of accounting for why there were exceptions and why there were idioms. Because of idioms, a grammatically correct usage can be an incorrect or ill-formed phrase in a language. And we know that ultimately it is the idiomatic command that is the most complete command of the language.

Chomsky's model of transformational grammar, and its limitations, have taught us three important things about language. First, the idea of competence is a logical construct, albeit a necessary one. We really have only performances of the language before us. Competence is a hypothesis constructed to account for the immense variety and creativity in language. We feel it is there, but cannot put our finger on it. We can describe discrete performances in language, but cannot adequately describe competence. Grammar reveals its own negative structure as a set of rules that helps up to become aware of what is not a well-formed performance. Yet somehow performances interact with competence in spite of grammar, since idiomatic performances are possible and can change grammar over a period of time.

Second, while grammar can describe performance texts and delve into competence, it ends up relating differently to competence than it does to performance. While grammar has a relationship to competence, its relationship is closer to, and much more dependent on, performance. Grammar is therefore a helpful though not fully adequate tool for describing competence.

Third, this study shifts again the relation of grammar to language as such. Grammar is not the norm of language, generating all possible performances. Yet it does have a normative function, one progressively developed as language performances multiply.

Let us apply this model to the problem of Christian tradition. Tradition is analogous to the entire language system. Faith is analogous to language competence. Theology and the expressive tradition (liturgy, wider forms of praxis) are analogous to language performance. The loci of orthodoxy (however construed: Scriptures, creeds, councils, confessions, magisterium) represent a grammar, mediating competence and performance.

Competence is the beginning point. Christian competence is that faith into which each Christian is baptized. It is the source of our relation to God and is open not only to the learned and wise, but (like language) to the foolish and the child as well. It is the source of Christian performances.

Faith, real and inexhaustible, infinitely creative, cannot be totally described. What we have of faith for descriptive purposes is not that unseen world, but the world of Christian performances—theological expression in all the rich variety discussed in chapter 4. That would include the expressive tradition in liturgy, prayer, art—the full range of Christian praxis. Any of these performances can be correct (well formed), yet none gives an exhaustive account of faith. Nor can all the performances be easily harmonized into a single whole. While they may not contradict each other, they exist in wide variety. There is no one performance that can subsume all the others. In terms of the discussion presented here, this is how the model would speak of the variety of local theologies. Many Christian performances have already been recorded, but new ones are always possible.

What of normativeness in all of this? The loci of grammar in Christian tradition would be the loci of orthodoxy.[21] These loci have grown up in the course of Christian history, beginning with the Scriptures. The fact that none of them (save the Hebrew Scriptures) was there in full form in the beginning shows how they have developed as responses to the performances of Christian communities. This is a not uncommon way of reading doctrinal history: doctrinal formulation emerges after the fact, in response to Christian performances proposed. And just as grammar is more successful in determining what is not a well-formed phrase than what is always a well-formed phrase, so too the loci of orthodoxy, even though sometimes positive in formulation, are really negative or delimiting in function. Creedal formulas set boundaries on belief but do not attempt to describe all possible combinations within those boundaries.[22]

To continue the analogy, the loci of orthodoxy do not, therefore, create theology for a community. Theology will not flow from these loci any more than performances flow from grammar. Thus while a kind of magisterial theology can be articulated, and is certainly correct, it of itself cannot be the theology of a community. To derive the community's theology solely from a magisterial (or biblical) theology is like trying to derive idioms from grammatical rules.

The loci of orthodoxy, like grammar, undergo transformation as performance texts (local-theology texts) change. Thus condemnations of heresy can be lifted or forgotten when circumstances have changed (one thinks of the Galileo case in Roman Catholicism).

This model addresses both the reading and the generation of local-theology texts. From this it should be obvious that local theologies (performance texts) cannot simply be derived from received formulas or from previous performance texts. Rather, their pattern of generation is parallel to that of other performance texts. Access to competence (Christian faith) is not reserved to theologians or older churches. Astonishing and well-formed performance texts can come out of the youngest of churches, just as young children can speak well-formed sentences never spoken before. Orthodoxy is not the source of texts so much as it is the guarantor of non-ill-formed performance texts.

But what of the tradition in all of this? In this proposal, tradition is the equivalent of the language system. Tradition is more than unarticulated faith, but it includes them. Tradition is more than the loci of orthodoxy, but it includes that. And tradition is more than the history of theology, but includes that. Without the competence of faith, the loci of orthodoxy are barren. Without the performance texts of communities, Christianity is mute.

Without the grammar of orthodoxy, the performance texts disintegrate into babble. Normativeness unexpressed is lodged in faith; normativeness expressed is lodged in the grammar of orthodoxy, which aids the community in discerning ill- and well-formed performance texts. But for the grammar to maintain its authority, it must be intelligible and credible. It must be adequate to competence and to performance.

A special word should be said here about the Scriptures as grammar. Given the place of honor among all types of normativeness in which they are held by all the churches, how can they be perceived as a grammar? Contemporary biblical scholarship offers an answer. On the one hand, the Scriptures can be studied as any other performance text in the history of Judaism or Christianity; and indeed, historical-critical exegesis has done so. But when the Scriptures are looked to for normative guidance, they are read differently from the way they are in a historical-critical setting. Often (but not always) they are read synchronically rather than diachronically in such normative settings. To that extent they constitute part of the grammar of orthodoxy. When the Scriptures are not looked to for normative judgment, they can be read as a performance text. I believe this approach to the Scriptures corresponds to the Roman Catholic position on the Scriptures as expressed in Vatican Council II's Dogmatic Constitution on Divine Revelation (*Dei Verbum*). The Scriptures are the firstfruits of the church, the beginning and head of the tradition process, rather than the source of the church itself.[23]

More of the implications of this theory of tradition could be drawn out, but the main lines of it should be clear. This theory can account for normativeness and for its development. It tries to respect the variety within the Christian tradition as well as its constant concern for orthodoxy.

CRITERIA FOR CHRISTIAN IDENTITY

For a Christian community struggling with the question of faithfulness to the gospel in its theology, the theory of tradition can form a useful backdrop to its work, helping to give a vision of the relation of faith, forms of normativeness, and theology. But there is a more concrete concern: Is the theology developing in this community genuinely reflective of the gospel, faithful to the Christian tradition? As was noted earlier in the chapter, there is a need to establish some criteria whereby Christian identity can be ascertained.

What has been presented thus far about the dynamics of tradition and the dynamics of culture would indicate that finding such criteria is not an easy task. Certainly no single criterion can be established, given the diversity of cultures and the complexity of the Christian tradition. Yet there must be some way of testing the theology that develops.

What follows is a proposal for a set of five criteria for establishing Christian identity. The five criteria have to work in consort. While failure to meet any one criterion can produce a negative judgment against the theology developed, all five are needed to arrive at a positive decision. The five are in fact well-known ones in the tradition; they are not new. Yet when related to the discussion on tradition presented here, they take on a new significance.

THE FIRST CRITERION: THE COHESIVENESS OF CHRISTIAN PERFORMANCE

In the discussion of contributions of tradition to the life of a community, it was noted that cohesiveness is one of the factors giving identity to a community. A study of the church tradition indicates that in the interrelation of its doctrines and symbols, there is a marvelous cohesiveness. The cohesiveness manifests a consistency, although not always consistency of a linear kind. The consistency is often one of balancing the great antinomies of life and death, good and evil, which mark human existence. One way of defining heresy is to see it as one doctrine or symbol taking a position that skews the rest of belief, even though it may exhibit a logical consistency. Arius' definition of the relation of Jesus to God is a case in point. While innerly consistent from a philosophical perspective, it undermined Jesus' role as the definitive revelation of God's salvific presence in history and, in so doing, wreaked havoc with any theology of grace and sacrament. The Council of Nicaea had to revert to a new meaning on an old word to define the relationship between Jesus and God: *homoousios.* Yet such a logical inconsistency was needed to preserve the greater coherence.[24]

The logic of the Christian tradition is often philosophically consistent, along the lines of the logic of Aristotle; but more importantly, it takes up within it the logic of symbol, which governs the generation of metaphor and metonymy. For that reason, the laws of transformation in semiotic systems may be more useful, ultimately, than any given philosophical logic in tracing the cohesiveness of a symbolic expression of the tradition.

Another way of approaching the building up of this cohesion is the notion of a hierarchy of truth: some truths of the Christian faith are more central to belief than others. Thus the truth that Jesus Christ is the definitive revelation of God's salvation is more central to Christianity than a Marian doctrine, although the latter may be closely related to the first. The church needs to grapple with this notion of a hierarchy of truths once again, as had been urged by Vatican Council II.[25]

Cohesion is in itself hard to ascertain. It is partly an analytical, partly an intuitive reality. But if the theological formulation finds itself clearly at odds with the rest of Christian doctrine or requires a radical shifting of large parts of it, there is a very good chance that it is not a well-formed Christian performance.

THE SECOND CRITERION:
THE WORSHIPING CONTEXT AND CHRISTIAN PERFORMANCE

One of the most powerful formulations of criteria for construing Christian identity in the tradition has been the principle *lex credendi, lex orandi* (the law of believing following the law of prayer). If the Lord is truly present in the community of word and sacrament, then what is expressed there is a touchstone for Christian identity. The worshiping context is not given over to enthusiasm alone; it is safeguarded by the place accorded to the Scriptures in that context.

The law of prayer has been invoked to ascertain Christian identity in the past. Again in the case against Arius, the use of the triune baptismal formula clearly indicated to Athanasius that Father and Son must be equal.[26] The hymnody of the Orthodox church has been a constant source of theology through the centuries.

Again this criterion can be difficult to use in and of itself. Yet what happens when the developing theology is brought into the worshiping context? How does it develop in the communal prayer of the church? What happens to a community that includes such in its prayer? This criterion, despite its less analytical character, is more easily used by a community than the first criterion given here, which often needs the help of the professional theologian.

From a different perspective, the reason for the importance of this criterion is reflected in the discussion of tradition earlier in the chapter: How does a performance relate to the ritual activity of affirmation and renewal of the tradition, an essential aspect of the tradition's enactment? A certain congeniality in the ritual context can help to affirm and refine the developing theology.

THE THIRD CRITERION: THE PRAXIS OF THE COMMUNITY AND CHRISTIAN PERFORMANCE

The theologies of liberation have reminded us once again that what Christians do is central to who Christians are. The concept of praxis reaches beyond mere action to include the reflection upon that action. "By their fruits shall you know them" has remained one of the oldest and clearest ways for discerning Christian identity. What happens to a community which follows out the theology that it has developed? This is showing itself again to be a particularly powerful criterion in dealing with responses to the gospel, which seem to call for violence. What happens to those who see this pathway as the genuine response to the gospel in this situation?

In terms of the theory of tradition we are reminded once again that we can come to know the competence of faith only through Christian performance. Where that performance moves beyond an intellectual formulation into engagement with its environment we discover its credibility or lack thereof. Along with the previous criterion this is one that can be more easily used by a local church.

THE FOURTH CRITERION: THE JUDGMENT OF OTHER CHURCHES AND CHRISTIAN PERFORMANCE

Catholicity and unity are traditional marks of the church of Christ. These can be formulated into a criterion for Christian identity: Is a local church willing to stand under the judgment of other churches in the matter of its Christian performance or does it close itself off, assured of its own truth? In polities such as that of the Roman Catholic Church, this is a prime criterion for Christian identity. Communion with all other local churches, of which the church of Rome has primacy, is central to Roman Catholic belief. A local church that closes itself off from both communion and judgment cannot fulfill this criterion.

There is a danger that this criterion will be applied in a one-way fashion. When this criterion is invoked, it is generally directed to the younger churches, to the small Christian communities, to the Independent Churches of Africa. But it should be remembered that the older churches in the North Atlantic community have the same obligation to communion and judgment. If they fail to respond to the challenge of the poor churches to their wealth and their complicity in oppression, they too can find themselves lacking in Christian identity.

THE FIFTH CRITERION: THE CHALLENGE TO OTHER CHURCHES AND CHRISTIAN PERFORMANCE

The correlative criterion to the fourth one is that a local community's theology should impel it to move outward from itself. It must make some contribution to the way in which the whole of the Christian church understands itself, either by affirming what is already known in the tradition or by extending it to new circumstances. Sometimes that contribution comes in the form of a challenge. Not only does a local church participate in communion and accept judgment, it must be willing to engage in the same for the sake of the other churches. If it looks only to its own concerns, its own environment, it will find itself closing in on itself, losing its catholicity and its unity with other churches. By achieving its mission it contributes to the cohesion of the tradition and its authority.

One concrete way in which this is carried out has been by the sending out of missionaries or by making workers available to other churches. If the theology developed in a local church impels its members to do this, there is a good chance that this criterion is being met.

This chapter has ranged over a wide number of problems and difficulties. Its purpose is to build up a framework wherein a local church can better come to terms with the tradition. It has looked at some of the common problems that local theologies confront, especially in those churches whose cultures have not been long part of the church. It has looked at what makes up a tradition and how it functions in human communities. It has tried to propose a theory of tradition that would go beyond any simple positivist model of transmission and would allow for what is known about how traditions function in both older and modern societies. And it has tried to use this as a

backdrop for development of a set of interlocking criteria, which, used together, would give a reasonable guarantee of Christian identity.

This remains the most difficult area in developing local theologies, at least
from a theoretical perspective. But it is also one of the most important. For
by assuring a genuine encounter with the tradition of the church, we are
surely brought into the presence of its saving Lord.

6

Popular Religion
and Official Religion

The late twentieth century has witnessed a resurgence of theological interest in popular religious forms of expression. For a long time popular religion was by and large denigrated by theologians as a way of expressing faith that needed to be overcome sooner or later by a more sophisticated understanding of the gospel. Devotions, processions, pious associations, and places of pilgrimage seemed to many religious leaders to be realities that would pass away with liturgical renewal and a more Word-centered spirituality. The conscientizing forces of liberation would replace the devotional patterns that for so long had marked the Christianity of the great majority of the population.

Reality, however, has turned out to be more complex than such prognostications. A host of forces have contributed to the rethinking of the role of popular religion as an authentic Christian response to the gospel.[1] Two of these especially can be singled out.

In the first wave of liberation theology in Latin America, a call went out for forming a new Christian community embodying the liberating power of the gospel and leaving the folk Christianity of the masses behind. Only with such a leaven could the whole loaf be leavened.[2] Such a notion of creating an elite within the mass of Christianity was certainly not new; similar sentiments had been echoed in church renewal in France in the immediately preceding decades.[3]

But liberation theology in that first generation wanted to be more than the vanguard of genuine Christian conversion in the Latin American context. It saw itself as a movement of the people as well. And it soon learned that in transforming the patterns of Christianity it could not ignore the longer-lived religion of the people. This has led to concentrated study on the whole phenomenon of how religion is lived and experienced by the great majority of the people of Latin America. Known most commonly as "popular religiosity," (*religiosidad popular*), the work of Latin American theologians and of sociologists has been immensely helpful to the world church in coming to a deeper understanding of what is probably one of the most prevalent forms of Christian experience.

A divergence between official ecclesiastical teaching and practice, and patterns of Christian behavior in the larger populace is not specific to Latin America. It has marked Christian life—and indeed life in other great religious traditions—everywhere. Popular religion has become increasingly the subject of study in Europe as well. Some of this has been under Marxist influence, particularly the influence of the thought of Antonio Gramsci.[4] Other modes of historiography, influenced by economics, sociology, or the approach of the *Annales* school in France, have also undertaken investigation of the religious activity and experience of the majority of the European population.[5] Concomitant to this has been the study of popular religion in other great religious traditions.[6]

Interest in popular religion is of special importance for developing local theologies. A close reading of the shape of popular religion gives us a unique perspective on the nature of religious activity and experience in concrete social contexts. It tells us something also of the role of religion in social change and in the continuing process of shaping identity in a particular cultural setting. To undertake the development of local theologies while rejecting or ignoring the religious patterns already present in a community suggests the very kinds of paternalism against which local theology has struggled. Hence to be able to develop an adequate local theology one must listen to the religious responses already present in the culture. Practices and symbolic networks have already taken shape. What do these say of life in that community?

A second reason for interest in popular religion in developing local theologies is more practical in nature. The previous local theologies that new theologies encounter usually have within them a good admixture of popular religion. Often this popular religion needs to be addressed along with the previous local theology, inasmuch as it may share the imported character of the theology. For example, Iberian popular religion has heavily influenced the popular religious patterns of Taiwan, the Philippines, and Latin America.

This chapter will review some of the major issues surrounding the use of popular religion in the development of local theologies, as well as look toward what the communities can teach us about future directions in the expression of Christian experience. It will begin by examining the definitions given to popular religion and what these say about perspectives and underlying assumptions about religion. From there it will move into the major interpretive frameworks that have been developed for understanding popular religion. This will lead to looking at a number of specific questions arising from such investigations and that are of significance to developing theologies in their concrete contexts.

WHAT IS POPULAR RELIGION?

A wide variety of terms are used for what is being called here "popular religion." Some of these reflect the different languages in which the discussion is being carried on; in other instances they imply quite different assumptions about the phenomenon being investigated. Because of these differences it is important to know where any given usage might be placed within the spectrum of opinion. At the same time this also reveals the variety of perspectives that are being taken on this phenomenon.

The term "popular religion" derives from the use of the adjective "popular" as it is found in its variants in the Romance languages. Literally it means "of the people" and can be used to mean of all people in general, or of one class of people (usually the poor, majority class) in particular.[7] It is not ordinarily used in the English sense of "popular" meaning "in fashion." When used in Latin American contexts, it generally refers to the poor, majority class. When used in North American contexts (as in "popular culture"), it refers to the majority, middle class.

A second term that is sometimes used is "folk religion." This derives from the Germanic adjective meaning "of the people." While it can be understood to carry the same meaning as "popular," it generally has additional overtones. Through the work initiated in Germany in the early nineteenth century by Herder and others, "folk" carries with it connotations of the lower strata of society, people who, in their simplicity, are the subjects of the authentic history of a nation. In the romanticized version of "folk," we have a body of wisdom in tales, proverbs, and lore, which has been preserved and transmitted orally from generation to generation. In the politicized version of "folk," we have a native purity and tradition relatively untainted by industrialization and modernization, which periodically asserts itself against the secularization process. It is conservative and often xenophobic in character, glorifying the life of the peasant as the ideal of a people.[8]

A third term is "common religion," suggested by the sociologist Robert Towler.[9] Similar to the two preceding concepts, it emphasizes the fact that the more theological or doctrinal understandings of religion are usually the province of but a small segment of the population, which has been entrusted with the maintenance of religious institutions. The religion of the greater part of the population will have various relationships to the religious institutions of that society, and those people will seldom identify all their religious experience with the social institutions. Towler goes on to suggest that common religion will be made up of the responses to a variety of needs within a population, upon which the religious traditions then build. Common religion forms a baseline of general experience, which is then specified by the institutional expression of religion.[10]

All three of these terms have their specific strengths and weaknesses. "Popular," the most common of the terms, captures a wide range of the concerns, but lacks a certain specificity. "Folk" has that specificity, but carries strong (and often negative[11]) overtones. "Common" has a sense similar to "popular" and is in some ways the most useful term, but it is also the least well known. In order to connect with the majority of the discussions going on, we shall use the term "popular" in this presentation.

From the use of all three terms—popular, folk, and common—it is clear that the phenomenon under investigation is not seen as independent from other realities. All three of these terms relate this form of religious expression to some other reality. By exploring these relational uses, we can get closer to some of the perspectives and assumptions coming into play.

Popular religion is sometimes contrasted with official religion.[12] If we take official religion to be those prescribed beliefs and norms of an institution promulgated and monitored by a group of religious specialists, then popular religion becomes those patterns of behavior and belief that somehow escape the control of the institutional specialists, existing alongside (and sometimes despite) the efforts at control of these specialists. In this view popular religion is seen as deviation from a norm. The task of official religion, then, is to bring popular religion into line with the established norm. The norm is understood to be a set of beliefs that then define a kind of practice. Popular religion in this sense is construed as having alternate beliefs or no clearly defined beliefs at all.

A second contrast is between popular and elite religion. "Elite" can be understood as either a cultural or a social category. When it is understood as a cultural category, it contrasts the more literate, verbal, and conceptually sophisticated approach of one group with the more illiterate, nonverbal, and often enthusiastic form of another ("lower") group. Most often it is also a social and economic category. The elite group will be identified with power and the control of resources, and the popular group will often be known simply as "the masses" of unlettered and disenfranchised people.[13]

"Elite" can also be used in another way to provide a third contrast, found in the older religious terms "esoteric" and "exoteric." This distinction refers to the quality and quantity of lore transmitted to the population. Certain doctrines and practices will be preserved for an initiated few, while a more general version will be transmitted to the majority. In the discussions of popular religion, this sense of "elite" is used in terms of theological sophistication of some believers over against the more rudimentary level of understanding of the great majority of adherents to a particular religious system.

These three contrasting uses of "popular" bespeak three different axes[14] along which popular religion is interpreted: institutional, social, and intellectual. While certainly not totally discrete categories, they represent distinctive conceptions of the major role of religion in society: as one of institutional organization, of social formation, of intellectual achievement.

What are we to make of all these different kinds of distinctions? It certainly alerts us to the fact that there is no comprehensive theory for grasping the reality under study. Indeed, it may be fair to assume, as some have, [15] that one can speak of different popular religions in the same cultural setting.

From the perspective of developing local theologies, a number of considerations emerge, which bear keeping in mind. First it is striking that none of these perspectives arises from the side of the phenomenon to be studied. The concern for popular religion seems to arise from the side of official or elite groups. This prompts questions about the audience and interest in studying popular religion: for whom is popular religion an issue? And why is it an issue for them? Is it a matter of analyzing popular religion in order to gain more effective control of it? This could be considered an interest of the officials of the institutional religion. Does an elitist group see it as an inferior product of the culture, which needs to be brought into the mainstream of "progress"? Does the presence of popular religion create a religious dissonance which intellectuals need to harmonize away? One of the reasons, perhaps, why the phenomenon of popular religion has remained intractable to theoretical analysis is that it is being viewed from an outside, and often inimical, perspective. It fails to fall into the categories that the dominant or intellectual class has prepared for it.

A second observation to be made is that religion seems to be construed here as a set of ideas, which then shape a particular practice. This is to a great extent a Western and intellectual bias. For the greater part of the world, religion is more a way of life than a view of life.[16] To try to isolate ideas and then derive the practice of a group from them may be putting the cart before the horse. This particular bias dates in the West especially from the time of the sixteenth-century Reformation with its emphasis upon the word of the Scriptures as normative entirely for Christian living. While it served as a useful corrective for Western Christianity, it does not function usefully as a criterion for understanding religion if employed separately and solely. It assumes a literate, idealist, and rational approach to life.

A third observation comes from the different categories identified above. It suggests that religion is immensely complex and inextricably woven through the fabric of human life. It is not a clear, isolated segment of social life. Any treatment of religion will have to have that kind of holistic approach called for in the analysis of the entirety of culture outlined in Chapter 3. To follow Geertz, religion itself calls for a "thick description." At the same time there is a need to be aware that religion has distinctive economic, political, and social ramifications, as well as the more familiar intellectual or ideational ones. When one analyzes popular religion it is important to know which semiotic domain—economic, political, social, psychological—is predominant in the consideration.

What does all of this mean for developing local theologies? It certainly calls for an adherence to some of the basic principles set out above, namely: trying to listen to the culture on its own terms; adopting a holistic pattern of description; remaining attentive to the audience and the interest of the questioner in each event. The sheer variety in the definitions of popular religion suggests something of the range of phenomena that come under that name. To that range of phenomena we are now ready to turn.

VARIETIES AND CHARACTERISTICS OF POPULAR RELIGION

Part of outlining the characteristics of popular religion is first to decide what will be included in the category. But without a somewhat comprehensive interpretive framework it is hard to know just what would constitute the boundaries of the category.

In the discussion of popular religion today, a wide range of phenomena is treated under the heading of popular religion. Some examples include: the religious activity of the illiterate majority in medieval and early modern Europe; the imported Iberian popular religion that has taken root in Latin America and the Philippines; the amalgams of African and European popular religion found in the Caribbean and in Brazil; the amalgams of African and European religion found in the African Independent Churches; the amalgams of Buddhist, Shinto, Confucian, and Christian elements in the new religions in Japan; United States civil religion; the dual religious systems among Native Americans in both North and South America, where the two systems are practiced side by side; the dual religious systems in sub-Saharan Africa, where the Christian religious system is returned to in times of crisis.

Other general forms could be added to this list, but this gives something of the range of phenomena that come under the heading of popular religion here. In this chapter we shall concentrate on the first three types mentioned; the amalgams and the dual religious systems will be taken up in chapter 7. Although there is no compelling reason for making this distinction on a theoretical level, there are some empirical ones. In the first three types, historical Western Christianity provides the paradigm in which the religious system is expressed and developed. In the latter cases, it shares the formation of the paradigm with other religious tradition. The case of American civil religion is separate from these considerations, since the debate continues to what extent it can be called a religious system, or to what extent the term "religion" is being used here in an extended sense.[17]

Therefore we shall concentrate on the first three mentioned. The investigations on these concentrate principally, although not exclusively, on the majority, poor population. The concentration is not exclusive because it seems that into the period of the western European high Middle Ages, there was no significant difference in the religious behavior of peasants and the aristocracy and most of the clergy. The economic and social distinctions did not seem to leave their mark on religious activity to any great extent.

A second preliminary consideration suggested by some investigators is a distinction between rural and urban popular religion.[18] When people migrate into cities from the countryside, the rural popular religion often undergoes a transformation. It may diminish in its frequency and cohesion of practice (secularization), it may take on new forms, or it may be replaced entirely by new religious systems (such as Pentecostalism in Brazil). In other instances it may remain relatively unchanged, since the so-called urbanization of many cities is often really a ruralization of urban centers because of the lack of an industrial base for the transformation of peasants into workers.

We shall address here primarily the rural forms of popular religion and their survivals in urban contexts, with some additional attention to new forms that develop. The majority of the research has been with the rural forms, and most investigators have developed their interpretive frameworks from the rural setting.

What are the principal characteristics of this kind of rural popular religion, shaped in its outward manifestations by historical Christianity? Manuel Marzal and Segundo Galilea[19] have each devoted attention to bringing together the principal characteristics of such religious activity and belief. Their descriptions are based on Latin American popular religion, but can be extended to cover most rural types elsewhere. Their designations can be summed up in the following eight points.

1. *God*: Popular religion begins with an image of God as provident, giving immediate reward and punishment for good and evil deeds in this world. God is at once gracious and stern, and immediately involved in the affairs of the world. Any extraordinary event, either for good or for evil, can be attributed to a decision on the part of God. There is no distinction between levels of causality. Thus if the priest drops the Host when I am about to receive Communion, it is no accident—God is displeased with me. If our region receives no rain, it is God's displeasure. If you find money along the road, God must be answering your prayers. Nothing really happens by chance; all living and nonliving reality is interconnected and controlled immediately by God. All is touched by his hand and is under his eye.

2. *Mediators*: Although God is intimately and concretely involved in the affairs of the world, he is seldom approached directly. Rather a host of mediators is invoked to intercede before God. Principal mediators are Jesus and Mary. While Jesus is seen as divine and not really of human estate, he is not considered quite the same as God. He is invoked especially as the baby Jesus (el niño Dios) and as the Crucified One.

Along with Jesus, Mary enjoys the most powerful mediation. Shrines to Mary usually outnumber those to Jesus. She is seen as the understanding Mother who knows how to approach God on behalf of her children. She appears often to her children, and these places of apparition (Guadalupe, Fatima, Lourdes) become sacred sites where miracles of healing often take place. Special images of her also have healing qualities. Sometimes these images are found (as in the case of Nossa Senhora de Aparecida in Brazil), or appear miraculously (as in the case of the image of the Virgin on the cloak of Juan Diego at Guadalupe), or are of ancient and unknown origin (Altötting in Bavaria, Montserrat in Spain). These images, too, can become the occasion for healings and wonders.

After Mary, there are other mediators, though none so powerful as she. Many have a certain circumscribed domain in which they work. Thus the patron or *santo* of a particular village will protect the people of that village in a special way. Saints Dominic, Francis, Martin, and James are examples of this. Sometimes a *santo* or a special image of the Virgin Mary becomes associated with an entire nation (Guadalupe with Mexico, Czestechowa with Poland). Often it is a specific statue or image, rather than the *santo* it signifies, that will carry this association. Thus if the statue of the *santo* is stolen or destroyed, a village may feel that it has been abandoned by its patron, and a complicated process will have to ensue before patronage is restored.

In addition to the local patron, some saints will become known for being able to protect or mediate certain things. Saint George is venerated, along with Saint Michael, as protection against lightning in parts of the Andes. Saint Agatha protects against fires in northern Europe. Again, a statue or some other form of image is necessary to make a proper intercession.

3. *Social Activities*: There is a strong communal dimension to popular religion. Celebrations are frequent and involve the entire rural community. Principal times for celebration include the feast days of important protectors of the community, anniversaries of miraculous events, significant moments of human passage (baptisms, marriages, funerals), and certain seasonal events (such as harvest celebrations among agricultural peoples). The first two types are celebrated by means of processions around the village with the image of the protector, as well as by feasting, dancing, and perhaps a market. Moments of human passage, especially births and marriages, also call for celebration with feasting and dancing. The fiestas, especially for the patron protectors, are sometimes arranged by special associations, with a rotation of persons in charge. They are often elaborate and constitute a major financial expense for the person in charge. The activities are seen as total events, and can last for several days. They include both prayer and social celebration.

4. *Devotional Activities*: There is also a private dimension to popular religion, built around the seeking of favors from God via the mediators. Individuals develop a personal cult or devotion to a particular image of the Virgin or to specific saints. The regularity of the cult or devotion assures that the Virgin or the saint will be familiar with the supplicant when need arises. Seeking favors is a major part of devotional religion. The favors include protection from evil forces, from illness, from unforeseen crises (sickness, marriage problems), as well as certain boons (a spouse, good crops, successful travel, success in business transactions). Often vows are taken or promises made by persons to engage in certain penitential or prayerful activities if protection is extended or the boon granted. Sometimes vows are in response to protection or favor received.

5. *Additional Mediations*: In addition to the activities just mentioned, there are other dimensions of popular religion that need to be mentioned. Blessings, and religious objects such as relics, medals, rosaries, and portable images play an important role in invoking divine power. Holy water, candles,

blessed palms, ashes, and penitential cords also must be counted among the apparatus of popular religion. Such concrete and tangible objects are necessary for assuring continuing contact with God and his mediators.

Processions, especially processions in pilgrimage, are clear indications of one's devotedness to the protectors and givers of favors who surround the throne of God.

6. *Associations*: Confraternities, sodalities, and other pious associations, dedicated to the Virgin or one of the saints, constitute an important part of popular religion. While they manifest the concrete devotion of their members to the patron, they also serve as the organizations that sponsor the major fiestas of the year. The rotating hosts acquire extensive social prestige and incur substantial expense in providing for the food and drink needed for these occasions. These groupings are essentially lay in character, although clergy may be invited to become members. Those that have official church sanction may also have a clerical moderator. Ordinarily, however, being a member of the clergy does not assure any special rank in these organizations.

7. *View of the World:* One cannot, of course, describe the view of the world underlying popular religion in any exhaustive manner. There are, however, some characteristics that deserve special mention: *(a)* The world is seen as an interconnected and controlled place. No bad deed goes unpunished, no good deed will be unrewarded, for God sees all. Because of this interconnection and control, there is a limited amount of room for human maneuvering. Some would see this as a certain fatalism about the prospects for human initiative; others, as a way of surviving under hostile circumstances. *(b)* Concerns are concrete, and requests for divine aid are usually directed at immediate needs. Since the world is a hostile place if one is not protected, a good deal of energy is directed toward assuring continued protection. *(c)* While concerns are to a large extent concrete, immediate, and this-worldly, there is a balancing concern for death and the afterlife. Death is a major preoccupation because of the high mortality rate in poor areas. It is not welcomed, except for the very old. Afterlife will reflect how one has lived here, and how one has fulfilled familial and moral obligations.

8. *Relation to Official Religion:* Popular religion intersects with official religion at many points. Official religion has clearly influenced the development of popular religion on many fronts. But there are some clear divergences. Among them are the following: *(a)* Prescriptions for religious activity of the official religion are not observed in popular religion, except where they coincide with popular religious activity. Thus the mandatory Mass attendance on Sundays and holydays for Roman Catholics is by and large ignored. Attendance at Mass is generally not considered important, except where it intersects with concerns of popular religion (patronal feasts, fiestas marking human passage). Sacramentally, baptism, marriage, and funerals are of importance in popular religion, along with First Communion. Communion and confession of sin are infrequent. *(b)* Clergy play an ambivalent role in popular religion. They are seen as mediators of divine power, but

only in specified areas. While they are needed for blessings, rites of human passage, and processions, their admonitions in other areas are often ignored. They do not exercise an authoritative role in directing the activity of popular religion. *(c)* Shrines play a more important role in the lives of those involved in popular religion than do church buildings, although the latter are important for the statues they house.

These characteristics have been painted in very broad strokes, which do not do justice to the variety within popular religion. But the characteristics noted are frequent in their occurrence. Together they constitute the framework for the religious experience of what might be the majority of Catholic Christians, and for that reason need to be taken seriously. With this we move to looking at some of the interpretations that attempt to develop a framework for understanding how popular religion functions.

INTERPRETING POPULAR RELIGION

How is one to interpret the phenomena that make up what we call popular religion? Its practices constitute what may be the major forum for religious experience for a majority of Catholic Christians and many Protestant and Orthodox Christians as well. Together these phenomena have provided a coherent communication system with the divine powers for many people over the centuries. They also offer a way for people in isolated areas to gather for extended periods of time in fiestas and other celebrations.

At the same time popular religion has been open to all kinds of abuse: idolatrous veneration of images, unrealistic and bizarre vows and promises made to saints, quarrelsome behavior in the associations. The fatalism in the world-view has kept the oppressed from dealing with the realities of their social conditions. The shadow side of popular religion is more than evident to many, especially to those functioning in official religion, or to those working for the liberation of the oppressed.

Interpretations have to take into account both the bright and shadow sides of popular religion. Some interpretations emphasize one aspect more than the others. The interpretations given here will be grouped by their emphasis on negative and positive aspects of popular religion.

NEGATIVE APPROACHES

For a long time, negative approaches dominated the interpretation of popular religion. They were essentially of two types: elitist and Marxist.

1. *Elitist Approaches:* Elitist approaches to interpreting popular religion were formulated principally by religious intellectuals interested in the reform of the church. They saw themselves as a small, informed group whose task was to enlighten the darkness of a popular religion that was situated somewhere between indifference and superstition. The urban working classes of Europe in France and Belgium had lapsed into indifference while their rural

cousins were locked in superstition.[20] Popular practice had strayed far from the meaning and commitment of gospel discipleship. The Christian commitment of most believers was to a kind of folk church that was of importance for birth, marrying, and burying, but carried little other sense of Christian value or virtue. These intellectuals saw evangelization and education leading to social action as the key to the dissolution of the folk church and the emergence of a genuinely conscious and committed Christian community. Among Catholics this action was seen as carrying out the best sentiments of church renewal; among Protestants, as returning to the ideals of the Reformation.

The strength of this approach is its close attunement to the gospel and its keen sense of Christian mission. It holds up an ideal of Christian commitment and service that invites a deeper realization of the mystery of Christ. Its sense of action presses toward the realization of a genuinely just society.

At the same time it shows some important weaknesses. It understands religion primarily in terms of ideas and a view of life, evidenced in its belief that verbal evangelization and more education will lead to a religious transformation. It is elitist in its self-assurance of its own command of the truth and its own plans for the reorganization of society. It intends to keep clear control of the process of change. It is interesting to note what happens when this elite is bypassed by other forms of renewal. The earlier renewal pioneered in France was in some ways superseded by Vatican Council II, and, as Bernard Lauret has documented, it left these intellectuals in a rearguard, integralist stance.[21]

The elitist approach to popular religion rarely is able to change popular religion much because it understands popular religion so abstractly and intellectually. A more concrete and comprehensive approach is needed if the elitist ideals are to be realized.

2. *Marxist Approaches:* Another negative approach comes out of a Marxist analysis. Such an approach would see popular religion as the false consciousness imposed by the ruling class upon the proletariat. This false consciousness is imposed in one of two ways. Either the ruling class directs the proletariat away from the real sources of social power to some putative otherworldly power, or it encourages the proletariat to engage in popular religious activities to achieve this-worldly success, which will never actually yield up the promised results. In both instances the actual relations of power and labor are obscured by a set of religious relations, which mask the genuine realities. From the Marxist perspective the majority are not poor or needy through the lack of resources, but because the ruling class has robbed the majority of the surplus value of their labor. To compensate for this loss the majority are allowed to believe in (or are encouraged to believe in) some reward in the afterlife for current deprivation and to seek out stopgap help in the meantime from their mediators. Church leaders are to be counted on to help maintain the illusion of power in popular religion.

The Marxist position calls for a transformation by destruction of the lies about access to power and for a politicization of the consciousness of the proletarian majority in order that they might see the genuine relations of power and labor that mark society. Only then can popular religion be changed: either to disappear altogether or to be transformed into genuine religion—depending on whether or not the analyst has a religious perspective. To quote an analyst (Francisco Vanderhoff) looking toward the transformation of religion: "one cannot 'evangelize' popular religion without demythologizing it, and one cannot demythologize it without politicizing its own environmentally conditioned sociopolitical relationships."[22] Of the two possible results of transformation of popular religion, atheistic Marxists have worked toward the former, and some members of the first generation of liberation theologians have worked toward the latter.

What are the strengths of Marxist approaches? Most notably they emphasize to what extent religious forms of expression are tied up with the totality of other social relationships. One cannot easily extricate religious activity from the rest of the human fabric and treat it independently. Second, Marxist analysts are correct in saying that some sectors of society have a special interest in seeing the proletarian majority of a society believe in a certain fashion, and want to keep things that way. Having their eyes turned toward heaven keeps them from analyzing the squalor of their current condition. Third, there is good reason to believe that religious change cannot come about with concomitant changes in the economic sphere. A new pattern of social relations has to emerge before more symbolic forms can change. The Marxist approach identifies important ingredients in the understanding of popular religion.

At the same time there are decided weaknesses in these approaches as well. The most common one encountered is that economic relations do not always unilaterally determine religious consciousness. Religious consciousness is a complex phenomenon that does not admit of such easy explanation. There are cases where religious belief has transformed economic relations. One thinks of the Iranian revolution of 1979 as an example. Second, the Marxist interpretation does not adequately account for a style of popular religion in precapitalist societies, shared across class lines, such as that of the early Middle Ages. Here there is no significant difference in the religion of ruling class and proletariat. Third, religion can reflect things other than economic relations. One thinks here of how Polish popular religion is tied to nationalism and the effect that has had on the Polish economic and social situation.

POSITIVE APPROACHES

There are also a number of readings of popular religion that take a neutral or more positive approach to the question. Five of these can be mentioned.

1. *The Baseline Approach:* The baseline approach derives from social psychologists such as Robert Towler.[23] It starts from the assumption that every culture has to meet a certain number of social and psychological needs if the culture is to sustain itself. A number of these (belonging, security, dealing with the dead, access to invisible power) will be resolved in a symbolic con-

stellation, which becomes the religion specific to that culture. Every culture has this kind of response. In addition to these responses, another series of symbolic responses is developed that addresses the more metaphysical issues facing humankind in a way that cuts across cultural barriers. Questions about the meaning of existence and the problem of evil and suffering would fit into this series of religious questions and answers. This second series of responses finds expression in the great literate religious traditions of the world (Christianity, Islam, Judaism, Buddhism, Hinduism). When this second series of responses comes into contact with the first series (the culture-specific religions), it selects some items from the first level for incorporation, reinterprets other elements, and so contextualizes itself in the culture.

With the baseline approach, popular religion is the first kind of religion in the culture, but one that has been reorganized by the entry of a world religion. From one point of view, what needs explanation in this scheme is not popular religion, but world religions. World religions become a specific derivative of the human religion-making function.

This approach would argue that popular religion could never be totally supplanted by the world religion; a certain baseline of human need will always have to be addressed. Moreover there is a limited range within which it can be transformed. For that reason any new religious form has the choice of remaining pure (and therefore small), or becoming universal (and having a popular variant of considerable magnitude). Even within renewalist movements like the Western sixteenth-century Reformation one finds the emergence again of such a popular religion.[24]

What are the strengths and weaknesses of this interpretive framework? A decided strength is that it takes popular religion as a phenomenon to be observed in its own right, not as a derivative from a world religion. It is neither derivative or deviant, but a phenomenon in its own right and of its own origin. It also helps to explain something of popular religion's resistance to change and certainly its resistance to annihilation—how elements of a people's baseline religion will survive for centuries despite the concerted efforts of religious leaders to extirpate them. The baseline-religion approach can also help to identify some of the basic human needs that any religious system will have to meet to win the adherence of a culture.

At the same time the baseline approach does have some shortcomings. First, the model seems to evidence a certain Western, industrial bias in that it sees religion primarily in terms of individual needs and behavior. It works out a decidedly psychological orientation that presumes an individualistic kind of culture. Second, while it reveals important insights into the nature of popular religion, and especially into its hardiness and perdurance over time, it does not provide a way of looking at it within the totality of culture and culture change.

2. *The Romanticist Approach*: There are two approaches to popular religion that could be called romanticist in their orientation. The first dates from nineteenth-century France, influenced by Jean Jacques Rousseau and the

Enlightenment.[25] This approach sees popular religion as the genuine religion of the people, but one that has been skewed by the church and its clergy. Were the restrictions and doctrines imposed by the church to be removed, a natural style of religion would emerge more conducive to the development and improvement of the human condition. Such a religion can be constructed by looking toward the popular religion among rural peoples and extracting from the popular religion those beliefs and practices commensurate with the natural human state of existence.

This kind of approach is too simple to attract many direct adherents today. Its bias is clearly against the church, and it assumes that popular religion has social organization of its own. A second problem is the lack of distinction between nature and culture. Religion is eminently cultural in form, and seemingly not the activity of the noble savage—if anywhere such might be found. While this approach does show some appreciation for popular religion, it seems to misconstrue radically the shape of culture and culture formation.

A second romanticist approach also owes its origins to the early nineteenth century, but more to Johann Gottfried von Herder than to the descendants of Rousseau. This approach, represented by theologians such as Juan Carlos Scannone,[26] starts with a unified and somewhat mystical concept of "the people" who are the subject of experience and cultural history. This concept of "the people" is incarnated especially in the poor majority who live a simpler and less alienated life. Their religious activity has definite and special value for the future of the human race because of their mystical relationship to this concept of "the people." Hence we need to listen to them closely in the process of the transformation of society. A study of their religion gives us special access to their vision of the world.

The advantage of this kind of approach is the seriousness with which it listens to popular religion in all its forms. It shows a deep respect for the poor majority who are the subjects of this history. A disadvantage is the romanticism of this view. Scannone not only sees the presence of the people in a particular culture, but envisions all of Latin America as having this mission to the rest of the church.[27] To see an entire continent as a single people disregards the genuine diversity of those people and carries strong chauvinistic overtones. A similar approach, which praised the German "people," was a major contributor to anti-Semitism and the rise of National Socialism in the 1930s, and such uncritical praise of "the people" can lead to such conclusions.[28] Liberationists also point out that the elements that are praised in this approach are particularly those which are oppressive to these same people and work toward their continued bondage. Besides lacking in cultural sophistication, this approach does not seem to provide the differentiation necessary to bring an end to the poverty and injustice that stalk so many of these privileged subjects of history.

3. *The Remnant Approach*: This approach sees popular religion in a culture as the previous, pre-Christian religion surviving in a transformed man-

ner. In contemporary Europe, which has been evangelized for over a millennium, or in Latin America, which has been evangelized for four hundred years, two things are evident. On the one hand, traces and elements of the old religion have survived intact, even to the point of continuing as an independent system in parts of Latin America. On the other hand, elements of the older system have been incorporated into Christianity. Thus older shrines now honor Christian saints; old customs are incorporated into Christian celebration. This process of incorporation has been part of the Christian ethos since at least the time of Gregory the Great who, in his instruction to Augustine of Canterbury, urged him to keep all that was not in direct conflict with the gospel.[29]

One thing that experience has taught is that evangelization is a much more gradual process than was once believed. Elements of the older religion remain for generations, even centuries, although Christianity may have been enthusiastically embraced. This points again to the complexity of the religious response.

What perspectives on popular religion does the remnant approach offer? It certainly emphasizes that much of what we call Christianity is actually composed of elements absorbed from local religions. Thus the Christianity brought to Latin America in the sixteenth century not only interacted with the local American religions, it also brought along Iberian pre-Christian elements into the new situation. An important implication of the remnant approach is that there is no such thing as "pure" Christianity; a culture receives faith with an admixture of cultural and religious elements. This becomes particularly important for understanding the history of countries like Brazil, which first was exposed to an Iberian Christianity, and then later to a Romanization of its Christianity, a pattern repeated earlier in a slightly different fashion for many of the countries of northern Europe.[30]

At the same time a mere identification of surviving elements and introduced elements will not be particularly helpful in ascertaining future direction of popular religion in a culture. While the surviving elements may point to areas of need not addressed by Christianity, there is usually not enough coherence to indicate anything like directions that might be taken.

4. *The Subaltern Approach*: Subaltern approaches are inspired by the reflections of the Italian Marxist Antonio Gramsci and have had a major influence on the analysis of popular religion in Italy.[31] Gramsci varied the classical Marxist approach to religion and proposed that the religion of the proletarian (or subaltern class, as he termed it) could not be understood entirely as having been imposed by the ruling class. While this is sometimes the case, and while sometimes subaltern religion will mirror the religion of the ruling class, at other times the subaltern class will develop its own form of religion in opposition to the wishes of the ruling class as a way of maintaining cultural identity. The work of Eugene Genovese on United States antebellum slave religion would be an example of application of this approach.[32]

In this form of subaltern religion, forms are often borrowed from the ruling class, but are given different meaning and roles within the subaltern system. In the case of the slave religion of North America, "crossing the River Jordan" did not refer to personal conversion, but to a wish to cross into the Free North. In the Caribbean and in Brazil, elements of Catholicism were wedded to Ibo and Yoruba religious systems of Africa to create new religious systems, which have by and large remained impervious to transformation by the ruling classes. They have remained a powerful source of identity to peoples in those areas; indeed, they often gain the adherence of rural peoples moving into urban areas in Brazil, the Caribbean, and North America.[33]

The subaltern approach highlights an important aspect of popular religion often overlooked, namely, that the symbolic world of a popular religion can provide one of the few resources of identity over which an oppressed people can exercise some control of their own. Pueblo peoples in the southwestern sections of the United States have used their old religion in this fashion, as a secret initiation transmitted to their children in order to maintain their identity in the midst of centuries of white domination. The secret, esoteric, inner side of subaltern religion can become the vehicle for liberation movements (such as the Mau-Mau revolts in East Africa in the 1950s) or can sustain people through long periods of silent suffering (such as the "hidden Christians" of Nagasaki during the Tokugawa period in Japan).

A second strength of the subaltern approach is that it sees popular religion as having an integrity of its own, which in turn implies an analysis somewhat independent of that of the religion of the dominant class. Its strength, its patterns of change, and its ability to endure have to be understood within the context of the subaltern class in its totality. A third strength that deserves mention is the extent to which the subaltern approach values the symbolic potential of popular religion, especially in its ability to forge identity for a people otherwise denied it by a ruling class.

The weakness of the subaltern approach lies not so much in what it does as in what it does not do. What of the religion of the ruling class and forms of popular religion to be found there? I would suggest that Gramsci's insight be extended to a wider context. One not only could investigate popular religion as a means of shaping identity with the subaltern class, but also could hypothesize that each class has its respective "popular religion." How religious activity is organized may have a lot to do with the resources available to a people. In other words, needs will cut across class lines, but response to needs will vary depending upon the resources available to a particular class. The invocation of the rubric of religion will vary across those lines, depending also on the resources available. Thus a poor family in South America may well know or understand how Western medical technology conceives of a certain disease, but if the resources of that technology are not available for responding to the disease, a vow at a shrine may be the only possibility open to them. In the same way different classes may have different responses to the same problem. A poor couple may light a candle to improve the quality of communication in their marriage, while their middle-class counterparts head for a weekend of Marriage Encounter workshop sessions.

This hypothesis suggests, then, that the same needs will receive different responses on different class levels. Some of the responses are rather clearly related to the amount of access to power that each class may have. The development of the small Christian community among the poor, with its Bible study, shows us how deeply evangelical popular religion can become. The quest of ever new spiritual techniques among the middle class in the United States shows us how unevangelical another form of popular religion can become. Because the popular religion of the middle and the upper classes tends to coincide with the religiosity of the clergy when it comes to the resolution of religious need, middle- and upper-class popular religion has not been recognized for what it is.

This hypothesis also provides a basis for explaining why Catholics who left their devotional practices behind in the wake of Vatican II became quite interested in charismatic renewal groups, in Marriage Encounter sessions, even in justice and peace issues. While the hypothesis does not account for the entirety of their interest, it does suggest that as people change class, or changes occur within a class, new forms of popular religion need to be found. The hypothesis of a class-specific popular religion can help us to respect the integrity of the variety of forms of popular religion, as well as help to identify the range of needs and solutions open to a society in the midst of social change.

5. *The Social-Psychological Approach*: Investigators in Brazil have addressed themselves to the phenomenon of Pentecostalism, the growth of the Afro-Brazilian cults, and what happens to rural religion when it comes into the city.[34] They would suggest as a model for understanding popular religion one that identifies social-psychological needs, and then sees how these interact with the economic, social, and political patterns in the environment. They trace much of the growth of urban cults to the problem of two cultures (Brazilian and European) not having achieved adequate integration. Edenio Valle, for example, suggests that the three doctrines of many Pentecostal groups—sanctification, the gifts of the Holy Spirit, and the awaited Second Coming of Christ—reflect three group-forming dynamics that account for the attractiveness of urban Pentecostalist groups to recent arrivals from the countryside. The doctrine of sanctification creates the sense of an elect group that allows its members to run away from the values of the bourgeois society whose resources are denied them. The doctrine of the gifts of the Holy Spirit gives them resources denied by that bourgeois society. And the imminent Second Coming justifies their gathering together in the city, despite their exclusion from the mainstream of urban life.[35]

This model is particularly useful in describing the kinds of change that popular religion sometimes undergoes in the move from the countryside into the city. It is less useful in helping to chart a pattern of change for the transformation of the situation for the disenfranchised, something that the Marxist model has been able to do more successfully. It also helps to explain the number and tenacity of conversions to new sects in Brazilian cities and provides a basis for the development of an explanation for similar situations elsewhere.

THE SEVEN APPROACHES IN SUMMARY

In summary, then, these approaches—two negative and five positive ones—provide distinctive ways of looking at the question of popular religion. Four of them make special contributions to understanding aspects of popular religion. If the observer is particularly interested in how a popular religious system blocks its participants from being freed from their oppression, then a Marxist model of explanation is the most helpful. If, on the other hand, one wants to discover what has made it possible for a people to survive an oppressive situation, then the subaltern approach is the most helpful. If one wants to locate which needs the popular religious system is addressing and meeting, then the baseline or the social-psychological approach is the most helpful. The baseline approach works better in rural settings; the social-psychological approach, in urban ones.

AREAS OF NEED AND POPULAR RELIGION

The seven approaches discussed in the previous section present seven frameworks for studying popular religion as a system. We can consider the question in a different way by looking at it from the point of view of the participants, rather than viewing the system as a whole. In this case, three sets of considerations need to be kept in mind.

1. *Psychological Considerations*: Questions of psychological needs are raised already in some of the approaches above, notably the baseline approach. One can pose the psychological question in terms of what an individual seeks from participation in popular religion.

The primary answer would be: access to power in times of crisis. In anyone's life, situations arise that are of crucial importance to an individual or to a group, over which little or no control can be exercised. The ability to respond depends to some extent on the resources available in one's class situation, but there are certain situations—sudden serious illness, natural catastrophes—over which no one can exercise control.

As was indicated in the discussion of the subaltern approach above, those with little material power will be more likely to need to invoke divine power to come to their aid than will those who have access to other forms of help. A correlate of this is that one cannot hope to initiate change away from such invocations of divine power until alternate ways of getting at the needed power are identified and provided. Those alternate ways may be either through other symbolic ways within religion (such as moving away from the use of holy water to intercessory prayer), or through the realignment of economic resources to achieve the same ends.

A second need in the psychological area is for multiple and direct mediations of this power. This is evidenced in the multiplicity of saints who are invoked for a variety of needs, sometimes in a highly specialized fashion. For the poor and the oppressed, there is certainly an awareness of the awesomeness of the power of God, but those whose sense of self-worth has been continually abused by a ruling class will not presume direct access to someone so exalted as God. More human forms of access are needed. And a multiplicity is needed, should one mode of access fail. The immediacy of a saint and the tactility of an image make for a clearer sense of communication. In other classes, a person may collect together a variety of forms of spirituality to achieve the same relationship with God. What this means pastorally is that mediation is necessary, and the mode of mediation must be commensurate with other social relations in the life of the one seeking help.

This leads to a third consideration, namely, the integrative nature of the religious process. One psychological task of religious symbolism is to help make the world a meaningful place. One cannot interchange religious symbols casually as though they were interchangeable parts of different machines. Images of God, of Christ, of Mary reflect other social relationships in a person's life. The image of Christ as brother may work in a middle-class setting where one is in a position to initiate all kinds of voluntary associations, but not in class situations where the powerful are feared and distrusted.

2. *Social Considerations*: One of the major changes that can occur in the popular religion of an individual or a family happens when it moves from the country to the city. In other words, an alteration in social relations will call for changes in the religious semiotic system as well. On the surface it may seem that the social pressure of conformity to particular religious patterns, gone now in the city, was the major factor holding the popular religious expression together. But the reasons are often deeper. If the patterns of popular religion no longer give a symbolic unity to the rest of life, they can die. We are often caught in patterns of suggesting a rural spirituality with its emphasis on the unity of work, family, and social relations to an urban people who find work, family, and social relations as operating in quite different spheres. Religious universes crumble for a reason, and that reason is most often that they are no longer integrative of the rest of social relations.

By the same token, the Marxist analysts are probably right when they say that the world-view and patterns of popular religion cannot be changed without a concomitant change in the economic relations. Religious symbols will continue to mirror, however obliquely, other relationships with the lives of people. To change an understanding of God and ways of relating to him, there must also be a change in our understanding of social relations in that same world.

Finally, the pace of change must be commensurate on the sides of both popular religion and social relations. If social change comes too quickly, previous religious practice can collapse. If new religious practice outpaces social change, it can lead to utopianism, idealism, and cynicism. While the development is seldom entirely even, there is nonetheless a limit to the amount that the two can be separated in their mutual development.

3. *Religious Considerations*: Much of the analysis of popular religion given here has been from psychological and social dimensions. This could lead to the conclusion that religious considerations are reducible to either or both of these. But popular religion is more than a psychological or social reflex. It has its own deeper dynamic. If popular religion is a legitimate form of contextualization of the experience of God, then it cannot be reducible in and of itself to another reality. Its concreteness is reflected in its embeddedness in psychological and social relations, but the phenomenon is more complex than this. All religious behavior has need of multiple mediations, but it also springs from multiple motivations. Karl Rahner holds that alongside all these variegated psychological and social relations lies a deep-seated need for completion and salvation to be found only in God.[36] God is not just a psychological or social cipher, but represents a reality transcending the finitude of the human condition, a reality to which individuals in human society are called. That, too, cannot be forgotten.

For this reason, with real justification, Segundo Galilea has suggested that we see popular religion as a spirituality.[37] This term has become an acceptable one for describing the form of religion taken in the middle class; it should be extended to other classes as well. To think of popular religion as a form of spirituality allows us to appreciate its subtleties and its depths, while raising questions about its shortcomings and pursuing lines for its future development.

Finally, one must realize that conversion is a gradual and a concrete process. While a group may accept the words of the Scriptures rather quickly, the full apprehension of them can take a very long time. Even peoples who have been evangelized for centuries have difficulty hearing parts of the Scriptures or conforming themselves to the challenge of the gospel. The evangelization of most cultures has been selective at best—better at some things than at others. We should not be applying, therefore, criteria to the poor majority to which the rich minority are not willing to live up.

PASTORAL APPROACHES TO POPULAR RELIGION

One can agree with Michael Singleton that, in respecting popular religion in a culture, letting the people be is not the same as letting them alone.[38] To speak at all of a pastoral approach to popular religion implies that some sort of pastoral intervention is likely. Perhaps more than anyone else, Segundo Galilea has worked at developing pastoral approaches to popular religion.[39] These will be incorporated into some suggestions here:

1. A first principle to keep in mind is: Does the popular religion of a particular group need to be changed at all? For whom is it a problem? Often it needs change because the local pastor feels uncomfortable with the practice. If this is the only reason for a change, perhaps the change should be on the part of the pastor.

2. Religion is best understood as a way of life rather than a view of life. A religious world-view is reflective of a way of living. Recent literature in the Catholic area of Christianity is beginning to recapture the notion of Catholicism as a particular Christian ethos that expresses itself in sacramentality, multiple mediation, and concreteness.[40] What this means pastorally in terms of popular religion is that one must first look to what is done before one tries to understand what is said.

3. Popular religion is not just something for the poor and dispossessed, but represents the form of religion in a specific class. All the class relations have to be taken into account in assessing the meaning of religious forms and in initiating change to transform them.

4. Do the practices of popular religion enhance the identity of a group and bring it more into conformity with images of identity present in the Christian tradition? Do the practices lead to a challenge to adhere more closely to Christian values? Do they free members to be more Christian?

5. Do the practices of popular religion have the edge of judgment; do they open new horizons toward a fuller human existence? Where do they land on the question of justice?

6. Do the practices lead to a freedom commensurate with freedom as understood in the culture? "Freedom" is a culture-specific word; it can mean individual freedom to choose from a wide variety of resources, or it can mean fuller participation in the social complex of the culture. Westerners have to be particularly careful about imposing their concepts of freedom on others.

7. Do the practices help individuals to recognize the sin in their lives and in the fabric of structures in the community? How do the religious practices help to reinforce the best values of the popular religion?

POPULAR RELIGION AND LOCAL THEOLOGIES

One of the major tasks often faced in the developing of a new local theology is the question of dealing with the previous local theologies in the community. Often these theologies were brought along by those who did the first evangelization and became embedded in the popular religion of that community. Sometimes these previous local theologies continue to undergird a popular religion that hampers the general development of the community or hinders that development in more outright fashion. For example, the clinging of many African communities to pre-Vatican II patterns from the Roman liturgy hinders the development of a more authentic local response in prayer and celebration and may perpetuate patterns of colonialism at the same time. How does one change these patterns?

If one takes the considerations offered in this chapter and thinks back to what was said on this subject in chapter 2, one would conclude that it is unlikely that those patterns can be changed to any great extent in Africa until Africans are given back their own sense of identity and self-worth and until they are allowed to look to their own culture as an ideal equal to that of Europe and white culture. That transformation depends to a large extent on a change in the economic relationships whereby the North Atlantic communities keep Africa in a state of underdevelopment. Keeping in Africans this sense of subservience and underdevelopment is necessary in order to maintain the relations of economic exploitation. Until this cycle is broken, it is difficult to change the popular religion involved.

One tool for changing that pattern has been the development of the small Christian communities. When people discover that their baptism gives them a voice in responding to the challenges of the gospel, when leaders listen to what their communities say in such circumstances, then the dimensions of the religious symbolic universe begin to shift as the people gain a sense of their own autonomy.

Local theologies are, in many ways, the expressions of popular religions. To develop local theologies, then, one must listen to popular religion in order to find out what is moving in people's lives. Only then can local theologies be developed and the liberating power of the gospel come to its full flower.

7

Syncretism and Dual Religious Systems

THE PROBLEMS OF SYNCRETISM AND DUAL RELIGIOUS SYSTEMS

In chapter 6, questions of popular religion and previous local theologies were taken up and investigated from a number of different perspectives. A popular religious system often exists prior to the development of a local theology in a culture and becomes an additional factor with which a local theology has to deal. It was also noted that the popular religion that develops in a culture (provided that it was not wholly imported) reflects a kind of local theology.

There are two other kinds of manifestations of religious belief and activity that also need to be looked at for themselves and how they affect the development of local theologies: syncretism and dual religious systems.

Syncretism, as the etymology of the word suggests, has to do with the mixing of elements of two religious systems to the point where at least one, if not both, of the systems loses basic structure and identity. The term derives from the study of the religious ferment in the Mediterranean basin at the beginning of the Common Era, when competing cults borrowed heavily from one another and were constantly reshaping themselves into new forms.

Christian literature regarding syncretism has always taken a negative stance toward the phenomenon. Anything that would dilute or substantially alter the basic structures of Christianity was combated strongly. The importance of keeping the gospel message pure and unadulterated has been a constant concern of the Christian church.

The missionary movements from the seventeenth century onward raised the questions about syncretism again, as Christianity encountered new cultural settings. In a special way the highly developed and literate traditions throughout Asia raised questions for Christian identity.

The problem of the Christian church disappearing into some syncretistic amalgam was not the only problem that needed to be faced, however. The Rites Controversy in China had already resulted in a strict position being taken on that issue well into the twentieth century.[1] There was also the phenomenon of peoples in cultures borrowing elements from Christianity and incorporating them into their own religious structures. The thousands of African Independent Churches, with the emphasis on healing, ecstatic behavior, and exorcism, began to spring up throughout that continent, and there was little that the established churches could do about it.[2]

Most recently that shift in perspective, which has led to the development of local theologies, has raised the old questions of syncretism in a new way. How thoroughly contextualized does a local church intend to become? Are there limits to contextualization? Can it reach a point where the gospel message is lost or communion between the churches is no longer possible? In the whole contextualization movement, should the Independent Church movement be seen as the ultimate outcome of contextualization rather than as some aberration? These are hard questions, which local theology is going to have to face.

It is fair to say that, from the perspective of the local church, the literature on syncretism coming from meetings of churches and from theologians has not been genuinely helpful. Theological and ecclesiastical literature takes on a uniformly negative tone when addressing syncretism.[3] Local churches share those concerns, but do not find in that literature much that would be of help in facing their local problems. Research by historians of religion, studying the syncretistic systems of Western classical antiquity, and by cultural anthropologists, studying contemporary syncretistic systems from the perspective of cultural accommodation and change, offer more of a possibility.[4]

One of the options for responding to the syncretistic possibility has been to take a rigid line on the question of any cultural accommodation whatsoever. But that, too, has had its unfortunate consequences, one of which has been the development of dual systems.

The problem of dual systems has been known to local church leaders for a long time and has come to the attention of anthropologists more recently. Theologically there has not been much reflection on the phenomenon. In dual systems a people follows the religious practices of two distinct systems. The two systems are kept discrete; they can operate side by side. Sometimes one system is followed more faithfully than the other (as in Africa, where people will follow the Christian system, but retain certain elements of a traditional system); in other instances the two systems may be followed almost equally (among Native Americans of the North American southwest, among Quechua and Aymaran peoples in the Andes, and among peoples in Japan, Taiwan, and southern Asia). Conversion to Christianity has usually meant putting all other religious systems aside, but in these instances significant parts or even the entirety of a second system is maintained.

How is a local church to deal with this phenomenon? Dual-system situations are notoriously intractable to any strategy to change them. What do they tell us about Christianity and about local theologies?

The purpose of this chapter is to look at these phenomena in order to see what might be done pastorally with them, and what implications they have for developing local theologies. The investigation will begin by trying to set out some of the different kinds of syncretism and dual-system phenomena commonly encountered. From that, some of the questions or issues arising from these phenomena will be presented. Then models will be presented for understanding and dealing with these systems, followed by some reflection on what this can mean for local theologies and for the entire church.

THE VARIETIES OF SYNCRETISM
AND DUAL RELIGIOUS SYSTEMS

In his study of syncretism in Western classical antiquity, Helmer Ringgren came to the conclusion that a precise definition of syncretism is, in the long run, not helpful as a research tool.[5] The phenomenon is amorphous and subject in its interpretation to the judgment and temperament of the investigator. When, for example, does a syncretistic system effectively become a new religion and lose the syncretist label? The basis for such a decision often follows criteria other than those used for studying the syncretistic process itself. Those who have themselves studied syncretistic systems or who have had to work with them understand Ringgren's point. There can be a clear point, say, when Christianity loses its identity in a syncretistic system. But at exactly what point is that actually reached?

Rather than attempt a definition of syncretism at the outset (although anthropologist Louis Luzbetak's "a theologically untenable amalgam" is a workable one, from a theological perspective[6]), let us begin by describing briefly three sets of phenomena, all of which would generally be considered syncretistic, and then we shall do the same for dual systems. These can then form a background for directing the discussion with more precision.

THREE KINDS OF SYNCRETISM

The first kind of syncretism to be looked at here is widespread along the northeastern coast of South America and throughout many islands in the Caribbean. The syncretism is between Christianity and West African religions of the former slaves. Christian deity and saints are amalgamated into the Yoruba or Ibo pantheons and communicated with along the lines of African ritual. The syncretistic systems claim thousands of adherents: Umbanda, Macumba, Batuque in Brazil; Voodoo (Vaudun) in Haiti.[7] These Afro-Brazilian and Afro-Caribbean systems represent the principal form of religious activity for their adherents. Developed first among the slave populations of Brazil and the Caribbean, they now attract many Native American people in Brazil as they migrate into the cities. Haitian refugees have carried their religion with them to North America, so that Voodoo is now a thriving cult in New York City. The adherents to these systems may have nominal affiliation also with Christianity, but more likely see themselves separate from Christianity; some take an inimical posture toward it. God, Jesus, Mary, the archangels Michael, Gabriel, and Raphael, the saints Sebastian and George figure especially prominently in the Brazilian systems, identified with *orixás* (spirits or deities) in the Yoruba pantheon. Certain Catholic elements (statues, holy water, candles, even the consecrated Host) will be sought out for the rites to enhance the power of the ritual action.

A second type of syncretism blends Christian and non-Christian elements, but uses the framework of Christianity for its organizations. Such would be the case with the Independent Churches in Africa (of which there are tens of thousands), and groups such as the Rastafarians in Jamaica.[8] Throughout Africa, men and women have had visions that have caused them to found a church. There is generally a heavy use of Christian elements. In East Africa, Roman Catholic vestments are especially prized. The Bible receives reinterpretation according to the vision of the founding member. Ritual singing and dancing, centering on healing, exorcism, and ecstasy, make up the principal group activity. Ritual follows African lines.

The Rastafarians believe Ras Tafari (later Emperor Haile Selassie of Ethiopia) to be their leader and the chosen prophet of God, although the emperor would have nothing to do with them. The Rastafarians separate themselves from the Christianity they received and wear distinctive clothing, braid their hair into dreadknots, and use in their ritual their own music, known to a wider audience as reggae. Similar movements involving other figures can be found elsewhere in the world.

The Melanesian cargo movements also look to the deliverance of the people and borrow heavily from Christian symbolism and apocalyptic theology to express their belief. In the cargo movements (from the neo-Melanesian *kahgo* = Western goods, money, and technology), a prophet foresees the return of the ancestors, bearing the white nations' goods. The whites will then be driven out of Melanesia, and Melanesians will live forever on the goods their ancestors have brought them. To achieve the return of the ancestors, certain rituals, revealed to the prophet, have to be carried out. An example of a cargo movement still active is Daniel Yaliwan's Peli Association.[9]

In a third type of syncretism, the religious system is highly selective in its appropriation of Christian elements. Some of the New Religions *(Shinkō Shukyō)* in Japan have a great veneration for Jesus. In one particular cult Jesus shares an altar with Muhammad and the Buddha. In a similar manner Christian marriage ceremonies have become very popular in Japan among large segments of the population. Engaged couples will take instructions and allow themselves to be baptized in order to have a Christian wedding ceremony, even though they have no intention of further practice as Christians subsequent to the wedding ceremony.

These three forms of syncretism represent three foci around which many syncretistic phenomena can be grouped: (1) where Christianity and another tradition come together to form a new reality, with the other tradition providing the basic framework; (2) where Christianity provides the framework for the syncretistic system, but is reinterpreted and reshaped substantially, independent of any dialogue with established Christianity; (3) where selected elements of Christianity are incorporated into another system.

THREE KINDS OF DUAL SYSTEMS

In the first kind of dual system, Christianity and another tradition operate side by side. This is a common phenomenon among many Native American groups in North and South America. South America and parts of the southwestern United States underwent an initial evangelization effort during the Iberian invasions in the 1600s. Many of these areas were then left without clergy for two centuries, with contact being reestablished in the nineteenth century. When this contact was reestablished, the old religion did not disappear, but continued to operate alongside the reintroduced Christianity. Thus among the Aymara in Peru and Bolivia, Christianity and the old Aymaran religion were practiced side by side. People follow both sets of rituals and see no contradiction in doing so. Among the Pueblo peoples in the southwestern United States, this is also common, although in this instance the old rites are often kept secret from outsiders. Anthropologist Alfonso Ortiz, a Tewa from the San Ildefonso Pueblo in New Mexico, recounts that, when someone dies, the Catholic funeral is held first. When the Catholic priest leaves the gravesite, the Tewa priest takes over for the next ceremony.[10] While there may be some amalgamation of the deities of the two systems, these systems function essentially independently of each other.

In a second kind of dual system, Christianity is practiced in its integrity, and selected elements from another system are also practiced. Often those elements are perceived by Christian leaders as incompatible and even contradictory to Christianity. Thus Christians in rural West Africa often will maintain sacrifices at a shrine to a local spirit or deity. In times of distress, this dual practice becomes especially evident. There are not only prayers to the Christian deity, but recourse to local priests and healers for their intercession with local deities as well. It is as though the people wish to exhaust all possible channels of mediation. While the dual practices appear clearly contradictory to the Christian leadership, local members do not see the contradiction.

A third kind of dual system has been called "double belonging."[11] This occurs in Asia, where a particular religious tradition and citizenship in a nation are seen as inextricably bound up. Can one really be Burmese or Thai without being Buddhist? Or Taiwanese without being Taoist? Or Japanese without being Shinto? These religious patterns are so deeply woven into the culture that it is no longer possible to discern easily what is religion and what is culture. And so people are raising the question of whether one can be Buddhist and Christian at the same time in South Asia, or whether all Taoist practices have to cease in order for one to be a Christian.

These three kinds of dual-system situations point to three sets of relationships. In the first set, Christianity and the other tradition are perceived as two distinct religious traditions, with both being practiced side by side. In the second set, Christianity is primary, with some selection of elements from a second tradition, which is nonetheless practiced separately from Christianity. In the third set, what constitutes religion in each of the systems becomes problematic as Christians try to remain faithful both to Christianity and to their national identity.

These six situations pose a number of questions about how to understand syncretism and dual systems and what those understandings mean for Christian practice. It is to those issues and questions that we now turn.

Some Issues and Questions

1. *What is the nature of conversion to Christianity, and how long does it take?* When syncretistic or dual systems appear, the first response is to fault the evangelization work that preceded baptism as being incomplete or inadequate. This may sometimes be the case. But local church leaders will tell us that sometimes they are as surprised by the reemergence of the older systems as anyone.

What is it that actually happens in the conversion process? One can account for the rational, conscious activity, but there appears to be much going on at an unconscious level as well. What does a convert understand to be the point of conversion? We still do not understand many things about the conversion process.[12] To understand conversion better will help us to account for why Christians move to syncretistic or dual-system practices. What is their understanding of their own identity as Christians in such instances?

2. *How we are to understand religion itself?* Throughout this presentation it has been repeated that religion is more than a view of life—it is also a way of life. The more closely we look at Christian religious activity in all its forms, the more we have to ask about the nature of religion itself. Is "religion" ultimately a Western or a Christian category? It cannot be insignificant that so many languages of the world do not even have a word for what we call "religion." For many peoples it is a way of being and living so tied up with being part of a particular culture that it is impossible to imagine living that way outside the culture. When Christianity comes into the situation, Christianity is not seen as replacing that way of living in the culture, but as enhancing it, giving it a link to the larger world, enhancing access to the sources of divine power, providing better insight into what one has been doing already. To say to people in those circumstances that Christianity is a "religion" means that it is something extra to add to the local situation, not something different. This is particularly the case when there is no word for religion in the local language.

The Barthian distinction between faith and religion does not get us out of this difficulty.[13] It is helpful for speaking about renewal of religious activity within a culture where Christianity is already prevalent, but otherwise it assumes that Christian faith is a disincarnate reality, above and beyond the human realities of religion. How effectively can we preach the Word Made Flesh in disincarnate terms? The faith-religion distinction is most certainly a cultural distinction of the West, and perhaps only of one form of Protestant Christianity.

What is clearly imperative is to come to a better understanding of what is meant by religion. The model in many people's minds is an American one in which a citizen chooses a church from among the hundreds of voluntary associations possible. This is not a helpful model in most of the world.

In both syncretism and dual systems, the understanding of religion has to be better thought through. What may appear to be syncretism may have something to do with how one construes the limits of incorporation of cultural elements. It may have something to do with thinking about such choices disjunctively (as either-or) instead of conjunctively (as both-and).

3. *If religious traditions are forces within a culture for the development of world-view and group boundary, can these traditions be easily forsaken?* Can one live in Poland or Spain and not be Catholic in some sense if one wants to participate fully in the life of the country? The same would hold in Buddhist or Muslim theocracies. In the questions of syncretism and dual systems, one touches some of the most significant dimensions of the theory of contextualization. If contextualization is about getting to the very heart of the culture, and Christianity is taking its place there, will not the Christianity that emerges look very much like a product of that culture? Or (to follow out the "heart of the culture" image) are we going to continue giving cultures the equivalent of an artificial heart—an organ that can do the job the culture needs, but one that will remain forever foreign? Syncretism and dual religious systems raise the question for Christians of how serious we really are about contextualization. Do we really mean what we say, or is it a subterfuge for carrying on a translation model of evangelization under a different name?

4. *What about change?* It is not simply a matter of pursuing the cultural pathways in a single-minded way, for the gospel is about change, about conversion of ways, mind, and heart. Hence, if the gospel is truly introduced into a culture, it will have to effect change. A genuine preaching of the gospel will always change the culture, and that change involves more than calling individuals back to the behavioral norms of their culture. It is a change of horizon, which has to have social implications and symbolic implications as well. From a semiotic perspective, one cannot introduce a new message into a culture without creating change in the sign systems.

An implication of this fact is that the culture is going to be faced with a situation of change when the gospel becomes part of that culture. Not only do the gospel and the church have to come to terms with the culture; the culture has to come to terms with the gospel and the church. A less than successful coming together of these two realities can be at the root of syncretism or the dual religious system.

5. *Syncretism and dual religious systems are problems for only certain members of the church. What can we learn from this fact?* It is obvious that many Christians are able to live with syncretism or dual religious systems without any real difficulty. While they probably should have some problems with syncretism or participating in two religious systems at once, the fact of the matter is that they do not. To write it off as simply a matter of laxity on the part of those Christians is too facile. Laxity could well come into play, but could hardly account totally for so widespread a phenomenon. Are we being told something about the nature of religion? Would the baseline model of popular religion be helpful for reorganizing our thoughts on this? Does the need for multiple mediations or routes of access to divine power play into this? Is "pure" Christianity seen as something only for foreigners? Or for certain classes or groups within the culture?

6. *If one follows out this perspective from the other side, another feature emerges: How did Christianity develop its incarnate character?* The usual term for explaining culturally specific practices in Christianity is that they have been "borrowed." Or it is sometimes said that there has been an "influence" from outside. For example, it would be hard to imagine the imagery of Christian eschatology, angelology, and demonology without considering the Persian influence upon Judaism. Where do the Christian feasts of the dead *(Todos Santos,* the Polish *Wigilia)* come from? Christianity, like other traditions, has a long history of absorbing elements from the cultures in which it has lived: Hellenistic, Germanic, Celtic, Syrian "influences." Is our problem now that this same process is continuing, but that things are happening too quickly and many more cultures are involved? A related question that has to be asked is: Who determines what is proper and improper borrowing?

There are other questions that could be explored here. But even with these something important is beginning to emerge. One of the reasons that the syncretism question and the dual-system question are so hard to deal with is that they ask some very hard questions, in turn, about the nature of the identity of the older churches. One cannot ask questions about evangelization, conversion, religion, and the like without calling into question the nature and quality of the identity of the existent Christian community. To resolve the questions about syncretism and about dual systems will mean, no doubt, some significant changes in the way of life for those churches who perceive the problem. That is indeed an uncomfortable prospect, but may be one of the great challenges and gifts that those younger churches can give to their older counterparts.

A MODEL FOR UNDERSTANDING SYNCRETISM

There have been various points of departure for understanding syncretism. It has been spoken of as an inconsistency, in which conflicting ideas and practices are brought together without coherence.[14] It has been called the result of an incomplete existential (deep-level) encounter between two cultures.[15] It has been suggested that it be read as part of the dynamics of culture change.[16]

Let us add yet another model to this list, drawing upon the semiotic description of culture outlined in chapter 3. The model has two distinctive features. First, it looks at the syncretistic process from the point of view of the culture, rather than from the side of the incoming church. This seems to be consistent with the contextualization stance in local theologies advocated throughout this presentation. Second (and perhaps less distinctively), it sees syncretism as a series of solutions at which a culture arrives as a result of trying to incorporate new messages, codes, and sometimes signs into the culture.

By taking the perspective of the receiving culture rather than that of the incoming church, we can get a better sense of which options are most likely to be engaged within the culture, given the range of incorporative possibilities. If the encounter between church and culture is often an incomplete one, the reason for that could well be that the church does not adequately understand the culture. Starting from the culture's perspective is a firmer base from which to envision the whole dynamic.

By looking at the whole from the dynamic of social change, we have a better chance of accounting for why some cultures become highly syncretistic whereas others quickly embrace the Christian message as their own in the form in which they have received it. In other words, we can get a better idea of when we are likely to have one or other form of syncretistic response and what would need to be done to change that when desirable.

The range of syncretistic possibilities, then, can be seen as four points on a spectrum, representing four incorporative responses to the new datum, Christianity. The responses are incorporative; that is, they are four ways in which the culture tries to incorporate the datum into its life, integrating it into the sign systems of the culture, so as to maintain the authority and credibility of its own culture.

The first such mode of incorporation is to play upon the *similarities* between the sign systems of the culture and that of Christianity. In this case, the elements in the invading culture are seen as analogous to those in the receiving culture. For example, the petitionary prayers, litanies, and holy water of Catholic Christianity seemed similar to the traditional garden magic in Melanesia, which helped to expedite the acceptance of Christianity there. In other instances, the Christian doctrine of the communion of the saints paralleled local veneration of ancestors, sacraments of healing and reconciliation seemed similar to local methods of exorcism and adjudication, and so on. Here the signs in the Christian system seemed similar to signs in the local system, and those Christian signs could then be taken over into the local system according to its own codes, and so could come to bear its own messages. Thus the signs of Christian grace, the sacraments, come to be understood as signs of local power, bearing the local messages about power.

Missionaries and leaders of young churches welcome those parallels in sign systems in the first instance, not always realizing that the signs can now be bearing quite different messages. This is the situation where, to all intents and purposes, Christianity has been fully accepted in the culture, judging from the practice of new Christians. But gradually it becomes evident that the understanding of traditional Christian beliefs and practices is at variance with the tradition. This is one difficulty with the translation model of local theology, as was discussed in chapter 1.

From the perspective of the local culture, this manner of incorporation provides the easiest accommodation of the foreign elements intruding upon it. The culture's own messages, and to a great extent its own codes, have remained intact, and the receiving culture may even believe that it has understood the intent of the incoming church.

A second form of incorporation is *filling gaps*. In this situation the invading culture provides signs and often codes for dealing with a problem not adequately accounted for in the dominant sign system of the receiving culture. Ichiro Hori has pointed out that one of the reasons that Buddhism was successful in Japan was that it could deal better with the spirits of the dead *(goryō)* than could local Shinto systems.[17] In a variant on this, sometimes the invading culture creates gaps that were not in the system before, gaps unable to be accounted for by the traditional sign system. Such was the case in the introduction of nineteenth- and twentieth-century technology into the late Stone Age cultures of Melanesia. Matteo Ricci and his associates followed this pattern in sixteenth-century China, by introducing Western inventions and technology.

Codes, as well as signs, are usually involved in filling gaps. In other words, not only a sign to carry the meaning, but the way of organizing the meaning is introduced into the culture. In these situations it is much easier to introduce messages as well, since the pathways developed by messages within the culture do not seem to cover the same territory.

A third form of accommodation is *indiscriminate mixing*. This happens when the receiving culture is at a low level of social and cultural organization, when it is particularly susceptible to new sign systems with their codes and messages. This situation occurs especially when the receiving culture finds itself in duress, when the credibility of its sign systems is being attacked. In these situations, whole new sign systems can be incorporated into the culture totally. Thus the introduction of Buddhism into northern China was to a great extent successful because of the disarray of the state at that time. Itinerant Indian monks, using exhibitions of magical practices, were able to win a hearing at court.[18] That Buddhist monks brought "Chinese learning" to the court in Japan expedited the introduction of Buddhism there.[19]

The difficulty with entering a culture under these circumstances is that the receiving culture will continue to find ways to maintain itself, and often will reconstitute the sign systems entering the culture to fit the entire pattern of the culture. The receiving culture, though in a stressful state, often proves more resilient than was first obvious. Indiscriminate mixing often results.

Part of it comes from the disparate attempts of the receiving culture to maintain itself. Thus in the China of the aforementioned period, Indian Buddhism did not end up gaining ascendancy, but came to be mixed with Confucian ethics and political organization and with Taoist aestheticism. In situations where the receiving culture looks especially to the codes for healing and redress in the invading culture (in the case of Christianity as the invading culture, to its rites of healing, access to power, and apocalyptic sign systems), the mixing will be especially acute.

This third kind of incorporation is the one most identified by Christians as syncretistic. In the first kind of incorporation, it may at the beginning escape the notice of Christians how their sign system is being incorporated into the local culture's sign system, since parallels are being played upon. In the second instance, the Christians may be lulled into premature dreams of contextualization by the way their signs and codes are being accepted. Only in the third type of incorporation do the dynamics become clear. Then it becomes more obvious that the Christian deity or the Virgin Mary is being interpreted as a local deity. In point of fact, the first two types of incorporation are also syncretistic; it is only that the results of the syncretism take much longer to become evident.

The fourth point on this spectrum of incorporation is *domination.* In this situation the sign system in the local culture has been so weakened that the sign system of the invading culture takes over completely, replacing the local sign system. A form of evangelization long prevalent in the history of Christianity saw this form of entry into the culture as the ideal one. The signs, codes, and messages of the local culture are swept away in favor of the complete sign system of the invading culture. There is no matching of signs, no filling of gaps, no danger of mixing. Western Christianity simply replaces the local system. Much of the rhetoric of nineteenth-century missionary groups, connecting Christianity with empire, fell into this category.[20] This seems to have happened in some places, notably in Micronesia, where almost no evidence of the older system remains today.

When looked at consistently from the perspective of the receiving culture, then, what has been called syncretism by Christians can be seen as fitting into a larger pattern of culture change. The changes in signs, codes, and messages are related to the resilience of the local culture. African religion was better preserved in Brazil and in the Caribbean than in the United States because slaves lived in greater concentrations. The average slaveholder in the United States owned twenty-five Africans, whereas plantations with a thousand or more slaves was the rule in Brazil.[21] In Brazil this allowed a better chance of the Africans' maintaining their own sign system, using Christianity to fill gaps or to double their power through doubling of deities in patterns of similarity. In Africa and Melanesia the stress to which Western societies subjected local cultures resulted in more indiscriminate mixing, the taking over of Western symbols and using them in vastly different ways, looking for patterns of healing, and latching onto apocalyptic patterns within Christianity.

The cargo movements in Melanesia, movements of different prophets in Africa, the Ghost Dance religion in North America—all point more to this third type of syncretistic activity.

Thus syncretism is not an isolated phenomenon. It is a way of reading the incorporative attempts of a local culture from the perspective of the receiving culture. The tables turn when an erstwhile invading culture finds itself invaded, and members of its own culture seek out similarities, fill gaps, and adopt other rites of healing. This happened in the United States and Europe during the 1960s and 1970s. During that time those cultures experienced extraordinary stress upon their sign systems. New religious movements, using elements from Asian religions, began to claim the adherence of Christians and Jews. It was the same pattern as before, but now played out on the former invading culture. To make such a statement as this is not to say that those new religious movements are of equal value with Christianity; it is only to say that the same structural dynamics are at work.

A MODEL FOR UNDERSTANDING DUAL RELIGIOUS SYSTEMS

A parallel model can be developed for understanding the functioning of dual systems. This model sees dual systems growing out of culture contact. But whereas the model of understanding syncretism emphasized the incorporative, harmonizing attempts of the receiving culture, a model for dual systems would emphasize the conflictual aspect of cultures coming into contact. British social anthropology catches this second aspect well when it speaks of "culture clash" rather than "acculturation."

Again, the perspective taken here will be that of the local, receiving culture. This provides for a more coherent perspective on the different types of dual systems. There are four perspectives available to the local culture, any of which can contribute to the growth of a dual-system situation.

In the first instance, *the encounter with the invading culture is incomplete.* The receiving culture does not feel that the invading culture's sign system is addressing the same things that its own sign system addresses, whatever the contrary protestations of the invading culture might be. As a result the two never come into serious contact. The invading sign system remains "foreign"; it does not effectively penetrate either the world-view or the group-boundary-formation process of the receiving culture. It is held at arm's length.

This can happen through lack of sufficient or sustained contact (as in the case of a brief period of evangelization followed by withdrawals of missionaries and church support systems), or through the failure of the sign systems to make contact with one another (which may be a way of looking at the situation in Japan, where many missionaries never achieved the linguistic ability to bring about a genuine contact). Thus Christianity may be allowed into the culture, and even be tolerated, but it never becomes part of the culture. It becomes a form of protocol for dealing with foreigners. The decision to tolerate Christianity once again in Japan at the time of the Meiji Restoration in the nineteenth century was motivated largely by this latter concern: if one wanted Western technology, one had to appear friendly to their religious system as well.[22]

In the case of some Andean cultures, where Christianity exists today as part of a dual system, the cultures had had a history of maintaining themselves against invaders before. The Spanish hegemony simply replaced the Incan hegemony over the Quechua system. And so the Spanish religion had to be outwardly practiced and tolerated, but it remained something foreign.

A second perspective giving rise to dual systems is closely related to the last example. In this instance *the presence of the invading culture actually enhances the value of the sign system of the local culture.* The outsiders are seen as militarily more powerful, but symbolically inferior. Thus it becomes a point of pride to keep the two sign systems separate, even while giving the necessary obeisance to the sign system of the invading culture. This would explain the tenacity of the dual system among the Pueblos in the American Southwest. The traditional religion is seen as superior to that of Christianity, but the people have no choice but to maintain an outward adherence to Christianity. This thought motivated many of the Plains American groups as well. Jews in medieval Europe often found themselves in the same situation with Christianity, forced to hear the weekly sermon and even sometimes to be baptized. In such instances the perceived inferiority of the invading system (Christianity, in these instances) actually enhances the status and strengthens the credibility of the local sign system.

From a third perspective *the local culture accepts the sign system of the invading culture, but believes that there are still problems that the invading culture's sign system does not adequately handle.* For those problems and issues, segments of the old system are maintained. Thus some forms of Christianity have been perceived as not dealing adequately with intercession for immediate and concrete needs in the culture. And so older patterns of magical intercession, divination, and even witchcraft survive. The Christian deity may be all-powerful, but that deity does not relate to that dangerous section of bush outside the village as well as a local deity does. Hence the need to maintain relations with the local deity. Christianity can seem too abstract, too concerned with words, and not sufficiently able to meet the day-to-day needs (Protestant Christianity suffers from this accusation more often than Catholic forms of Christianity). For that reason, certain aspects of the old system will perdure, even for centuries, alongside Christianity.[23] Those that most directly touch human need have the best chance of making that kind of survival.

From a fourth perspective *the invading sign system and the local sign system are seen as dealing with two different things.* This is similar in perspective to the first option outlined here. It may be the key for addressing the question of double belonging. It arises out of observations like: How can I venerate my ancestors by praying for them as Christians do, since my ancestors were Buddhist? Only the Buddhist rites provide proper veneration.

Is there a Buddhist way of being Christian, or a Hindu way of being Christian? Those two great traditions have been able to accommodate Christianity, but Christianity does not seem able to accommodate them. Does the ability to accommodate, which those systems have, indicate their superiority, since to deal with something only by excluding it can be understood as a sign of weakness? These are difficult questions for a Christian to respond to, since they are addressed not so much to the doctrines of Christianity as to Christian exclusivist thought patterns. Are those thought patterns essential to Christianity, or do they represent certain cultural categories only?

Thus dual systems can be seen as arising from perceptions on the part of the receiving culture that the invading culture's religious sign system is alien, inferior, inadequate, or not to the point. Thus the encounter never really takes place. Pressing harder for the encounter to take place will be unsuccessful as long as those bigger questions remain unanswered.

DEALING WITH SYNCRETISM AND DUAL RELIGIOUS SYSTEMS

The models presented for dealing with syncretism and dual systems suggest some practical considerations for approaching these phenomena. Some of those considerations have already been alluded to above. It might be helpful to rephrase them in terms of basic principles.

1. Good evangelization will also bring about culture change. If the message of the gospel is genuinely heard in the local culture, that message must find a place among the most fundamental messages of that culture, with concomitant change in codes, signs, and the entire sign system. In the midst of our concerns for contextualization, we must not be lulled into thinking that contextualization will leave the culture untouched and simply affirm the good values there. Christ can be found in culture, but making that discovery explicit will have consequences for the culture.
2. Syncretism and dual systems are ultimately not about theology, even though that may seem to be the case on the surface. They are about the entirety of the religious sign system. Thus, resolving the fact that Saint George is equated with the Quechuan lightning deity will not be done by theological argument, but by looking at the entirety of the sign system— which social relations it maintains, what problems it solves, what benefits accrue from keeping things as they are. To conflate syncretism and theology is to reduce religion solely to a *view* of life, forgetting that it is also a *way* of life.
3. Connected with the second principle is a reminder that what "religion" means varies from culture to culture. In the United States it refers to a private voluntary association. In the northern Mediterranean area one can be somehow Catholic simply by being born into the culture. Religion, again, cannot be reduced simply to a set of ideas.

4. The question of interest has to be raised again here as well. For whom is syncretism or a dual system a problem? And what will constitute the resolution of that problem?
5. The conversion process, we now know, is much slower than we had first thought. While genuine and sincere commitment can be made on the part of those baptized, there are many other factors involved, which take longer time for resolution and incorporation into a culture. Thus what appears to be syncretism or a dual system may be but reflective of the stages of the conversion process.

These reflections by no means resolve the thorny problems surrounding syncretism and dual systems. But these perspectives can help us in gaining a more holistic approach to the question and allow for resolutions that respect the situation of those cultures in which they are found. It is a reminder, too, that the firm foundations we experience today were not easily achieved. No doubt they may have looked like a dangerous syncretism to an earlier generation.

Notes

PREFACE

1. Karl Rahner, "Toward a Fundamental Interpretation of Vatican II," *Theological Studies* 40 (1979): 716–27.
2. Literature devoted to an examination of this earlier version includes Ernest Ranly, "Constructing Local Theologies," *Commonweal*, Nov. 11, 1979, pp. 716–19; Joseph Spae, "Missiology as Local Theology and Interreligious Encounter," *Missiology* 7 (1979): 479–500; Klauspeter Blaser, "Kontextuelle Theologie als ökumenisches Problem," *Theologische Zeitschrift* 36 (1980): 220–35; Louis Luzbetak, "Signs of Progress in Contextual Theology," *Verbum SVD* 22 (1981): 39–57; Krikor Haleblian, "Contextualization and French Structuralism: A Method to Delineate the Deep Structures of the Gospel" (Ph.D. dissertation, Fuller Theological Seminary, 1982); idem, "The Problem of Contextualization," *Missiology* 11 (1983): 95–111.

1. WHAT IS LOCAL THEOLOGY?

1. Joseph Gremillion, e.g., speaks of regions in the global church, bound together by geography and common economic problems, in his "North American Ecclesial Consciousness in Its Global Context," *Proceedings of the Catholic Theological Society of America* 38 (1981): 113–124.
2. Decree on the Church's Missionary Activity (*Ad Gentes*), 22; see also the Pastoral Constitution on the Church in the Modern World (*Gaudium et Spes*), chap. 2; Paul VI, Apostolic Exhortation, On Evangelization in the Modern World (*Evangelii Nuntiandi*).
3. Krikor Haleblian, "The Problem of Contextualization," *Missiology* 11 (1983): 95–111.
4. Gustavo Gutiérrez, *A Theology of Liberation* (Maryknoll, N.Y.: Orbis Books, 1973).
5. A good example of such reconstruction of early Christianity is Elisabeth Schüssler Fiorenza, *In Memory of Her* (New York: Crossroad Publishing Co., 1983).
6. However, Australian anthropologist Clement Godwin has made a case for the acceptability of the term within the social sciences in *Spend and Be Spent* (Bangalore: Asian Trading Corporation, 1977).
7. Avery Dulles introduced this idea in his *Models of the Church* (New York: Seabury Press, 1974), and it has been applied since that time to other areas of theology. Dulles himself has done this in his *Models of Revelation* (New York: Crossroad, 1983).
8. Charles Kraft, *Christianity in Culture* (Maryknoll, N.Y.: Orbis Books, 1979).
9. Placide Tempels, *Bantu Philosophy* (Paris: Présence Africaine, 1969). It was first published in Flemish in 1944.

10. See Victor Ochoa's series of articles under the heading "La cosmovisión Aymara," in *Boletín de Instituto des Estudios Aymaras,* 1978–79; Esau Tuza, "A Melanesian Cosmological Process," *Catalyst* 8 (1978): 244–58.

11. Thus G. Reichel Dolmatoff's informant in the conclusion of *Amazonian Cosmos* (Chicago: University of Chicago Press, 1971).

12. Charles Nyamiti, *African Theology: Its Problems, Nature and Methods* (Kampala, Uganda: Gaba Institute, 1971); idem, *The Scope of African Theology* (Kampala, Uganda: Gaba Institute, 1973).

13. Allocution to the Convocation of the Bishops of Africa in Kampala, Uganda, July 31, 1969; the text quoted can be found in *Acta Apostolicae Sedis* 66 (1969): 577.

14. Vincent Donovan, *Christianity Rediscovered* (Notre Dame, Ind.: Fides/Claretian Books, 1978; Maryknoll, N.Y.: Orbis Books, 1982).

15. See the four volumes of reflections published by Ernesto Cardenal, the pastor of the community, *The Gospel in Solentiname* (Maryknoll, N.Y.: Orbis Books, 1976–82).

16. Two important works have been A. B. Lord's study of Yugoslav folk poets, *The Singer of Tales* (Cambridge, Mass.: Harvard University Press, 1960); and Jan Vansina, *Oral Tradition: A Study in Historical Methodology* (Chicago: Aldine Publishing Company, 1961).

17. John Henry Newman, *On Consulting the Faithful in Matters of Doctrine* (New York: Sheed and Ward, 1961), is a classic text in this subject. Reception, a concept borrowed from nineteenth-century German legal research, remains an underdeveloped aspect of theology. Its basic point is that doctrinal formulation requires not only magisterial promulgation, but also positive reception by the faithful.

2. MAPPING A LOCAL THEOLOGY

1. For field theory in the social sciences, see the later work of the psychologist Kurt Lewin, such as his *Field Theory in the Social Sciences* (Westport, Conn.: Greenwood Press, 1975). Much more work has been done in systems theory, for which see especially Ludwig von Bertalanffy, *General Systems Theory* (New York: Georges Braziller, 1969); Ervin Laszlo, *Introduction to Systems Philosophy* (New York: Gordon & Breach, 1972).

2. *Codex Iuris Canonici,* can. 213. For an examination of some of the problems and issues involved, see Edward Schillebeeckx, ed., *The Right of a Community to a Priest* (Concilium, vol. 133, 1980).

3. Clifford Geertz presents this idea in a number of essays collected in his *The Interpretation of Cultures* (New York: Basic Books, 1973).

4. Declaration on the Relation of the Church to Non-Christian Religions (*Nostra Aetate*), nos. 2–3; see also Dogmatic Constitution on the Church (*Lumen Gentium*), no. 16.

5. Robert Schreiter, "The Anonymous Christian and Christology," *Missiology* 6 (1978): 29–52.

6. Tissa Balasuriya, *The Eucharist and Human Liberation* (Maryknoll, N.Y.: Orbis Books, 1979).

7. There has been some debate as to whether or not African proverbs would make a sound basis for an African theology. What argues for such a usage is their pervasive presence in African conversation. However, others argue that they are often pessimistic in tone, and so inadequate carriers of the message of salvation. This is a debate that

cannot be entered into here, but one that does need to be pursued. One thought could be added: wisdom literature (of which proverbs are a part) is often pessimistic in nature. The wisdom literature collected in the Old Testament (Qoheleth, Ben-Sira) has many such pessimistic tones.

8. James Cone, *The Spirituals and the Blues* (New York: Seabury Press, 1972).

9. Dogmatic Constitution on the Church, *Lumen Gentium*, no. 26.

10. See Elaine Pagels, *The Gnostic Gospels* (New York: Random House, 1981). Her argumentation raises an important question about whether some Gnostic groups came to be considered heterodox for reasons of doctrine or because of the need for a more centralized control.

11. David Tracy, *The Analogical Imagination* (New York: Crossroad Publishing Co., 1981), chap. 1.

3. The Study of Culture

1. Raymond Facélina, "Une théologie en situation," *Revue de Sciences Religieuses* 48 (1974): 320, makes use of this phrase in developing a theology for Berber tribes in North Africa.

2. In an overview of contemporary theories of culture, Roger M. Keesing makes this point: "And what universals there are may turn out to be—most interestingly, at least—universals of process, of logic, of structure, of organizational principles, rather than of substance," "Theories of Culture," *Annual Review of Anthropology* 3 (1974) 86.

3. The question of native exegesis, i.e., description and analysis of a culture by a member of that culture, has been studied most extensively by Claude Lévi-Strauss and his associates. An earlier discussion was begun by the linguist Kenneth Pike with his distinction of "emic" (from the inside) and "etic" (from the outside) analyses of cultural systems. The terms are derived from "phonemic" and "phonetic," respectively. See Kenneth Pike, *Language in Relation to a Unified Theory of the Structure of Behavior* (The Hague: Mouton, 1967). For a presentation of the current discussion, see Marvin Harris, "History of the Significance of the Emic-Etic Distinction," *Annual Review of Anthropology* 5 (1976): 329–50.

4. Alfred Kroeber and Clyde Kluckhohn, *Culture: A Critical Review of Concepts and Definitions* (Cambridge, Mass.: Peabody Cultural Museum, 1952), lists 150 definitions.

5. Perhaps the best single description of this as a way to understand identity can be found in the discussion of "group"and "grid" in Mary Douglas, *Natural Symbols* (New York: Random House, 1970). See also her *Cultural Bias* (London: Royal Anthropological Institute, Occasional Paper no. 34, 1978), and *Essays in the Sociology of Perception* (London: Routledge and Kegan Paul, 1982).

6. Both Keesing, "Theories of Culture," and Maurice Freedman, *Main Trends in Social and Cultural Anthropology* (New York: Holmes and Meier, 1979), raise this criticism. For a different approach, see also Clifford Geertz, "Ritual and Social Change: A Javanese Example," in his *Interpretation of Cultures* (New York: Basic Books, 1973), p. 143.

7. This is a principal critique of the Frankfurt School of Social Criticism. See, e.g., Jürgen Habermas, *Erkenntnis und Interesse* (Frankfurt: Suhrkamp, 1968); idem, *Zur Logik der Sozialwissenschaften* (Frankfurt: Suhrkamp, 1970).

8. See, as examples, Louis Luzbetak, *The Church and Cultures* (Pasadena, Calif.: William Carey Library, 1976); David Hesselgrave, *Communicating Christ Cross-Culturally* (Grand Rapids, Mich.: Zondervan, 1978). Much of the analysis in the now defunct *Practical Anthropology* followed functionalist lines.

9. See notes 6 and 7, above, on this matter.

10. Roy Rappaport, *Pigs for the Ancestors* (New Haven, Conn.: Yale University Press, 1968) is a significant attempt in this area. See also Rappaport's later writings on the relation of ritual and environment: "The Sacred in Human Evolution," *Annual Review of Ecology and Systematics* 2 (1971): 23-44; "Ritual, Sanctity, and Cybernetics," *American Anthropologist* 73 (1971): 59-76; "The Obvious Aspects of Ritual," *Cambridge Anthropology* 2 (1974): 3-68; "Liturgies and Lies," *International Yearbook for the Sociology of Knowledge and Religion* 10 (1976): 75-104. For an early programmatic essay, see Åke Hultkrantz, "An Ecological Approach to Religion," *Ethnos* 31 (1966): 131-50.

11. Marvin Harris, *Cultural Materialism* (New York: Random House, 1979), is the most articulate statement of this approach, including a critique of other approaches to culture from his materialist perspective. Arend van Leeuwen, "Op weg naar een economische theologie," *Tijdscrift voor Theologie* 13 (1973): 391-406, tries to ground a theology upon materialist principles.

12. Harris, *Cultural Materialism*, pp. 242-53, summarizes his research in this area. He frames his analysis in terms of the cost-benefit ratio. To eat the meat of the cow and to grow cattle for beef is too expensive ecologically, but the cow is also the mother of the bullock, the principal traction animal in Indian preindustrial cultures. Thus keeping the cow sacred (i.e., taboo for eating) makes it available for the production of much-needed bullocks.

13. Some of Claude Lévi-Strauss's principal theoretical writings are collected in two volumes, entitled *Structural Anthropology* (New York: Basic Books, 1958 and 1975).

14. Notably, among the Russians, the folklorist Vladimir Propp and the literary critic Viktor Shklovskij. See the discussion of the contribution of Russian formalism to structuralism in Frederic Jameson, *The Prison-House of Language* (Princeton, N.J.: Princeton University Press, 1973).

15. See particularly Lévi-Strauss, *Les structures élémentaires de la parenté* (Paris: Plon, 1949), and *La pensée sauvage* (Paris: Plon, 1962).

16. Lévi-Strauss' programmatic essay "The Structural Study of Myth" has been anthologized in many places and is included in the first volume of his *Structural Anthropology*. The "overture" to his *The Raw and the Cooked* (New York: Harper & Row, 1970) is also of great importance in this area.

17. For some brief histories of this "genealogy," see Jonathan Culler, *The Pursuit of Signs* (Ithaca, N.Y.: Cornell University Press, 1981), and the essays in R. W. Bailey, L. Mateijka, and P. Steiner, eds., *The Sign: Semiotics around the World* (Ann Arbor, Mich.: Michigan Slavic Publications, 1980).

18. Thus David Kronenfeld and Henry Decker, "Structuralism," *Annual Review of Anthropology* 8 (1979): 536.

19. For an overview, see D. Jean Umiker-Sebeok, "Semiotics of Culture," *Annual Review of Anthropology* 6 (1977): 121-35; and the series "Advance in Semiotics," edited by Thomas Sebeok, from the University of Indiana Press.

20. This prospect was raised specifically by the secretary of the Association for the Study of Semiotics, Umberto Eco, "Looking for a Logic of Culture," in Thomas

Sebeok, ed., *The Tell-Tale Sign* (Lisse, Netherlands: Peter de Ridder Press, 1975), pp. 9-17.

21. Irene Portis Winner, "Cultural Anthropology and Semiotics," in Baile, Matejka, and Steiner, eds. *The Sign*, p. 336.

22. So argued by Dan Sperber, *Rethinking Symbolism* (Cambridge, England: Cambridge University Press, 1975), on the basis of his research in Ethiopia. The critique does not seem to have had much effect.

23. See the discussion collected in Josue Harari, *Textual Strategies: Perspectives in Post-Structuralist Criticism* (Ithaca, N.Y.: Cornell University Press, 1979), especially Harari's lucid introduction (pp. 17-72).

24. One finds anthropologists such as David Schneider and Eric Schwimmer preferring this term. See the latter's short-lived (1973-1974) *Journal of Symbolic Anthropology*, replaced in 1977 by the *Yearbook of Symbolic Anthropology*.

25. Roland Barthes, *Système de la mode* (Paris: Editions du Seuil, 1967); idem, *Mythologiques* (Paris: Editions du Seuil, 1957).

26. Geertz, "Thick Description: Toward an Interpretive Theory of Culture," in Geertz, *Interpretation of Cultures,* p. 5.

27. Ibid., p. 17.

28. See Geertz's essays "Religion as a Cultural System" and "Ideology as a Cultural System," in Geertz, *Interpretation of Cultures,* pp. 87-124, 193-233; "Art as a Cultural System," *Modern Language Notes* 91 (1976): 1473-99; "Commonsense as a Cultural System," *Antioch Review* 33 (1975): 5-26.

29. Geertz, "Thick Description," p. 30.

30. Kurt Lewin, *Field Theory in the Social Sciences* (Westport, Conn.: Greenwood Press, 1975).

31. Published in Jan van der Eng and Mojmir Grygar, eds., *Structure of Texts and Semiotics of Culture* (The Hague: Mouton, 1973), pp. 1-28.

32. Most notably by Irene Portis Winner and Thomas G. Winner, "The Semiotics of Cultural Texts," *Semiotica* 18, no. 2 (1976): 101-56.

33. See note 14, above, and also Viktor Ehrlich, *Russian Formalism: History-Doctrine* (The Hague: Mouton, 1965).

34. Lotman et al., "Theses," in van der Eng and Grygar, eds., *Structure of Texts,* thesis 6.0.0.

35. A. M. Pjatigorskij, "Nekotorye obščie zamečanija otnositel 'no rassmotrenija teksta kak raznovidnosti signale," in Karl Eimermacher, ed., *Teksty sovetskogo literaturovedčeskogo strukturalizma* (Munich: Fink, 1971), pp. 78-88.

36. Paul Ricoeur, "The Idea of the Text," in David Rasmussen, *Mythic Symbolic Language and Philosophical Anthropology* (The Hague: Mouton, 1973).

37. See especially Jurij Lotman, "On the Metalanguage of a Typological Description of Culture," *Semiotica* 14, no. 2 (1975): 97-123.

38. Some examples: Peter Bogatyrev, *Functions of Folk Costume in Moravian Slovakia* (The Hague: Mouton, 1971); Jurij Lotman, *Analysis of the Poetic Text* (Ann Arbor, Mich.: Ardis Publishers, 1976); B. A. Uspenskij, *The Semiotics of the Russian Icon* (Lisse, Netherlands: Peter de Ridder Press, 1976), Jurij Lotman, *Structure du texte artistique* (Paris: Gallimard, 1970).

39. Lotman, "On the Metalanguage"; V. V. Ivanov and W. M. Toporov, "The Invariant and Transformation in Folklore Texts," *Dispositio* 3 (1976): 203-70.

40. Geertz, "Thick Description," p. 9.

41. For two examples, see Algiren Greimas, "Les jeux des contreintes sémiotiques," in his *Du sens* (Paris: Seuil, 1970); M. I. Lekomceva and B. A. Uspenskij, "A Description of a Semiotic System with Simple Syntax," *Semiotica* 18, no. 2 (1976): 157–69.

42. Paulo Freire, *Pedagogy of the Oppressed* (New York: Herder and Herder, 1970).

43. The classic story of the French anthropologist Marcel Griaule, in his account in *Conversations with Ogotemmeli* (New York: Oxford University Press, 1974), provides a touching story of his move from the exoteric to the esoteric world of the Dogon of Mali.

44. Lotman et al., "Theses."

45. See especially the works of Peter Berger in this regard, notably *The Heretical Imperative* (New York: Doubleday, 1980).

46. See Turner's discussion in his *Dramas, Fields and Metaphors* (Ithaca, N.Y.: Cornell University Press, 1974).

47. Vladimir Propp, *Morphology of the Folktale* (Austin: University of Texas Press, 1968), is the classic locus for this discussion.

48. P. Bouissac, *Circus and Culture: A Semiotic Approach* (Bloomington: Indiana University Press, 1976), gives an important discussion of this concept.

49. For studies in metaphor, see Paul Ricoeur, *La métaphore vive* (Paris: Seuil, 1975), and the older P. Stutterheim, *Het Metafoor* (Amsterdam: H. V. Paris, 1941).

50. James Fernandez, "The Mission of Metaphor in Expressive Culture," *Current Anthropology* 15, no. 2 (1974), 119–45, and Edmund Leach, *Culture and Communication* (Cambridge, England: Cambridge University Press, 1976), are the best studies of the relation of metaphor and metonymy in culture texts.

51. See Robert Nisbet, *History of the Idea of Progress* (New York: Basic Books, 1979), for a discussion of this problem.

52. Besides Lotman, "On the Metalanguage," and Ivanov and Toporov, "The Invariant and Transformation," Pierre Maranda and Elie Köngäs Maranda, eds., *Structural Analysis of Oral Tradition* (Philadelphia: University of Pennsylvania Press, 1971).

53. William Burrows, *New Ministries: The Global Context* (Maryknoll, N.Y.: Orbis Books, 1980), discusses this in terms of Papua New Guinea.

4. THEOLOGY AND ITS CONTEXT

1. Daniel von Allmen's thoughtful article, "The Birth of Theology: Contextualizing as the Dynamic Element in the Formation of New Testament Theology," *International Review of Mission* 64 (1975): 38–52, is often pointed to as such a blueprint.

2. James Dunn, *Unity and Diversity in the New Testament* (Philadelphia: Westminster Press, 1977), develops this point well.

3. See Julius Gross, *Entstehungsgeschichte des Erbsündendogmas,* 2 vols. (Munich: E. Reinhardt, 1960–63).

4. Alexis Kagame, *La philosophie bantu comparée* (Paris: Présence Africaine, 1976).

5. O. Bimwenyi-Kweshi, *Discours théologique négro-africain: Problème des fondements* (Paris: Présence Africaine, 1980).

6. For the prehistory of the sociology of knowledge, see Kurt Lenk, *Ideologie*

(Neuwied: Luchterhand, 1961), pp. 15–51; Lewis Coser, "Knowledge, Sociology of," *International Encyclopedia of the Social Sciences* 8: 428–35.

7. Karl Mannheim, *Ideology and Utopia* (New York: Harcourt, Brace and World, 1955); idem, *Essays on the Sociology of Knowledge* (Oxford: Oxford University Press, 1952).

8. See Geertz's important essay, "Ideology as a Cultural System," in *Interpretation of Cultures* (New York: Basic Books, 1973), pp. 193–233.

9. For the historical background of this distinction, see Alois Grillmeier, "Vom Symbolum zur Summa: Zum theologiegeschichtlichen Verhältnis von Patristik und Scholastik," *Kirche und Überlieferung* (Freiburg: Herder, 1960), pp. 119–69.

10. For background on this distinction, see Wolfhart Pannenberg, *Theology and the Philosophy of Science* (Philadelphia: Westminster Press, 1976), pp. 7–14; Gerhard Söhngen, "Die Weisheit der Theologie durch den Weg der Wissenschaft," *Mysterium Salutis*, 5 vols. (Einsiedeln: Benziger, 1965) 1: 905–77; and the useful historical section of Johannes Beumer, *Theologie als Glaubensverständnis* (Würzburg: Echter, 1953).

11. Claude Lévi-Strauss, *The Savage Mind* (Chicago: University of Chicago Press, 1966), chaps. 7 and 8. Also the "Overture" to his *The Raw and the Cooked* (New York: Harper & Row, 1970).

12. Roy Wagner, *Habu: The Innovation of Meaning in Daribi Religion* (Chicago: University of Chicago Press, 1972), especially Part 1.

13. James Fernandez, *Bwiti: The Religious Universe of an African People* (Princeton, N.J.: Princeton University Press, 1982); also his programmatic essay, "The Mission of Metaphor in Expressive Culture," *Current Anthropology* 15 (1974): 119–45.

14. See especially Alfred Lord, *The Singer of Tales* (Cambridge, Mass.: Harvard University Press, 1960); Jan Vansina, *Oral Tradition* (Chicago: Aldine Publishing Company, 1961). *Semeia*, no. 5 (1976), was devoted to a study of oral literature and exegesis. Walter Ong, *Orality and Literacy* (New York: Methuen, 1982), gives an overview of the literature.

15. See Claude Lévi-Strauss, "How Myths Die," in the second volume of his *Structural Anthropology* (New York: Basic Books, 1976), pp. 256–68.

16. Augustine, *De trinitate* IV, Praef.

17. See Griaule's remarkable *Conversations with Ogotemmeli* (New York: Oxford University Press, 1975).

18. Thomas Aquinas, *Summa theologiae* I, a. 1.

19. Bernard Lonergan, *Method in Theology* (New York: Herder and Herder, 1972). For an overview of some of the recent approaches to creating alternative foundations for a critical fundamental theology, see Helmut Peukert, *Wissenschaftstheorie-Handlungstheorie-Fundamentale Theologie* (Düsseldorf: Patmos, 1976).

20. Helpful sources here are Martin Grabmann, *Die Geschichte der scholastischen Methode* (Freiburg: Herder, 1909); Yves Congar, *A History of Theology* (New York: Doubleday, 1968); G. R. Evans, *Old Arts and New Theology* (New York: Oxford University Press, 1979); J. de Ghellinck, *Le mouvement théologique du XIIème siècle* (Brussels: Universelle, 1948); M. D. Chenu, *La Théologie comme science au XIIIème siècle* (Paris: J. Vrin, 1957).

21. For a history of the term "praxis," see Nicholas Lobkowicz, *Theory and Practice* (Notre Dame, Ind.: University of Notre Dame Press, 1968).

22. Of the many works now available in liberation theology, Gustavo Gutiérrez's *A*

Theology of Liberation (Maryknoll, N.Y.: Orbis Books, 1973) can still be singled out as a classic in the genre. For a sense of what is happening in liberation theology on different continents, see the proceedings of the Ecumenical Association of Third World Theologians (EATWOT), all published by Orbis Books: *The Emergent Gospel* (1978); *African Theology en Route (1979); Asia's Struggle for a New Humanity* (1980); *The Challenge of Basic Christian Communities* (1981); *Irruption of the Third World* (1983); *Doing Theology in a Divided World* (1985).

5. TRADITION AND CHRISTIAN IDENTITY

1. The problems of Augustinian anthropology vex not only non-Western cultures. Western feminists have pointed out how that anthropology has contributed to a history of misogyny in Christianity.

2. Philip Gibbs, "Kaunala Tape: Toward a Theological Reflection on a New Guinea Initiation Myth" (M.A. thesis, Catholic Theological Union, 1977).

3. Pierre Maranda, ed., *Mythology* (Harmondsworth, England: Penguin Books, 1972), p. 7.

4. Communication from Spiritan missionaries working in Kenya and Tanzania.

5. For a history of some of the exegesis on this passage, see Bruce Vawter, *On Genesis* (New York: Doubleday, 1977); for the structuralist analysis of this passage, see Gibbs, "Kaunala Tape."

6. Augustine's command of Greek was tenuous, and following the Latin translation of the time, he translated the *eph'hō* in Romans 5:12 as a relative phrase referring to Adam, rather than as a conjunction, which is the more likely rendering. For the history of this, see Stanislaus Lyonnet, "Le Sens de *eph'hō* en Rom 5, 12 et l'exegese des pères grecs," *Biblica* 36 (1955): 436–56.

7. Eugene Hillman, *Polygamy Reconsidered* (Maryknoll, N.Y.: Orbis Books, 1975); on related issues, see Michael Kirwen, *African Widows* (Maryknoll, N.Y.: Orbis Books, 1979).

8. For a presentation of some historical positions as they are read by church authority, see Francisco Urrutia, "Can Polygamy Be Compatible with Christianity?" *African Ecclesiastical Review* 23 (1981): 275–91.

9. The scandal is only part of the problem. The woman and her children are often excluded from the social services of the society because there is no marriage.

10. A good discussion of the questions of limits can be found in Charles Taber, "The Limits of Indigenization in Theology," *Missiology* 6 (1978): 53–80.

11. On this matter, see Meinrad Hebga, *Sorcellerie . . . Chimère dangereuse?* (Abidjan, Ivory Coast: Inades, 1979); idem, *Sorcellerie et prière de délivrance* (Abidjan, Ivory Coast: Inades, 1982). The history of Emmanuel Milingo, former archbishop of Lusaka, presents a cautionary tale in this regard. His involvement in healing rites seems to have been the prime factor that led to his removal as archbishop of the Zambian capital.

12. Thus William A. Christian, *Local Religion in Sixteenth Century Spain* (Princeton, N.J.: Princeton University Press, 1981).

13. Edward Shils, *Tradition* (Chicago: University of Chicago Press, 1981), traces this transition back to an interest in the question of tradition.

14. The critiques of the Frankfurt school of sociology and social criticism took special leadership in this regard. For a summary of this work, see Jürgen Habermas, *Theorie des kommunikativen Handelns*, 2 vols. (Frankfurt: Suhrkamp, 1982).

15. Some of the neo-conservative response to this analysis has been to eschew these developments and call for a return to simpler societies. See, e.g., Theodore Roszak, *Where the Wasteland Ends* (New York: Doubleday, 1973). In a more refined vein, see Daniel Bell, *The Cultural Contradictions of Capitalism* (New York: Basic Books, 1974); Robert Nozick, *Anarchy, State and Utopia* (New York: Basic Books, 1974).

16. Mary Douglas speaks of group-boundary and world-view formation as "grid and group" in *Natural Symbols* (New York: Pantheon, 1970).

17. Richard Sennett, *Authority* (New York: Random House, 1981).

18. An enlightening study in this regard is Bryan Wilson, *The Noble Savages* (Berkeley: University of California Press, 1975).

19. *Commonitorium*, II, 5.

20. I draw here especially on Chomsky's *Aspects of a Theory of Syntax* (Cambridge, Mass.: MIT Press, 1965). Chomsky's theory of transformational grammar went beyond this early formulation, but the principles of competence and performance developed here continue to inform his later work on human creativity.

21. The word *loci* is being used here in the sense in which it has been used in Christian theology since Melchior Cano.

22. I have developed this idea in "The Specification of Experience and the Language of Revelation," *Concilium* 113 (1979): 57–65; and in "Jezus als paradigma van God en parabel van menselijkheid," in A. Willems, H. Häring, T. Schoof eds., *Meedenken met Edward Schillebeeckx* (Baarn: H. Nelissen, 1983), pp. 58–67.

23. Vatican II, Dogmatic Constitution on Divine Revelation (*Dei Verbum*), nos. 8–10.

24. See the discussion of this in J. N. D. Kelly, *Early Christian Doctrines* (London: Adam and Charles Black, 1968), p. 235.

25. Vatican II, Decree on Ecumenism (*Unitatis Redintegratio*), 110–11.

26. Athanasius, *Contra Arianos* 2, 41f.

6. POPULAR RELIGION AND OFFICIAL RELIGION

1. Maximino Arias reviews the reason that led to a change in attitude to popular religions, in "Religiosidad popular en América Latina," *Iglesia y religiosidad popular en América Latina* (Bogotá: Secretariado General del CELAM, 1977), pp. 17–37.

2. See, e.g., the discussion in *Mensaje* (March–April 1965), "¿Religión de masas, religión de elite?" involving Juan Luis Segundo, Renato Poblete, and others.

3. The history of this discussion is reviewed in Bernard Lauret, "Die Diskussion über die Volksreligion in Frankreich," in Karl Rahner et al., eds., *Volksreligion-Religion des Volkes* (Stuttgart: Kohlhammer, 1979), pp. 141–55. This discussion continued in Europe into the late 1970s, with the distinction being made between a "folk church" and a "committed church." See the articles devoted to the topic of popular religion in *Tijdschrift voor Theologie* 17, no. 4 (1977).

4. References to religion are scattered throughout Gramsci's *Quaderni del Carcere*, 3 vols. (Torino: Einaudi, 1964–75). For an exposition of Gramsci's sense of popular religion, see Arnaldo Nesti, "Gramsci et la religion populaire," *Social Compass* 22 (1975): 343–54.

5. I am thinking here especially of the work of Philippe Braudel, Jacques Le Goff, and Emmanuel LeRoy Ladurie. The latter's *Montaillou* (Paris: Pleiades, 1974) is particularly well known.

6. The literature is extensive. For a bibliography on Chinese folk religion, see

Alvin P. Cohen, "Bibliography of Writings Contributory to the Study of Chinese Folk Religion," *Journal of the American Academy of Religion* 43 (1973): 238–365. See the discussions of various religious traditions in P. H. Vrijhoff and J. J. Waardenburg eds., *Official and Popular Religion* (The Hague: Mouton, 1979).

7. Of the many discussions of the term "popular" see especially the Introduction to Vrijhoff and Waardenburg, *Official and Popular Religion;* and Waldo Cesar, "O que è 'popular' no Catolicismo Popular," *Revista Eclesiástica Brasileira* 36 (1976): 5–18.

8. Wolfgang Huber, "Ökumenische Perspektiven zum Thema 'Religion des Volkes,' " in Rahner et al., *Volksreligion*, pp. 165–73, especially p. 166, explores this history.

9. Robert Towler, *Homo Religiosus: Sociological Problems in the Study of Religion* (New York: St. Martin's Press, 1974).

10. Ibid., p. 156.

11. Huber, "Ökumenische Perspektiven," p. 167.

12. See the discussion on the term "official" in the introduction to Vrijhoff and Waardenburg, *Official and Popular Religion*.

13. While the term "the masses" comes from Marx's writings, it is used widely by intellectuals to contrast their experience with that of the great majority of the population. See notes 2 and 3 above.

14. Cesar, "O que è 'popular' . . .," pp. 10–13.

15. Thus Huber, "Ökumenische Perspektiven," p. 172.

16. I develop this point in a response to Stanley Samartha, in Gerald Anderson and Thomas Stransky, eds., *Christ's Lordship and Religious Pluralism* (Maryknoll, N.Y.: Orbis Books, 1980) pp. 52–58.

17. Since Robert Bellah's introduction of the term "civil religion" in 1968, there has been a good deal of controversy around the topic. See Bellah's own discussion of it in *The Broken Covenant* (New York: Harper & Row, 1975).

18. Segundo Galilea makes this distinction in his *Pastoral popular y urbana en América Latina* (Bogotá: CLAR, 1977), and in his *Religiosidad popular y pastoral hispano-americana* (New York: Northeast Pastoral Institute, 1981).

19. Manuel Marzal, "Investigación y hipotesis sobre la religiosidad popular," in *Pastoral y lenguaje* (Bogotá: IPLA, 1973); Galilea, *Pastoral popular*.

20. Bernard Lauret, "Die Diskussion über die Volksreligion in Frankreich," p. 142.

21. Ibid., pp. 151–52.

22. Francisco Vanderhoff, "Die Volksreligion im sozialen und ökumenischen Kontext Lateinamerikas," in Rahner et al., *Volksreligion*, p. 50.

23. Towler, *Homo Religiosus*. Sri Lankan theologian Aloysius Pieris developed a similar position in "Towards an Asian Theology of Liberation: Some Religiocultural Guidelines," *Zeitschrift für Missionswissenschaft und Religionswissenschaft* 63 (1979): 161–82. See also Virginia Fabella, ed., *Asia's Struggle for Full Humanity* (Maryknoll, N.Y.: Obis Books, 1980), pp. 75–95.

24. See the studies on Reformation popular religion in Bernard Plongeron, ed., *La religion populaire dans l'Occident chrétien* (Paris: Beauschesne, 1976); and in G. J. Cuming and Derek Baker, eds., *Popular Belief and Practice* (Cambridge, England: Cambridge University Press, 1972).

25. See the discussions in Plongeron, *La religion populaire*.

26. Juan Carlos Scannone, "Volksreligion, Volksweisheit, und Volkstheologie in Lateinamerika," in Rahner et al., *Volksreligion*, pp. 26–39, as an example of this.

27. Ibid.

28. Huber, "Ökumenische Perspektiven," pp. 167–68.

29. The Venerable Bede, *Historia Ecclesiastica Gentis Anglorum*, I, 27.

30. Eduardo Hoornaert, *Formação do Catolicismo Brasileiro 1550–1800* (Petropolis, Brazil: Vozes, 1974), has developed this argument extensively.

31. Enzo Pace, "The Debate on Popular Religion in Italy," *Social Analysis* 40 (1979): 71–75, reports on the state of the question there.

32. Eugene Genovese, *Roll, Jordan, Roll: The World the Slaves Made* (New York: Basic Books, 1974).

33. Edenio Valle, "Condicionamentos sociais do catolicimo popular," *Revista Eclesiástica Brasileira* 36 (1976): 171–88; idem, "Psychologie und Volksreligiosität: Elemente für eine pastorale Reflexion in Brasilien," in Rahner et al., *Volksreligion*, pp. 54–75.

34. Valle, "Psychologie und Volksreligiosität"; Yvonne Vehlo, *Guerra de Orixà: Um estudo de ritual e conflito* (Rio de Janeiro: Zahar, 1975).

35. Valle, "Psychologie und Volkreligiosität," p. 65.

36. Karl Rahner, *Hearers of the Word* (New York: Herder and Herder, 1969).

37. Galilea, *Religiosidad popular*, pp. 49–53.

38. Michael Singleton, *Let the People Be: Popular Religion and Religion of the People* (Brussels: Pro Mundi Vita Bulletin no. 61, 1976).

39. Galilea, *Religiosidad popular*, pp. 49–53.

40. Rosemary Haughton, *The Catholic Thing* (Springfield, Ill.: Templegate Publishers, 1979); Johannes Metz, *The Emergent Church* (New York: Crossroad Publishing Co., 1981).

7. Syncretism and Dual Religious Systems

1. For a brief history of the Rites Controversy, down to the reversal in stance under Pius XI and Pius XII, see F. A. Rouleau, "Chinese Rites Controversy," *New Catholic Encyclopedia* 3: 611–17.

2. Harold Turner's *Bibliography of New Religious Movements in Primal Societies* (New York: G. K. Hall, 1977) provides the literature on this subject.

3. The influential work of Hendrik Kraemer deserves mention in this regard. See his *De Wortelen van het Synkretisme* (The Hague: Boekencentrum, 1937) and his *Religion and the Christian Faith* (London: Lutterworth, 1956).

4. R. D. Baird reviews some of these issues in "Syncretism and the History of Religions," *Journal of Religious Thought* 24, no. 2 (1967–68): 42–53; and more recently J. H. Kamstra, *Synkretisme op de Grens tussen Theologie en Godsdienstfenomenologie* (Leiden: E. J. Brill, 1974).

5. Helmer Ringgren, "The Problems of Syncretism," in Sven Hartman, ed., *Syncretism* (Scripta Instituti Donnerano Aboensis, III) (Stockholm: Almqvist and Wiksell, 1969), pp. 7–14.

6. Louis Luzbetak, *The Church and Cultures* (Pasadena, Calif.: William Carey Library, 1976).

7. For descriptions of these systems, see Roger Bastide, *The African Religions of Brazil* (Baltimore, Md.: John Hopkins University Press, 1978); Alfred Metraux, *Voodoo in Haiti* (New York: Schocken Books, 1972).

8. For descriptions of the Independent Churches, see the literature in Turner, *Bibliography*; on the Rastafarians, see Tracy Nicholas, *Rastafari: A Way of Life* (New York: Doubleday, 1979).

9. On the Peli Association, see Michael Knight, "The Peli Ideal," *Catalyst* 5, no. 4 (1975); for a general description of cargo movements, see Peter Lawrence, *Road Belong Cargo* (New York: Humanities Press, 1967).

10. Alfonso Ortiz, *The Tewa World* (Chicago: University of Chicago Press, 1969), introduction.

11. See, e.g., Joseph Spae, *Buddhist-Christian Empathy* (Chicago: Chicago Institute of Theology and Culture, 1980).

12. Harvey Conn, ed., *Conversion* (Boston: Alba House, 1981), is a helpful contribution to the understanding of the conversion process.

13. A good review and critique of Barth's distinctions can be found in Donald Dawe, "Religion as a Problem for Christian Theology," in Donald Dawe and John Carman, eds., *Christian Faith in a Religiously Plural World* (Maryknoll, N.Y.: Orbis Books, 1978), pp. 83–107.

14. Thus Baird, "Syncretism and the History of Religions."

15. J. H. Kamstra, *Encounter or Syncretism: The Initial Growth of Japanese Buddhism* (Leiden: E. J. Brill, 1967), pp. 5ff.

16. Luzbetak, *The Church and Cultures,* pp. 239–48.

17. Ichiro Hori, *Folk Religion in Japan* (Chicago: University of Chicago Press, 1968).

18. This history is recounted in Arthur Wright, *Buddhism in Chinese History* (Stanford, Calif.: Stanford University Press, 1959).

19. Joseph Kitagawa, *Religion in Japanese History* (New York: Columbia University Press, 1962).

20. For a study of some of that language, see Lawrence Nemer, *Anglican and Roman Catholic Attitudes on Mission* (St. Augustin, Germany: Steyler, 1981).

21. Thus Eugene Genovese, *Roll, Jordan, Roll: The World the Slaves Made* (New York: Random House, 1976).

22. Kitagawa, *Religion in Japanese History*, p. 185.

23. See, e.g., Keith Thomas, *Religion and the Decline of Magic* (New York: Scribner, 1971), which is a study of the survival of pre-Christian magic and healing rites in seventeenth-century Puritan England.

Index

Abelard, Peter, 90
Adaptation models of local theologies, 9–12, 13, 16
Ad Gentes, 2
Africa: and adaptation models, 11; and church tradition, 35, 77; contextualization in, 1, 13; and the doctrine of original sin, 96, 97, 100; dual systems of belief in, 40, 145; exorcism and healing in, 99; liberation theology in, 2; oral theology in, 84; polygamy in, 3, 97–98; popular religion in, 127, 142–43; proverbs in, 31, 160–61; syncretism in, 145, 154, 155; Western rituals in, 27; wisdom theology in, 87. *See also* Independent Churches of Africa
Afro-Brazilian cults, 138, 146
Afro-Caribbean cults, 146
Afterlife, 64, 65, 69, 130
Allmen, Daniel von, 164
Altars, 67, 112, 147
Ambrose of Milan, 86
Analogy, 85–86
Anselm, 89
Anthologies, 82–83, 84
Anthropology, 41, 42–49, 53
Apartheid, 35
Apocrypha, 82
Aquinas, Thomas, 88, 89, 90
Arias, Maximino, 167
Aristotle, 88, 90, 118
Arius, 118, 119
Art, 43, 52, 55, 63, 66, 67, 115
Asia, 1, 2, 10, 26, 87, 92, 145, 148
Asmat people, 14
Athanasius, 119
Audience of theology, 36–37
Augustine, 60–61, 85, 86, 96, 97, 100, 166

Authority, 108, 110, 113
Aymara, 145, 148
Bacon, Francis, 78
Baird, R.D., 169, 170
Balasuriya, Tissa, 30
Bantu peoples, 9, 77
Baptism, 2, 27, 97, 129, 130, 143, 149, 156, 158
Barth, Karl, 82, 89, 149–50
Barthes, Roland, 53
Baseline approach to popular religion, 133–34, 139, 151
Basic Christian communities. *See* Small Christian communities
Bastide, Roger, 169
Bede, Venerable, 169
Bell, Daniel, 167
Bellah, Robert, 168
Berger, Peter, 164
Bertalanffy, Ludwig von, 160
Beumer, Johannes, 165
Bible: and adaptation models, 10–11; and christocentrism, 30; commentaries on, 84; and contextual theology, 29; and the development of local theologies, 20, 76; and liberation theology, 33; and local churches, 96–97, 100, 101, 103; and local cultures, 141, 147; and orthodoxy, 116, 117; and the Reformation, 126; and small Christian communities, 16, 24; theology as a variation on, 80–85; and tradition, 109, 110, 111, 115, 119; and the translation model, 7, 8
Bimwenyi-Kweshi, O., 77
Blacks, 3, 4, 13, 27, 100
Black theology, 31, 78, 102–3
Boethius, 88
Bogatyrev, Peter, 163
Bolivia, 9, 26, 148